The Little Black Book

Prentice Hall Series in Innovative Technology

Dennis R. Allison, David J. Farber, and Bruce D. Shriver   *Series Advisors*

The Little Black Book:

Mail Bonding with OSI Directory Services

Marshall T. Rose

Performance Systems International, Inc.

Prentice Hall
Englewood Cliffs, New Jersey 07632

Library of Congress Cataloging-in-Publication Data

Rose, Marshall T.
    The little black book : mail bonding with OSI directory services /
Marshall T. Rose.
        p.   cm. -- (Prentice Hall series in innovative technology)
    Includes bibliographical references and index.
    ISBN 0-13-683210-5
    1. Electronic mail systems. 2. Computer network protocols.
I. Title. II. Series.
TK5105.73.R67 1992
384.3'4--dc20   91-22709
                                                        CIP

Editorial/production supervision: Mary P. Rottino
Cover design: Wanda Lubelska Designs
Pre-press buyer: Mary E. McCartney
Manufacturing buyer: Susan Brunke
Acquisitions editor: Paul W. Becker

 © 1992 by Prentice-Hall, Inc.
A Simon & Schuster Company
Englewood Cliffs, New Jersey 07632

The publisher offers discounts on this book when ordered
in bulk quantities. For more information, write:
        Special Sales/Professional Marketing
        Prentice-Hall, Inc.
        Professional & Technical Reference Division
        Englewood Cliffs, New Jersey 07632

Printed in the United States of America
10 9 8 7 6 5 4 3 2 1

ISBN   0-13-683210-5

Prentice-Hall International (UK) Limited, *London*
Prentice-Hall of Australia Pty. Limited, *Sydney*
Prentice-Hall Canada Inc., *Toronto*
Prentice-Hall Hispanoamericana, S.A., *Mexico*
Prentice-Hall of India Private Limited, *New Delhi*
Prentice-Hall of Japan, Inc., *Tokyo*
Simon & Schuster Asia Pte. Ltd., *Singapore*
Editora Prentice-Hall do Brasil, Ltda., *Rio de Janeiro*

for Duck Soup

Contents

List of Tables

List of Figures

Foreword

Marshall Rose has achieved fame for his ability to build implementations in the face of fuzzy specifications and political firefights. As the *Internet/OSI Combat Engineer*, he has withstood opposition **and** friendly fire (regardless of your point of view). His books are noted for an intriguing combination of implementation experience, lucid description of theory, and soapboxes.

The Little Black Book merits the attention of all who are interested in directory services. It documents the struggle to build an *operational* distributed service, including applications which are faithful to the distributed model. This isn't a mere implementation exercise, it involves innovation at all levels, from basic X.500 mechanisms to applications which are seen by the users as carrots, not sticks. Progress and evolution need starting points; this is one.

While the engineering can be written off as a product of his ge- | soap... | nius, the organizational and political progress recorded in the *The Little Black Book* is noteworthy. In addition to harnessing the work of many talented individuals, Marshall may even have contributed to the *completion* of registration plans. Of course, it might be that he just wanted to get on to the fine lunches and dinners. | ...soap |

Paul V. Mockapetris
Seal Beach, California

Preface

Networks, whether telephone, physical delivery (postal), transportation, or computer-communications, all build *infrastructure*: they support interaction between the users connected to the network. In a computer network, electronic mail is perhaps the best example of this. However, infrastructure-enhancing services, such as electronic mail, also require an underlying infrastructure, one which maps names into addresses and numbers.

This is a book about one particular technology which can be used to provide this underlying infrastructure: *Directory Services*. In brief, a Directory allows both people and programs to find out information about other users in the network. For example, a person might use the Directory to find someone else's electronic mail address, a program might use the Directory to find the network address of another process, and so on.

Of course, directory services are always built in the context of a protocol suite. A *protocol* is simply a set of rules used by computers to communicate with each other, and a *protocol suite* is a group of these protocols all related to a common framework. In the last decade, there has been much interest in standards-based, or so-called open, systems for computer-communications. There are in fact two: the current *de facto* standard for open systems, the Internet suite of protocols (commonly known as "TCP/IP"), and the *de jure* standard OSI suite, which some hope will become the open protocols of the future.

The OSI approach towards directory services, which we'll simply term "The Directory," is quite ambitious: it is intended to serve the needs of many diverse classes of applications throughout the globe, at the site, LAN, WAN, enterprise, and internet-level. In contrast, the Internet approach towards directory services is much more focused, and today provides very useful service in the limited problem domain that it was intended to serve.

The Little Black Book concentrates only on the OSI approach, which has yet to achieve its promise, and may not do so for several years (if ever). However, because the Internet suite of protocols is pervasive throughout networking, it would be folly for us to completely ignore the services that this suite can provide, even though it does not contain a technology in direct competition with the OSI Directory. As such, throughout the discussion, some Internet concepts and observations will appear.

In contrast to my earlier works, this book places its emphasis on the services offered by the protocols, rather than the protocols themselves. To be sure, we'll give some consideration to the protocols, but primarily as a means of understanding the services which they make possible.

In my view, a paradigm shift has finally begun to occur in networking, in which protocols are becoming less interesting, to be replaced by a strong interest in services and the applications based on those services. Perhaps it has always been this way, and I've been entirely too focused for the last decade. In any event, the remainder of this preface is a personal note explaining why this book (and the other two) were written, so you might wish to skip ahead to page xxviii where some suggestions are given on how to use this book.

In many ways, completion of this book has nearly "closed the circle" of my efforts in computer-communications.

I got involved with networking at the University of California at Irvine (UCI), in 1980, when Einar A. Stefferud ("Stef") of Network Management Associates, my University mentor and now long-time friend, set me to work on e-mail systems. In particular, I spent a lot of time working with a very forward-thinking Internet mail system, called The Rand Message Handling System (MH). The people who designed MH at Rand (Bruce Borden, Stockton Gaines, and Norman Shapiro) had developed an imaginative approach towards message-handling, and with some help from Stef, a colleague at UCI named John L. Romine, Norman Shapiro, and MH advocate Phyllis Kantar, I set about fleshing out a few of the concepts. MH is still used quite heavily today, over a decade after its introduction. Although I spent five years hacking on it, I think that all the major credit for MH goes to Borden, Gaines, and Shapiro for coming up with the brilliant ideas, and to John and Phyllis for persevering. John still maintains MH to this day; as for myself, I simply delete any unsolicited mail about MH, unless it comes from John! After my five year immersion in MH, I was burnt out on Internet mail.

Next, at the Northrop Research and Technology Center, I found myself moving towards being more interested in OSI technology.[1] A colleague, Dwight E. Cass, and I began work on building a development environment for OSI applications, which led to several years work on the ISO Development Environment (ISODE). Appendix C contains an overview of ISODE, along with some rather self-serving retrospections on the state of computer-communications.

Due to a series of poor judgements on my part, ISODE is now both a reference implementation of the core aspects of OSI, and the basis for several national and regional pilots in OSI services. As with MH, I made the mistake of working on something (primarily in my spare time), which became widely-distributed and modestly-used, and now I'm on the hook to provide a modicum of support for the ISODE junkies of the world. Unfortunately, unlike the situation with MH, I can't just jump ship, since I seem to be lashed to the mast. (I hope you won't get the impression that I alone work on ISODE. That impression is patently wrong: substantive contributions are made by a large number of individuals, around the globe; however, I'm the person stuck with the ultimate responsibility for the integrity of the source tree.) At this point, I'm probably doing ISODE more harm than good, by simply not bothering to return most of the phone calls I get about it.

So, by the time this book is in print I will have transferred responsibility for ISODE to my colleagues at X-Tel Services Limited. Since they have been key participants in ISODE effort, and they have a greater expertise with many parts of ISODE than myself, I think this will be best for all concerned.

As a technology, OSI shows great promise, but also has some show-

---

[1]While working on MH, I had dismissed X.400, the OSI technology for Message Handling Systems, as the product of a demented mind, hopelessly out of touch with reality. History has proven me wrong, though the jury is still out as to how wrong!

stopping flaws. The promise is very seductive, but the actual delivery seems to always be postponed. After the initial work on ISODE (which Dwight and I completed in 1987), I kept working on things because I thought that ISODE could aid in the introduction of OSI technology into the market. (Note that I wrote "introduction" and not "adoption" or "dominance.") My agenda for ISODE was for it to become an educational tool, and in that respect, I suppose it has been somewhat successful. Of course, tossing code over the fence isn't enough. So, I ended-up writing *The Open Book*, which emphasizes a practical perspective to OSI, as taught to me by experience with building ISODE.

However, writing the book was not really my idea. One day I got a call from another of my University mentors, Professor David J. Farber of the University of Pennsylvania, who also, coincidentally, is a series editor at Prentice-Hall. (Although, in my opinion, he is one of the founding-fathers of networking in the US, Professor Farber is perhaps best known for his "farberisms." Take a look at the footnote on the bottom of page 221 for an example.) The conversation went something like this:

> "Marshall, you have to write a book on OSI."
>
> "Dave, I am burnt out on OSI. I don't want to write a book."
>
> "Marshall, trust me. This will take two weekends of your time, no more."
>
> "Dave, I don't believe you."
>
> "Marshall, trust me. Four weekends, max."

Against my better judgement, I acquiesced, and in early 1990, four *months* (of nearly full time work) later, the first draft of *The Open Book* was completed.

For all of its hype, OSI technology is a very dry subject. I have never been happy with the false image of intellectual respectability that some have tried to superimpose on the computer-communications field and in particular on OSI, so I decided that *The Open Book* would have fragments of personal opinion interjected throughout. These fragments were included primarily to remind the reader that OSI was not handed down on stone tablets, but also to keep the reader's interest and (more importantly) to allow me to vent my frustration at having tried to implement a lot of this stuff.

Of course, most professional texts have opinion, they just don't label it as such! So, I introduced a typographical convention termed a *soapbox*. Look for text bracketed between the symbols $\boxed{\text{soap}\ldots}$ and $\boxed{\ldots\text{soap}}$, which appear in the margin. Although I always strived to present a balanced set of perspectives, I felt that the soapbox notation added just the right tone that I wanted to convey. (This whole Preface should probably be in a soapbox, but it's the Preface, so I think most people expect it to be a personal perspective anyway.)

I caught a fair bit of shrapnel from a lot of the OSI purists who were outraged that I would drag their dirty laundry out of the closet, simply by pointing out the things that did not work. And, I suppose, by having tried to implement this stuff, I had an unfair advantage over them. My favorite rebuttal to *The Open Book* came in the form of a book review written by a participant in the British Standards Institute, and a long-time OSI proponent. The first time I read the review, I was simply mystified by the criticisms. Then, when I got to the end and read the affiliation of the reviewer, I thought to myself "Of course! This was written by a Standards person" (Note that capitalization of the word "Standards".) So, I read it a second time and really quite enjoyed myself. Later, when asked about the review, my comment was simply that *The Open Book* was not written for Standards people. I don't want to sound condescending, but the Standards community was simply not my intended market segment. Fortunately for me, there were also a lot of the "good OSI'ers" who were glad to see someone cut through the nonsense and talk about OSI in a straight-forward fashion.

I also caught some shrapnel from the Internet purists, who were even more outraged that I could present their camp as anything less than the Eden of networking. Urban legend has it that one member of the Internet management structure, upon reading *The Final Soapbox* in *The Open Book* became so enraged that the veins on his neck were sticking out like the quills of a porcupine. This surprised me a bit, since I thought I had portrayed the Internet camp in a much more favorable light. (Technically, they often shine quite brightly, and this commands my respect and admiration.)

About a year before that manipulative call from Dave, I got involved with Internet network management. Of course, I was viewed with a lot of suspicion, since I think that the majority of the Internet community views me as some kind of OSI bigot. In any event, there were two technologies competing to be the basis of network management in the Internet. One was a home-grown protocol, built in the finest of Internet traditions — discuss, implement, evaluate, rediscuss, and so on. The other was based on the OSI network management framework. If ever OSI has a "dark side," then, in my opinion, network management (or "Systems Management" in their vocabulary) is the hands-down winner. An ad hoc committee was formed to evaluate the situation, and I was invited to participate as an OSI "expert." Having spent some time interacting with the champions of the OSI approach, it was clear to me that their approach was a non-starter.

While not particularly knowledgeable (then or now) on network management, I know bad design, particularly when I see it on a viewgraph and not in product. Fortunately in those days I was working closely with Keith McCloghrie now of Hughes LAN Systems, a real network management guru who was also invited on the committee. The outcome of the meeting was that the home-grown protocol would be evolved once again, and that a common framework for the two approaches would be developed, in the hopes that someday, perhaps the OSI approach might prove useful.

A working group was formed to oversee the next step of evolution, the result of which is now called the Simple Network Management Protocol (SNMP). I was selected as chair of the working group, because of some mis-guided notion that I would provide balance as an OSI person. My goal was simply to let the real experts (Keith and the four engineers who designed the home-grown protocol, Professor Jeffrey D. Case of the University of Tennessee, James R. Davin of the MIT Laboratory for Computer Science, Mark S. Fedor and Martin L. Schoffstall of Performance Systems International) have free rein, while I threw obstacles in the path of the OSI network management types. So, the others got to do the substantive work (they were more qualified), and I got to play the heavy (which, given my physique, was a rather apt role).

Less than a year later, two things were clear: first, that the OSI approach truly was a non-starter (no products to speak of, and dwindling vendor support); and, second, the incredible success that SNMP attained which led to an information-gap. As chair of the working group, I felt an obligation to answer the basic SNMP questions which pop up on the mailing lists. But, by early 1990, the same 20 questions were being asked by different people every other week. This left me with a choice: I could either write up some canned scripts that shot back blanket answers, or I could get a book published about SNMP. Well, the rest of the SNMP cadre where busy writing code, managing networks, and/or running companies. After a chat with my publisher at Prentice-Hall, Paul W. Becker (who, at that time, was still reeling from having discovered what a soapbox was — some six months after the publication of *The Open Book*), I decided to undertake the project, and completed the first draft of *The Simple Book* in mid-1990.

Since publication, the number of messages asking the usual questions has dropped dramatically. Of course, it's impossible to show a direct cause; but regardless, my problem is solved for the present. Unfortunately, Internet network management has become highly politicized (an unfortunate first for the Internet community), and I hang on as chair of the SNMP Working Group primarily to provide damage control and adult supervision.

At Performance Systems International, my primary task these days is to oversee a project offering a White Pages service to the Internet community. The service is based on X.500 technology, and this has lead to a great deal of effort in evolving from a prototype implementation into a production service, and the job is not done yet! However, I think enough has been learned about the Directory to put together a book which takes a practical perspective towards the topic.

Originally, I wanted to write a book on both electronic mail and directory services, to complete the circle of my experiences. I was going to call it *The Postal Book*. However, after grinding through it for a few months, I decided that such a project was a fundamental error in judgement: I doubted my competence to write a book that dealt with electronic mail to the same level of depth and insight that

I had mustered with *The Open Book* and *The Simple Book*. In brief, I decided that I had just been out of day-to-day e-mail hacking for too long, and that if I wrote on electronic mail, it would start to look like the books written by other people on the topic. Perhaps this is prideful, but I have felt that the distinguishing characteristics of my books is that they read like they are written by someone with "the wisdom of the trenches." If readers like this perspective, then my publisher is happy. If not, then I suggest that perspective readers vote with their feet. Regardless, by being out of the inner loop of e-mail for five years, I simply felt that I could not meet the same level of intensity that my previous efforts had wrought. If only Dave had made a phone call some five years earlier!

Fortunately, in the area of the Directory, I have been in the inner loop, perhaps too much so, for nearly three years. So, I changed the name of this book to the title it now has, and started writing with a renewed frenzy.

In many ways, I view this book as another educational exercise, but instead of presenting the balanced view of OSI with *The Open Book*, or avoiding the "dark side" of OSI with *The Simple Book*, *The Little Black Book* presents the "good side" of OSI — the Directory.

Some might argue that Message Handling is the gem in OSI's crown, and I will certainly agree that, at present, MHS is the most credible of OSI's applications. However, MHS is at a significant disadvantage — it has serious competition: the creaky old Internet mail system is dominant throughout much of the world, and gaining even more popularity. It may not be able to directly handle multiple body parts like MHS, nor may it be able of directly deal with multi-media content like MHS, but Internet mail technology works really well and gets the job done: it delivers (no pun intended). This is because it is a *tractable* technology (the implications of which are discussed in a Soapbox starting on page 7).

To date, history has shown that for all of its advantages on paper, most of the MHS implementations around have equivalent or less functionality than their Internet counterparts. I will admit to liking the potential services that MHS makes available, but if most of the implementations offer only exchange of text messages and the user-interfaces are less powerful than the ones I use with the Internet suite, then why bother? MHS's only citable advantage is that it is "internationally agreed upon." Somehow, this fails to excite me.

Now, in contrast, the Directory has no direct competition! There is no protocol in the Internet suite which is intended to offer services like those of the Directory. Thus, my feeling is that this represents a tremendous opportunity for OSI to deliver something useful, in an area where there isn't an installed base to compete against. Of course, OSI and Internet purists may scoff at my opportunistic approach, but frankly, if OSI can't be sold on the basis of offering useful service, then the situation is simply hopeless. Although I had hoped a few years ago that MHS would be the wedge OSI would use to gain acceptance, I've now pinned my hopes on the Directory as a more likely winner.

Well, if you've struggled through this much of the Preface, you've earned the right to read the good part: this is my last book for a long, long while. Writing is very difficult for me, and frankly, had Dave not tricked me into writing the first one, I would have felt no inclination at all to do the other two. In late 1992, a revision of *The Open Book* will be published, but after that the books go into maintenance mode. I was burnt out on OSI when I wrote *The Open Book*, burnt out on Network Management when I wrote *The Simple Book*, and am *really* burnt out before even starting on *The Little Black Book*.

However, there's this evil rumor going about that my next project will be on network security and titled *The Closed Book*. There is no truth to this rumor. I know nothing about network security, I want to know nothing about network security, and if I have any say in the matter, I will learn nothing about network security in the future.

And now for some really good news: after publication of *The Simple Book* a few people commented how much they enjoyed soapboxes, and then went on to express minor discomfort at the relative lack of them in the second book. So, I've included quite a few soapboxes in *The Little Black Book*. In fact, I made a special "soapbox editing" pass, with the help of some of my more mean-spirited friends. Of course, soapboxes are really meant to be instructive, but a little dig here and there really seems to get the point across!

How to Use this Book

This book is intended to serve both as a graduate-level text and also as a professional reference. It is expected that the reader has a modest background in networking.

The first part of the book, Chapters 1 and 2, presents an introduction to the problem domain and a broad overview of the technology platforms used for a solution. The first chapter tries to motivate concern for the services we need as networking moves into the '90s, whilst the second chapter presents the collection of protocols which provide the infrastructure for these services.

The second part of the book, Chapters 3 through 6 deal with the Directory. Since our motivation for looking at the Directory is how it can help users find out information about other people, a recurring focus throughout this part will be that of a White Pages service.

Finally, as the book concludes, future trends are hypothesized in Chapter 7. In the appendices, the book contains a rather lengthy discussion of ISODE. In addition, ordering information for ISODE is given.

Instructors can build a two-semester course on this text, augmenting the text with parts of Chapters 6–10 of *The Open Book*.

Acknowledgements

I have always been fortunate in being able to build on my previous work and the work of others. In particular, I find it useful to synthesize reports and papers I have written as part of a project, in order to provide a better overall picture. Although the leverage is good, the unfortunate part about this comes about when trying to acknowledge all the sources that have provided much appreciated help. Einar A. Stefferud of Network Management Associates, has been a constant positive force. Although I don't get to interact with Professor David J. Farber of the University of Pennsylvania as much as I would like, his influence, albeit indirectly, is always appreciated.

It is fair to say that the basis for this book came largely out of my experiences at Performance Systems International. I happily credit Martin L. Schoffstall, Vice President and COO of PSI, for instigating and then providing continuing support for the White Pages Pilot. Many contributed to the software which made the pilot possible: Stephen E. Kille of University College London and Julian P. Onions of X-Tel Services Limited, have been constant contributors to ISODE, which provides the basic infrastructure. Colin J. Robbins, formerly of University College London and now of X-Tel Services Limited, and Stephen E. Kille, are the persons responsible for much of QUIPU, the Directory implementation used by ISODE. Many of the site administrators have also made good contributions to the pilot, in particular, Timothy A. Howes of the University of Michigan, and Peter Yee of the NASA Ames Research Center. In addition, after hearing a talk by Alfred J. Grimstad of Bellcore on the Directory, I was able to write a very concise description of DSA knowledge.

The hypothetical Freedonian national decision is based on a proposal, *A Contribution on a Naming Scheme*, put forth by Stef and myself to the North American Directory Forum (NADF), the US ANSI Registration Authority Committee, and the IETF OSI Directory Services Working Group, as the basis for the US national decision on Directory naming. There were actually several versions of this proposal, and I used one of the intermediate versions, which proved to be the most controversial as it illustrates a lot of interesting naming issues.

Work on ISODE started at the Northrop Research and Technology Center, and then moved with me to The Wollongong Group, NYSERNet, and Performance Systems International. When at NYSERNet, and at Performance Systems International, ISODE work is partially supported by the US Defense Advanced Research Projects Agency and the Rome Air Development Center of the US Air Force Systems Command under contract number F30602–88–C-0016.

Finally, there have been many reviewers who have spent considerable time pouring over countless manuscripts to help me produce the snappy prose contained herein: Geoffrey S. Goodfellow of Anterior Technology, Stephen E. Kille of University College London, Keith McCloghrie of Hughes LAN Systems, Paul V. Mockapetris who is currently assigned to the US Defense Advanced Projects Research Agency (DARPA), Julian P. Onions and Colin J. Robbins both of X-Tel Services Limited, and Einar A. Stefferud of Network Management Associates.

Ole J. Jacobsen, Editor and Publisher of ConneXions — The Interoperability Report® was kind enough to perform the copy-editing on *The Little Black Book*. His efforts brought this work to print in time for the INTEROP® conference and trade-show of 1991.

The title for *The Little Black Book* is derived from a title suggested by the well-known *Cynic of the Internet*, Dr. Paul V. Mockapetris. Back when I thought this book was going to discuss both electronic mail and directory services, Paul suggested that I use the title *The Mail Bonding Book*, which would be quite apt. However, my publisher still exerts a modicum of control over my writing (which no doubt is a great surprise to him), so I modified Paul's idea slightly.[2] Actually, I get all my best jokes from Paul, but he rarely allows me to attribute these to him, owing to the respectable image he is required to maintain. This is a great loss to many of us, since Paul has one of the quickest wits I've ever seen.

---

[2]Despite the change in this book's focus, there is a little bit about electronic mail interacting with directory services, so I kept Paul's idea for a hook.

And finally, Cheetah, my awesome cat, continues to be a sheer terror. (I suspect that this is true of any strong-willed, hyper-intelligent, 12 kg, feline with razor-sharp fangs and extremely powerful back claws.) Although he is getting on in years, he remains as rambunctious as ever!

/mtr

Mountain View, California
May, 1991

Chapter 1

Introduction

One purpose of computer networks is to provide *infrastructure* among users who work together as a community. For example, the electronic mail service offered by computer networks provides a means for users to collaborate towards some common goal. In the simplest cases, this collaboration may be solely for the dissemination of information. In other cases, two users may work on a joint research project, using electronic mail as their primary means of communication.

Most network services are based on the implicit assumption that each user can supply *infrastructural information* to facilitate interactions through the network. For example, electronic mail services expect that an originator can supply addressing information for all the intended recipients. It is not necessarily the task of electronic mail, per se, to provide this infrastructural addressing information to (or for) the user.

The assumption that each user can supply such information works fine in small environments, particularly those where infrastructural information is not difficult to obtain and remember. However, the model does not scale well. Consider the case when the membership of a network consists of hundreds of thousands of users belonging to thousands of organizations. It is no longer reasonable for a single user to obtain and provide all this information, except in very limited circumstances. Further, it is likely that some of the information changes frequently (e.g., on a monthly basis), due to personnel and other resource movement. The goal of a *White Pages* service is to provide the necessary information, and to mask the complexity of infrastructural information.

The kind of White Pages service we are interested in relies on some kind of network-based Directory. However, for the remainder of this chapter, the discussion is focused entirely by "the high view." After this motivation, we'll look at how the technology is designed and realized.

1.1 White Pages in the Real World

The White Pages service in the telephone system provides an excellent model. In the telephone system, the listed user is a person, enterprise, or organization. To find some infrastructural information associated with a listed user (e.g., a telephone number), the name is looked up in the telephone book. Upon finding the name, the telephone number is listed nearby.

We note that telephone books also include other information such as a partial postal address of each user. This is an important issue: the telephone white pages book contains more than one kind of information. In fact, if a user of the telephone system had to consult one book for telephone numbers and a second book for postal addresses, the service would be much less valuable. For example, if there are two entries which are similar (e.g., both entries have the same first initial and last name), then additional information may help the user to determine which entry is the desired listing.

At the next level, we see that most telephone books include two parts: the White Pages, and the equally familiar Yellow Pages. The Yellow Pages contains essentially the same information as the White Pages, but rather than indexing by the name of each user, the Yellow Pages index by the products or services offered by each listed user.

Given the scope of the telephone system (both in terms of size and number of autonomous administrations), everyone recognizes that it would be impractical to have a single telephone book for the world, an entire nation, a large region, or even a single city. Typically, there is a telephone book for each local geographical area. Since telephone system usage tends to dramatically favor local calls over long distance calls, local telephone books are commonplace. Telephone books for remote areas are found only in small quantities. Of course, there is no reason, other than economics, why any particular set of users might not be listed together in a specialized White Pages service.

This leads to the last aspect of the telephone system's white pages service, the operator-assisted listing service, commonly known as *directory assistance* or *directory enquiries*. If a telephone book isn't available, the user places a phone call to ask for assistance in retrieving the desired information. In addition to making remote information readily available, the operator-assisted listing service has another interesting feature: *approximate matching*. It is not uncommon to have partial or even incorrect information about a user, when trying to determine that user's telephone number. The combination of personnel and computers which provide the listing service usually employ phonetic matching and other heuristics to try to generate a list of entries, of which one might be the "correct" entry.

1.2 White Pages in the Computer World

A White Pages service in a computer environment performs a role quite similar to that of the telephone system's white pages service. To begin, information from the telephone book (name, postal address and telephone number) is available from the White Pages service. Further, the "local" White Pages information is maintained by each organization, e.g., an internal telephone directory is typically available.

Because local information is made available through the White Pages service, this argues for both distribution of information and access control: each local organization will wish to maintain its own "part" of the information in the service. It is reasonable to expect that every organization has some directory information that should not be openly published.

In addition to containing infrastructural information for the network community, the White Pages service may also contain other network information for listed users of the network. Of these, perhaps the most notable is a user's electronic mail address. Other information, to support authentication and authorization, might also be available. For example, the White Pages service might keep track of the network nodes for which each user is permitted access.

Whilst there is a clear distinction between White and Yellow Pages in the telephone system, this distinction is often blurred when applied to networking technology. There is a single service, which supports a common class of queries which search on different attributes (of which only one need be an entry's name). Thus, perhaps the term *Rainbow Pages* is more apt.

Programs which run in the network make use of the White Pages service for other purposes. For example, a sophisticated network management program might use the White Pages service to obtain information about the computers attached to a particular physical network (e.g., contact information for the system administrators of those systems) in order to perform some task (e.g., notify administrators of problems).

This simple example illustrates the variety of services the White Pages might offer. First, the network management program asks the

White Pages service to identify the computers it is interested in. This
is probably done with a Yellow Pages type of query — a search on one
of the attributes of the entries for listed computers. Second, for each
computer identified, the "administrator" attribute will be retrieved.
The value of this attribute is the name of a person, or the role of a
person, which in turn is a pointer to another entry in the White Pages
service. Thus, the White Pages service is again queried either for the
"electronic mail address" attribute for each administrator, or perhaps
a phone number for voice contact.

In order for programs, rather than people, to make use of the
White Pages service, it is essential that the information be rigor-
ously structured: associated with each attribute is a set of procedures
defining how operations such as matching, exact or approximate, are
performed.

Ultimately, a White Pages service might be the unifying facility for
both system and network administration: local databases (password
files, configuration files, and so on), can be generated automatically
from the infrastructural information available from the White Pages
service. By providing a common framework, a powerful set of tools,
and some semi-intelligent programs, administrators may be able to
configure and maintain all resources in the network. This scenario is
beyond the scope of the *The Little Black Book*, though it is a very
probable application in the medium term.

1.3 Roadmap

The discussion in *The Little Black Book* will look at a single technology for providing a White Pages service, namely the emerging OSI Directory. Further, attention will be given to a pioneering implementation of the Directory, QUIPU, developed at University College London.

The next chapter introduces the Internet and OSI suites of protocols. This provides some context for the discussions which follow.

Next, we introduce the concepts behind the Directory and then examine how the service is accessed. Following this, algorithms employed by the user in order to interrogate information are presented. Finally, the nature of a distributed Directory is explored. Throughout the exposition, special attention will be given as to how one might establish a global White Pages service using the Directory.

Finally, *The Little Black Book* speculates as to where things might be going with the Directory.

Some readers of either *The Open Book* or *The Simple Book* have `soap...` noted that no chapter is complete without a soapbox. Not wishing to disappoint those readers who are soapbox fans, let's consider a question that often comes up:

> *Is Marshall T. Rose really pro-OSI or anti-OSI? After all, he criticizes so much of OSI, and in discussions with OSI "experts" he often subjects them to a severe verbal thrashing. On the other hand, he writes all this OSI software and runs a very large OSI pilot project.*

The answer is that I consciously try to be neither pro-OSI nor anti-OSI; my goal is to be pro-market.

My belief is that the ultimate goal in computer-communications is to deliver useful service. I also believe that many people seem to lose sight of this. Although many feel that OSI has a *raison d'être* in and of itself, this might be considered to be a rather *techno-centric* perspective. In the pragmatic sense, both the OSI and Internet suites exist *solely* as a means of building user services.

To temper this, it must be emphasized that

> *The problems of the real-world are remarkably resilient*
> *towards administrative fiat.*

Thus, citing "successful" publication of implementation agreements for OSI technology, well-intentioned government mandates for OSI and other bits of "excellent progress" are largely unimpressive: I believe that users probably want a robust market with competing mature products that solve their problems. Users may be willing to put up with the standardization process, but *only* if it is a means towards the end of a robust market. standards, per se, are probably of no interest to users without robust products which implement those standards.

Over the last decade, there has been some experience with OSI around the globe, but, from my perspective, production-quality products delivering really useful service have been sadly lacking. I think this is also true, to a lesser extent, with the Internet suite of protocols. Of course, the Internet suite is much less ambitious and much more focused than the OSI effort. The key advantage of the Internet approach is that it produces *tractable technology*, which is the fundamental building block for a mature market. Consider:

- an important characteristic of a mature market is the competition of robust products;

- in order to develop robust products, it is necessary to deploy the technology in a large number of operational environments and subsequently "harden" it; and,

- in order to deploy technology, it is necessary to be able to implement that technology within a reasonable time-frame.

Although anything can be viewed as "a simple matter of programming," experience has shown that simpler technologies are more tractable, and in being so exhibit a greater likelihood of being implemented in a timely fashion. Clearly, the technology comprising the Internet suite of protocols is much more tractable than the corresponding OSI technology; and, just as clearly, the Internet suite has been widely-implemented, deployed in numerous operational environments, and has a tremendous number of mature products in market competition.

Thus, whilst I desire a lot of the more powerful services that OSI promises, I am disappointed when I see what actually gets delivered to the end-user. What good is a standard for multi-media mail if all anyone ever uses it for is sending textual messages? To be sure, some vendors of OSI software are breaking out of this mold, and there are now some products with greater functionality than their Internet counterparts. Even so, the investment required may be two or three orders of magnitude greater, and unless a lot of products implement the additional functionality, then it is unlikely that it will see widespread use!

Although ISODE started out as an effort to study parts of OSI, it became apparent at the end of the '80s that, for better or worse, it had to serve other uses. One of these uses was as a reference implementation. The idea is to make the core aspects of OSI widely available, by producing an implementation which is openly available. This means more experience with OSI can be gained in less time, and (here's the leap of faith) this may lead to greater understanding and ultimately to better products and services.

The downside to this theory is that, in practice, reference implementations tend to get widely used but infrequently extended in the field. (Although many vendors do a lot of posturing as to the software they bundle with their systems, there is apparently a predominant attitude to "shrink-wrap-and-ship" openly available software — see the soapbox starting on page 53 for an example). As a result, ISODE may put OSI in the hands of a lot of sites, but it's not clear how many of those sites use it to build better things, as opposed to the sites which simply use the features supplied with the system.

So, to answer the question at the beginning of this soapbox. When something in OSI shows promise — both in terms of new functionality and likelihood of deployment — I'm for it. If not, ...

⎯ ...soap

Chapter 2

Protocols for Open Systems

The need for standardized networking technology has long been recognized. Computers must adhere to a common set of rules for defining their interactions, i.e., how they talk to one another. How computers talk to one another is termed a *protocol*. Protocols defined in terms of a common framework and administrated by a common body form a *protocol suite*.

Conventional theory holds that a single, non-proprietary suite of protocols is required to achieve information mobility. To ensure that all computers within an enterprise can communicate with each other (regardless of their manufacture), there has to be exactly *one* protocol suite. The protocol suite has to be *open* so that no one vendor could have an unfair competitive advantage in the market.

In practice however, the market dictates that there are two non-proprietary protocol suites used for computer-communications: the Internet suite of protocols, and the OSI suite of protocols.

Although they started development at roughly the same time (the late-'70s), unlike OSI, the Internet suite of protocols has seen extensive deployment — throughout the world across the entire spectrum of user organizations. This is particularly interesting since only the OSI suite has received broad international support and governmental mandate. In contrast, the Internet suite has simply proceeded to dominate the market, based solely on its availability and the simple fact that it works! Because of this, many often refer to OSI as the future *de jure* standard for open systems, whilst the Internet suite is called today's *de facto* standard for open systems.

In this chapter, we consider both protocol suites in just enough detail to provide a background for the remainder of discussion in *The Little Black Book*. If you've read either *The Open Book* or *The Simple Book*, then you've probably seen a lot of this text before, and may wish to skip ahead to Chapter 3 on page 51. For the benefit of readers "coming in cold," the remainder of this chapter has been subtly focused on areas of particular interest to *The Little Black Book*.

2.1 The OSI Suite

In the '80s, Open Systems Interconnection (OSI) was perhaps the most ambitious undertaking in computer-communications. OSI is sponsored by the *International Organization for Standardization/ International Electrotechnical Committee* (ISO/IEC Joint Technical Committee 1) in joint activity with the *International Telephone and Telegraph Consultative Committee* (CCITT). The reference model for Open Systems Interconnection, was developed in the late '70s. Since then, the international and national standards arena has seen intense work in developing the OSI protocol suite.

It is impossible to consider a full treatment of OSI here. Indeed, *The Open Book* touched only on the core aspects and ran nearly 700 pages. For our purposes, we are interested in the application services which OSI offers. In order to understand these however, it is necessary to cover, what for many is old ground, and re-acquaint the reader with several facets of OSI: the OSI model, the OSI view of services, interfaces, and protocols, and the seven layers of OSI. Following this, we'll slow down to spend some time looking at the application-layer portion of OSI. In particular, we'll focus on the notation used to communicate data structures, along with the structure of OSI application-entities, since these two concepts permeate OSI Message Handling and Directory services.

Most of the material which follows is condensed from *The Open Book*. The author apologies for retreading this area, but feels it necessary to level the field for those readers who are not overly familiar with OSI.

2.1.1 Models, Conventions, and Notation

A model is simply a way of organizing knowledge to explain the way things work.

In OSI, a *Reference Model* is used to describe computer-communications. The Model is inherently abstract. It does not specify:

- programming language bindings,

- operating system bindings,

- application interface issues, or

- user interface issues.

The Model is intended solely to describe the external behavior of systems, independent of their internal constructions. From a communications standpoint, OSI says what goes on the wire and when, but not how computers are built to exhibit the mandated behavior.

OSI standards are grouped into pairs: one defines the *service* offered by some entity, and the other specifies the *protocol* used by that entity to offer that service. This is a well understood concept of abstraction. It allows individual entities to be constructed with little knowledge of other entities. There are two advantages to an architecture that localizes knowledge:

- undesirable interactions caused by side-effects are avoided, because the external behavior of an entity is well defined; and

- the internal construction of an entity may vary without affecting other entities — providing the former maintains its same external behavior.

The discussion now proceeds to consider how OSI services are described.

2.1.2   Services

An ISO/IEC technical report, [1], defines the conventions used when describing OSI services.

A *service* represents a set of functions offered to a user (typically a computer system) by a provider. As shown here in Figure 2.1, the service is made available through *service access points* (SAPs). From the user perspective, all of the qualities of the service are completely defined by the interface at the SAP. Thus, the provider may be viewed entirely as an abstract entity.

This particular example shows a two-user service. Although this is by far the most common kind of service in OSI, there are other possible services. For example, a multicast service involves multiple receivers of data sent by one user.

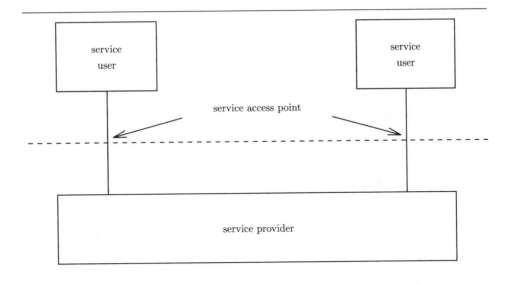

Figure 2.1: Service Users and Provider

It is not hard to imagine that the service provider itself might be composed of smaller entities, which in turn use the service immediately below as shown in Figure 2.2. In addition to introducing a new underlying service provider, this figure also explains how two entities combine to offer a new service: they use the services from below and they communicate using a protocol.

This is the fundamental concept known as *layering*: a relatively simple service may be augmented to offer more powerful services at the layer immediately above. This process may continue indefinitely, until the desired level of abstraction and power is reached.

In OSI, layers are numbered from the bottom up.

The term "layer-(N)" is used to refer to a generic layer. Similarly, "layer-(N-1)" refers to the layer immediately below, and "layer-(N+1)" refers to the layer immediately above.

Thus, the (N)-service provider consists of two (N)-service entities. These are also (N-1)-service users.

Each service offered by a provider can be characterized in terms of a *time sequence diagram*. In the diagram, a service consists of one or more *primitives* which are invoked by either the user or provider. In OSI, time sequence diagrams are used to denote the relationship

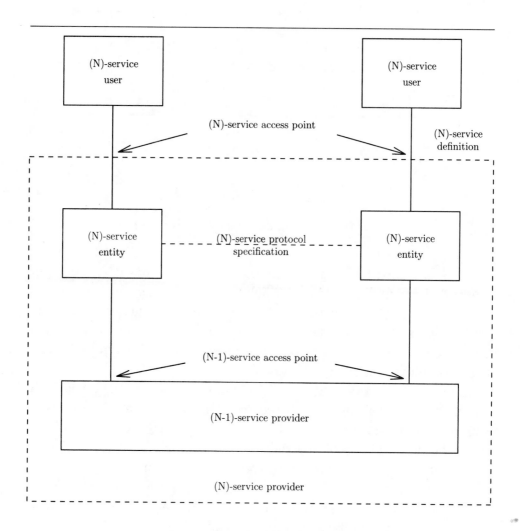

Figure 2.2: Service Layering

between the primitives which form a service and the order in which they occur.

In a confirmed service, for example, the .REQUEST primitive is used by the requesting user to initiate the service. This is ultimately delivered to the accepting user as an .INDICATION primitive, which in turn issues a .RESPONSE primitive, which is finally returned to the requesting user as a .CONFIRMATION:

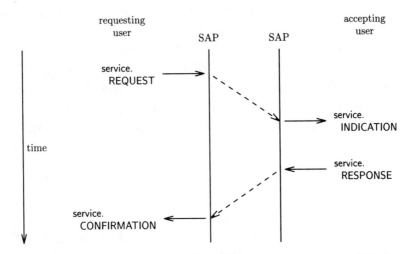

In contrast, an *unconfirmed* service involves no handshake:

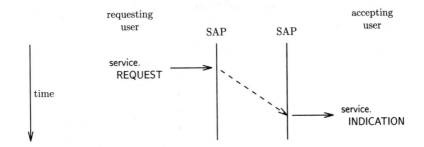

2.1.3   Interfaces

Next, the discussion considers the OSI formalism used to describe the interaction occurring when a service primitive causes information to pass from one layer to the next.

Suppose a service provider is asked to transfer some data to the remote service user. This user-data is termed a *service data unit*

(SDU). The service provider attaches a small header to the user-data, termed the *protocol control information* (PCI). The PCI identifies the data that is to be transferred.

The resulting object is termed a *protocol data unit* (PDU).

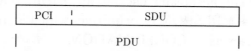

This is the unit of information that is exchanged by peers, implementing a protocol to offer a service.

Next, it is necessary to invoke the (N-1)-service provider to cause the data to be transmitted. To do this, *interface control information* (ICI) is (conceptually) attached to the PDU. The ICI identifies the service primitive that is to be invoked from the (N-1)-service.

The resulting object is termed an *interface data unit* (IDU).

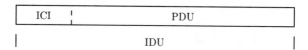

The (N)-service provider passes the IDU through the (N-1)-SAP. The (N-1)-service provider receives the IDU and breaks it apart into the ICI and an (N-1)-SDU. It then invokes the desired primitive based on the ICI. Note that from the perspective of the (N-1)-service provider, an (N)-PDU is precisely an (N-1)-SDU. All of these relationships are summarized here:

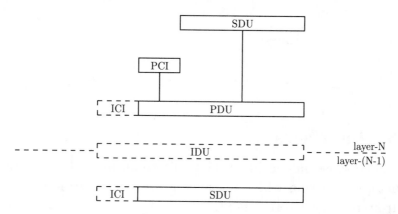

Once the data is transferred, the remote (N-1)-service provider generates an ICI and combines it with the received SDU to form an

IDU, and then passes IDU up to the remote (N)-service provider. This
is broken into the ICI and PDU, which in turn is broken into the PCI
and SDU. Finally, the SDU is delivered to the (N)-service user.

Of course, this is an excruciatingly abstract way to describe how a
user and provider interact through service boundaries. The distinction
between protocol control information and user-data in a PDU is a well-
known technique called *encapsulation*. This allows user-data to be
transparently transmitted. More familiar terms from other protocol
suites might be:

$$
\begin{array}{lcl}
\text{SDU} & = & \text{data} \\
\text{PCI} & = & \text{header} \\
\text{PDU} & = & \text{packet}
\end{array}
$$

The introductions of ICI and IDU are used simply to make the
notion of the SAP work; they are formalisms that permit a service
provider to offer multiple services and still have a single point of interaction. Indeed, many people do not particularly care for the notion of
an IDU. They prefer to think of the interface information as existing
in parallel with the data unit, but not attached. That is, they prefer
to keep the control and data aspects of the model separated.

It must be stressed that these service conventions are not intended
to have any impact on implementations. For example, the IDU mechanism for layer communication is essentially a message passing scheme.
Each message (the IDU) carries with it typing information (the ICI)
and data (the PDU).

It is important to understand that OSI, per se, never specifies the
notion of programmatic conformance to a service. That is, a designer
always has the responsibility (and freedom) to implement a service
faithfully. OSI makes no constraints as to how that service is implemented, as long as the services offered conform to the specifications.

2.1.4 Protocols

OSI service providers are described as *finite state machines* (FSMs).
The protocol machine for a particular service starts in an initial state.
Events, which are service primitives received from the user above or
the provider below, as they occur, trigger activity on the part of the
FSM. As a part of this activity, actions may be required (service

primitives issued to the underlying provider and/or the user), and possibly a new state is entered. Eventually the SAP becomes inactive and the FSM returns to the initial state.

Thus, when examining any OSI protocol, there are three things to be discussed:

- how the underlying service is used;

- the elements of procedure for the protocol, which define the behavior of the FSM; and,

- how PDUs are encoded.

Each OSI protocol specification defines these activities. In addition, each usually contains an annex that has a state table to describe formally the FSM composing the protocol machine.

2.1.5   The 7 Layers

Finally, with the necessary notational conventions out of the way, the discussion looks at the OSI Reference Model as defined in [2]. The Model divides the task of computer communications into seven functional layers.

There is no mystique to the choice of the number seven. Other protocol architectures have numbers of similar magnitude. The reader is strongly encouraged to read [3] for an insightful discussion on why the actual number of layers is not fixed and is largely unimportant.

The first four OSI layers form the lower-layer infrastructure of the Model. These provide the end-to-end services responsible for data transfer. The remaining three OSI layers form the upper-layer infrastructure of the OSI model. These provide the application services responsible for information transfer. The relation between these is shown in Figure 2.3.

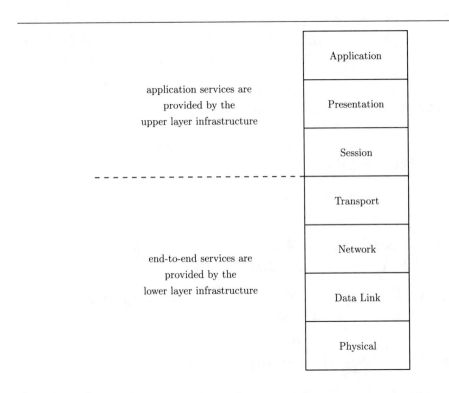

Figure 2.3: The OSI Reference Model

The discussion now considers the individual layers that compose the reference model. The descriptions will be brief.

Physical Layer (Ph): responsible for the electro-mechanical interface to the communications media.

Data Link Layer (Dl): responsible for transmission, framing, and error control over a single communications link.

Network Layer (N): responsible for data transfer across the network, independent of both the media comprising the underlying subnetworks and the topology of those subnetworks.

Transport Layer (T): responsible for reliability and multiplexing of data transfer across the network (over and above that provided by the network layer) to the level required by the application.

Session Layer (S): responsible for adding control mechanisms to the data exchange.

Presentation Layer (P): responsible for adding structure to the units of data that are exchanged.

Application Layer (A): responsible for managing the communications between applications.

2.1.6   Services Revisited

In OSI, the service offered by a layer is either *connection-oriented* or *connectionless*.

A connection-oriented mode (CO-mode) service has three distinct phases:

connection establishment: in which the service users and the service provider negotiate the way in which the service will be used. If successful, this results in a *connection* being established. Once a connection is established, this is an explicit binding between the two service users. All other service primitives occur in the context of this binding.

data transfer: in which the service users exchange data.

connection release: in which the binding between users is discarded.

In contrast, a connectionless mode (CL-mode) service has one phase: data transfer. Any and all options must be supplied for each and every primitive as there is no explicit ongoing relationship established between service users. Typically, each OSI layer provides a single CL-mode service using the verb UNITDATA. This is an unconfirmed service.

The OSI model is inherently connection-oriented. However, the first Addendum to the International Standard, [4], augments the model for connectionless-mode (CL-mode) transmission.

For historical reasons, OSI has been primarily interested only in connection-oriented services and protocols. Originally, only CO-mode versions of the services and protocols were defined. Then, the CL-mode lower-layers were defined. Finally, as of the end of 1988, CL-mode versions of the presentation, session, and transport services existed, but no OSI applications made use of them.

In contrast, both CO-mode and CL-mode versions of the data link and network service exist. The transport service may use either the CO-mode network service or the CL-mode network service in order to provide a connection-oriented transport service. Furthermore, either network service may use either data link service. The gist of this is simply stated: OSI application services are connection-oriented. The underlying end-to-end services presently offer a connection-oriented service, but may be internally composed of connectionless-mode protocols.

2.1.7 Abstract Syntax Notation One

At the application layer, the data structures exchanged by protocol entities are often quite complex. Therefore, OSI introduces a powerful, feature-rich formalism for describing these structures.

This formalism is termed an *abstract syntax*, which is used to define data without regard to machine-oriented structures and restrictions.

Presently, only one such language has been standardized, *Abstract Syntax Notation One* (ASN.1).

ASN.1 is used to describe objects at the higher layers of OSI. In the simplest case, it can be used to define the formats of the PDUs exchanged by OSI application-entities, but it can also be used to describe higher-level concepts, such as the actual composition of OSI application-entities.

Hand in glove with abstract syntax is the notion of a *transfer syntax*. Once data structures can be described in a machine-independent fashion, there must be some way of transmitting those data structures, unambiguously, over the network. This is the job of a transfer syntax notation. Obviously, a single abstract syntax could have several transfer syntax notations. But, as of this writing, only a single abstract syntax/transfer syntax pair have been defined in OSI. ASN.1 is used as the machine-independent language for data structures, and the *Basic Encoding Rules* (BER) are used as the encoding rules.

ASN.1 is a *formal* language, which means that it is defined in terms of a *grammar*. The language is defined in [5]. Some extensions to the language were more recently defined in [6]. The corresponding CCITT definitions may be found in [7]

It is clearly beyond the scope of *The Little Black Book* to present a thorough treatment of ASN.1; the reader should consult Chapter 8 of *The Open Book* for a detailed exposition of both ASN.1 and the BER. Thus, ASN.1 is presented here only as briefly as possible to give the reader a feeling for the concise expressiveness it provides.

Modules

A collection of ASN.1 descriptions, relating to a common theme (e.g., a protocol specification), is termed a *module*. The high-level syntax of a module is simple:

```
<<module>> DEFINITIONS ::= BEGIN

<<linkage>>

<<declarations>>

END
```

The `<<module>>` term names the module, both informally and possibly authoritatively (uniquely) as well. Think of the authoritative designation as allowing several modules to be placed in a library and then unambiguously referenced through the `<<linkage>>` term. Thus, modules can **EXPORT** definitions for use by other modules, which in turn **IMPORT** them. Finally, the `<<declarations>>` term contains the actual ASN.1 definitions.

Three kinds of objects are defined using ASN.1:

- *types*, which define new data structures;

- *values*, which are instances (variables) of a type; and,

- *macros*, which are used to change the actual grammar of the ASN.1 language.

Each of these objects is named using an ASN.1 word; however, ASN.1 uses an alphabetic case convention to indicate the kind of object to which the word refers:

- for a *type*, the word starts with an uppercase letter (e.g., `SearchArgument`);

- for a *value* (an instance of a type), the word starts with a lowercase letter (e.g., `rOSE`); and,

- for a *macro*, the word consists entirely of uppercase letters (e.g., `ATTRIBUTE`).

The keywords defined within the ASN.1 specification itself appear entirely in uppercase. This includes the built-in types, such as **INTEGER**.

Types and Values

An ASN.1 type is defined using a straight-forward syntax:

```
NameOfType ::=
    TYPE
```

Similarly, a value (more properly an instance of a data type) is
defined as:

```
nameOfValue NameOfType ::=
    VALUE
```

That is, first the variable is named (`nameOfValue`), then it is typed
(`NameOfType`), and then a value is assigned.

The simple types of ASN.1 include such things as integers, octet
strings, bit strings and the like. Beyond this, constructed types, which
combine simple types and previously-defined constructed types alike
can be built. Examples of this are sequences, sets, and choices. ASN.1
associates a tag with each data type, so that it can be identified
during transmission. Some types are standard throughout OSI, and
have *universal* tags. Other designations for tags include: *application-
wide*, which unambiguously identify a type within an ASN.1 module;
context-specific, which are used to resolve ambiguity in constructed
types; and, *private*, which refer to enterprise-specific types. All tags
consist of a class (universal, application-wide, context-specific, or private) and a non-negative integer. Thus, several application-wide tags
might be defined in a module, each with a different number.

In addition to using construction to define new data types, ASN.1
allows subtyping, which is used to define a new type in terms of a
refinement to an existing type. For example, subtyping can be used
to assign lower- and upper-bounds on the values that an integer might
take, or to "cap" the length of a string of octets, and so on.

Interesting enough, for the purposes *The Little Black Book*, the
most important ASN.1 type is the `OBJECT IDENTIFIER`. An `OBJECT
IDENTIFIER` is a data type denoting an authoritatively named object.
`OBJECT IDENTIFIER`s provide a means for identifying a particular object, regardless of the semantics associated with that object (e.g., a
standards document, an ASN.1 module, and so on).

An `OBJECT IDENTIFIER` is a sequence of non-negative integer values that traverse a tree. The tree consists of a *root* connected to a number of labeled *nodes* via edges. Each label consists of a non-negative
integer value and possibly a brief textual description. Each node may,
in turn, have children nodes of its own, termed *subordinates*, which
are also labeled. This process may continue to an arbitrary level of

depth. Central to the notion of the `OBJECT IDENTIFIER` is the understanding that administrative control of the assignment and meanings of the nodes may be delegated as one traverses the tree.

When describing an `OBJECT IDENTIFIER` there are several formats that may be used. The most concise textual format is to list the integer values found by traversing the tree, starting at the root and proceeding to the object in question. The integer values are separated with one or more space characters, and the whole thing enclosed between "{" and "}". Thus,

```
{ 1 0 8571 5 1 }
```

identifies the object found by starting at the root, moving down the tree to the subordinate node with label 1, then moving further down the tree to the subordinate node with label 0, and so on. The node found after traversing this list is the one being identified.

The root node has three subordinates:

- `ccitt(0)`, which is administrated by the International Telegraph and Telephone Consultative Committee (CCITT);

- `iso(1)`, which is administered by the International Organization for Standardization and International Electrotechnical Committee (ISO/IEC); and,

- `joint-iso-ccitt(2)`, which is jointly administered by ISO/IEC and CCITT.

Thus, at the first cut, the naming tree looks like this:

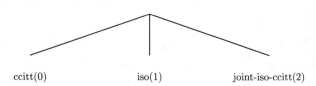

ccitt(0)   iso(1)   joint-iso-ccitt(2)

and, the administrative authority for each node is free to assign further subordinate nodes and optionally to delegate authority to others to name objects under those nodes.

The CCITT has defined four subordinates:

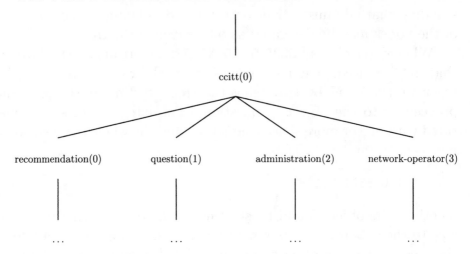

These are:

- **recommendation(0)**, which has 26 subordinate nodes, labeled **a** through **z**. Each subordinate corresponds to a series of CCITT recommendations. The committee responsible for a series of CCITT recommendations, such as the "X" series, is delegated responsibility for naming objects. Thus, 0.0.24 is the prefix used by the committee responsible for the "X" series.

- **question(1)**, which is assigned to particular Study Groups in the CCITT. Each CCITT Study Period occurs over four years. During each period, these groups meet to resolve "questions" of interest to the CCITT, such as defining OSI protocols. An **OBJECT IDENTIFIER** has been delegated for the use of each Study Group for each Study Period. The first Study Period in which objects were assigned was in 1984–1988. This is the *epoch* Study Period, taking value 0. The next Study Period is 1988–1992 which takes value 1, and so on. To calculate the **OBJECT IDENTIFIER** used by a particular Study Group at a given time, take the number assigned to the Study Period, multiply it by 32, and then add the number of the Study Group in question. Call this number **n**. The resulting **OBJECT IDENTIFIER** is 0.1.n. As a result of this "encoding," it should be clear that there can be no more than 32 Study Groups (numbered 0 to 31) operating during any given Study Period. If this were not the case, then duplication would occur since two different organizations would be authorized to assign objects under this prefix!

- **administration(2)**, which is assigned to the PTTs for each country. The value of the label assigned to each node is a *decimal country code* (DCC).

- **network-operator(3)**, which is assigned to the organizations running X.121 networks. The value of the label assigned to each node is a *Data Network Identification Code* (DNIC). In turn, each organization might further delegate their own subordinate nodes to customers.

The ISO/IEC has defined four subordinates:

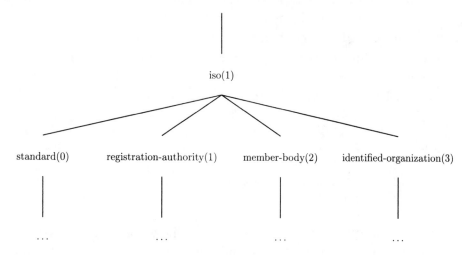

These are:

- **standard(0)**, which has a subordinate assigned to each International Standard. For example, the OSI file service, FTAM, is International Standard 8571. Thus, when FTAM defines objects, these start with the prefix `1.0.8571`. Each standard is then responsible for the naming hierarchy used under its assigned prefix.

- **registration-authority(1)**, which is reserved for use by OSI registration authorities, as they are created.

- `member-body(2)`, which has a subordinate assigned to each member body of ISO/IEC. The value of the label assigned to each node is a *decimal country code* (DCC). Each member body is then responsible for further organization of its respective naming space.

- `identified-organization(3)`, which has a subordinate assigned to any organization that ISO/IEC wishes to favor. This permits a way for any organization to name objects (even proprietary objects) without fear of collisions in the naming hierarchy.

Finally, joint committees of ISO/IEC and CCITT delegate naming authority under the `joint-iso-ccitt(2)` tree. This is particularly important in the area of initial standards development. For example, the standard **OBJECT IDENTIFIER**s for use with the Directory are allocated under this branch as the Directory standard was jointly developed. In order to coordinate matters, the American National Standards Institute (ANSI) is responsible for delegating authority under the `joint-iso-ccitt(2)` tree.

The **OBJECT IDENTIFIER** syntax is straight-forward:

```
Document-Type-Name ::=
    OBJECT IDENTIFIER

fTAM-1 Document-Type-Name ::=
    { 1 0 8571 5 1 }
```

In this example, the value declaration shows only the numeric values of the nodes. The textual values may also be used, providing that those strings are unambiguous:

```
fTAM-1 Document-Type-Name ::=
    { iso standard 8571 5 1 }
```

(An unambiguous string is one that uniquely names an immediate sibling of a node.) In order to promote readability, but not risk ambiguity, these two forms can be combined, as in

```
fTAM-1 Document-Type-Name ::=
    { iso(1) standard(0) 8571 5 1 }
```

or

```
ucl OBJECT IDENTIFIER ::= { ccitt data(9) pss(2342) 19200300 }
quipu OBJECT IDENTIFIER ::= { ucl 99 }
```

2.1.8   The Upper-Layer Infrastructure

The OSI upper-layer infrastructure is rich with functionality. It is hoped that this richness will allow applications designers and programmers to develop powerful applications for users of OSI networks. In particular, both OSI Message Handling and Directory services make extensive use of the upper-layer infrastructure, and in particular, the services of the OSI application layer.

In brief, the basic concepts of the upper-layer infrastructure are:

- the OSI transport service provides full-duplex circuits, offering a service similar to that of the eminently popular Transmission Control Protocol (TCP);

- the OSI session service builds on top of transport circuits by adding mechanisms that allow the user to *control* the dialogues between applications that are specific to a particular application task, e.g., if the application was message handling, then a dialogue might refer to sending a mail message, and the session service would provide mechanisms to restart a message transfer that had been previously interrupted; and,

- the OSI presentation service builds on top of session dialogues by adding mechanisms that allow the layer above to define the *structure* of data exchanged between applications, e.g., the body parts contained in a mail message.

2.1.9   The Application Layer Structure

The OSI application layer builds on the services provided by the upper-layer infrastructure.

Application Contexts

To begin, even after the layers beneath the application layer have built
a progressively higher-level of service, there are still services required
by OSI applications which are common to many of them. As a result,
the OSI application layer is divided into *application service elements*,
each with a particular function. To define an application protocol, one
combines different service elements and decides the rules for the ways
in which these elements interact with themselves and the underlying
OSI services (as seen through the presentation service). For example,
all connection-oriented applications establish an association with a
peer. The Association Control Service Element (ACSE) is responsible
for this task. Hence:

- all OSI applications must contain the ACSE in order to perform
  association establishment and release.

- all OSI applications contain definitions stating how the ACSE
  will be used (e.g., which other service elements might invoke the
  services of the ACSE); and,

- only the ACSE is allowed to invoke the connection establishment
  and release services of the presentation layer below.

The combination of all service elements that comprise the application,
along with the relationship between those service elements and the
underlying OSI services forms an *application context.*

It should be noted that in addition to making application protocols more tractable, the use of application service elements promote
reuse of application layer facilities. As with the OSI upper-layer infrastructure as a whole, from an implementation viewpoint this effect
can provide substantive leverage.

Application Entities

In an OSI environment, *application processes* are "things" which execute in the network environment and provide (presumably) useful
service to end-users. The OSI communications aspects of these processes are termed *application entities*. Hence, an application entity

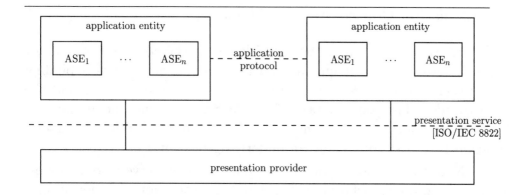

Figure 2.4: **The Structure of an OSI Application Entity**

is a "thing" composed of one or more *application service elements* (ASEs) which provide the particular application protocol defined by the application context.

Conceptually, we might view these relationships as shown in Figure 2.4. Note that each of the peer application entities is composed of precisely the same ASEs. Further, each ASE talks only with its peer in the remote application entity. To make sure that the application protocol data units are always delivered to the correct ASE peer, each ASE defines an *abstract syntax* to be used over the association. When data from an abstract syntax is given to the presentation layer, the data is marked with the appropriate presentation context so as to ensure correct delivery on the remote system.

There are several application service elements that may be part of an application context. Although several have been progressed or are being progressed through the standards process, only three are of interest to us here:

- association control;

- remote operations; and,

- reliable transfer.

Let's now take a look at these three service elements in a little more detail. As these are examined, other issues relating to the OSI application layer structure will be introduced.

Association Control Service Element

The Association Control Service Element (ACSE) is responsible for
association establishment and release. An association is a binding
between two entities, which are referred to as the *initiator* and the
responder. The primary task of the ACSE is to bind one application
entity to another across a network. This binding results in an association that is supported by an underlying presentation connection.

Note that although binding implies a client/server model for establishing the association, this needn't have the same relationship for
the services provided. It is perfectly reasonable for an initiator to bind
to a responder for the purpose of letting the responder request actions
to be performed by the initiator. This provider/consumer model is
contrary to the familiar client/server model in which the client connects to the server, and then the client proceeds to request actions to
be performed by the server.

The binding process is really two-step: first, the initiator determines which service it requires, and asks to have this service mapped
onto the application entities running in the network; second, based
on the initiator's communications requirements, an association will
be bound to one of those entities that becomes the responder.

The first mapping is actually two steps: first, the application must
derive the *application entity title* corresponding to the desired service;
and, second, this title must be mapped into a presentation address.
The first step is performed according to local mechanisms, whilst the
mapping in the second step is performed by the OSI Directory. For
our purposes, it is this mapping, in which the OSI Directory acts as
a "nameservice," which is of interest. The application provides the
application entity title of the desired service, which is registered in
the OSI Directory as an information object. A Directory read operation is performed to retrieve the `presentationAddress` attribute
of the object in question. In simplest terms, the OSI Directory acts
as rendezvous point for the initiator and responder. When a service
is to be offered in the network, the application which provides that
service registers itself and its address in the OSI Directory. Later on,
when another process wishes to use that service, the OSI Directory
is consulted to retrieve the appropriate addressing information. (As

might be expected, the application uses local knowledge to ascertain the address of the local Directory service — otherwise a bootstrap problem exists!)

The second mapping is performed by the initiator's transport provider, and is not germane to the discussion at hand. However, it is instructive to consider the causality of events which occur in between the time an application decides to establish an association and the initiator's transport provider is invoked. (Readers who are already familiar with this chain of events should skip ahead to page 39.)

Suppose that the application entity contains two ASEs: the ACSE and a generic FTAM ASE (FTAM is the OSI file service). When an association to the file service is to be established, the FTAM ASE generates a data object to initialize the remote FTAM ASE. This object is termed an **F-INITIALIZE-request** FPDU (file protocol data unit), and is defined in the abstract syntax for the FTAM protocol. The FTAM ASE then invokes the association establishment service of the ACSE, passing along this data. Thus, the FTAM ASE must signal both its own abstract syntax, along with an abstract syntax for the ACSE, to the presentation service. Since each file in FTAM is defined in terms of a document type which contains structuring definitions, the FTAM ASE might also request a presentation context for each document type that it wishes to exchange over the duration of the association. In this example, there are three document types specified.

The FPDU generated looks something like that shown Figure 2.5. (This is, of course, a conceptualization — real implementations of OSI will use compact binary encodings for these data structures! Throughout *The Little Black Book*, we'll use an extended form of ASN.1's value notation to represent data values. For example, **OBJECT IDENTIFIER**s are represented in a dot-notation because it makes them easier to read and write.)

Upon receiving the connection establishment request, the local ACSE generates a data object to initialize the remote ACSE. This object is termed an **AARQ** APDU (application protocol data unit), and, as you might expect, the APDU is passed as user-data when the ACSE invokes the connection establishment service of the presentation layer. From the perspective of the ACSE, which does not need to understand

```
{
   service-class {
      management-class, transfer-class,
      transfer-and-management-class
   },
   functional-units {
      read, write, limited-file-management,
      enhanced-file-management, grouping
   },
   attribute-groups { storage },
   ftam-quality-of-service no-recovery,
   contents-type-list {
      1.0.8571.5.3,    -- FTAM-3 document
      1.0.8571.5.1,    -- FTAM-1 document
      1.3.9999.1.5.9   -- NBS-9 document
   },
   initiator-identity "cheetah"
}
```

Figure 2.5: Example FTAM File Protocol Data Unit

the data types defined in the FTAM abstract syntax, the APDU looks
something like that shown in Figure 2.6.

Upon receiving the connection establishment request, the local
presentation entity generates a data object to initialize the remote
presentation entity. This object is termed a **CP-type** PPDU (presentation protocol data unit). Here, we see the use of the presentation
contexts: presentation context identifier 1 is used for the FTAM PCI,
contexts 3, 5, and 7 are used for the abstract syntaxes for the three
document types, and context 9 is used for the ACSE PCI.[1]

The presentation service serializes the PPDU, and passes the result, a string of 193 octets, as user-data when the presentation entity invokes the connection establishment service of the session layer.
From the perspective of the presentation service, the PPDU looks
something like that shown in Figure 2.7 on page 38.

Finally, upon receiving the connection establishment request, the

---

[1]Why the odd numbers? When establishing presentation contexts, odd values
are proposed by the initiator of a presentation connection, and even values are
proposed by the responder.

```
{
    application-context-name 1.0.8571.1.1,    -- iso ftam
    user-information {
        {
            indirect-reference 1,                 -- indicates FTAM PCI
            encoding {
                single-ASN1-type {
                    [3] '0370'H,
                    [4] '053700'H,
                    [5] '0580'H,
                    [6] '00'H,
                    [7] {
                        [APPLICATION 14] '28c27b0503'H,
                        [APPLICATION 14] '28c27b0501'H,
                        [APPLICATION 14] '2bce0f010509'H
                    },
                    [APPLICATION 22] "cheetah"
                }
            }
        }
    }
}
```

Figure 2.6: Example ACSE Application Protocol Data Unit

```
{
   mode {
      normal-mode
   },
   normal-mode {
      context-list {
         {                    -- ftam pci abstract syntax
            identifier 1,
            abstract-syntax 1.0.8571.2.1,
            transfer-syntax-list { 2.1.1 }
         },
         {                    -- FTAM-3 abstract syntax
            identifier 3,
            abstract-syntax 1.0.8571.2.4,
            transfer-syntax-list { 2.1.1 }
         },
         {                    -- FTAM-1 abstract syntax
            identifier 5,
            abstract-syntax 1.0.8571.2.3,
            transfer-syntax-list { 2.1.1 }
         },
         {                    -- NBS-9 abstract syntax
            identifier 7,
            abstract-syntax 1.3.9999.1.2.2,
            transfer-syntax-list { 2.1.1 }
         },
         {                    -- acse pci abstract syntax
            identifier 9,
            abstract-syntax 2.2.1.0.1,
            transfer-syntax-list { 2.1.1 }
         }
      },
      user-data {
         complex {
            {
               identifier 9,                 -- indicates ACSE PCI
               presentation-data-values {
                  single-ASN1-type {
                     [1] { 1.0.8571.1.1 },
                     [30] {
                        {
                           indirect-reference 1,
                           encoding {
                              single-ASN1-type {
                                 [3] '0370'H,
                                 [4] '053700'H,
                                 [5] '0580'H,
                                 [6] '00'H,
                                 [7] {
                                    [APPLICATION 14] '28c27b0503'H,
                                    [APPLICATION 14] '28c27b0501'H,
                                    [APPLICATION 14] '2bce0f010509'H
                                 },
                                 [APPLICATION 22] "cheetah"
} } } } } } } } } } }
```

Figure 2.7: Example Presentation Protocol Data Unit

local session entity generates a data object to initialize the remote session entity, and establishes a transport connection. If the transport connection is established, the data object is sent to the remote entity.

Reliable Transfer Service Element

The Reliable Transfer Service Element (RTSE) is responsible for bulk-mode transfers. Although the functionality of the session service provides for explicit checkpointing and connection recovery, many applications, whilst desiring the service (or a portion thereof), may find it daunting to manipulate these services directly. The RTSE is intended to hide the complexity of the session and presentation services to provide a simple transfer facility.

The RTSE itself can be used by other service elements. For example, in Message Handling Systems, the Remote Operations Service Element often uses RTSE, as the information exchanged may contain large electronic mail messages. Further, RTSE can use other service elements, such as ACSE. The idea is that RTSE provides an additional level of abstraction in which the rich functionality of the underlying services are provided without requiring knowledge of how to use them in detail.

Thus, an application might be configured as shown in Figure 2.8. In this example, the application context contains four service elements:

- ACSE, to manage associations;

- ROSE, to manage request/reply interactions;

- RTSE, to provide for bulk-data transfer; and,

- a *user-element*, which is responsible for orchestrating the application entity's actions.

This has two implications:

- the user-element uses RTSE services to manage the association, which, in turn, use ACSE services; and,

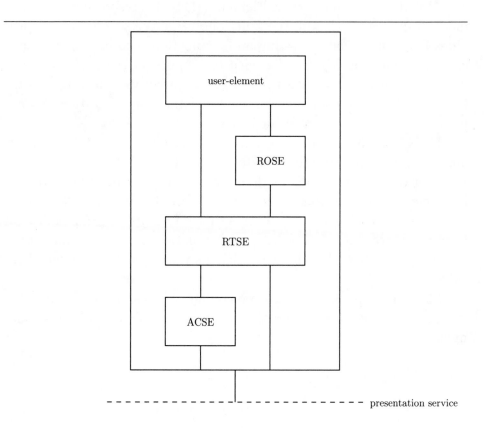

Figure 2.8: Application Entity containing the RTSE

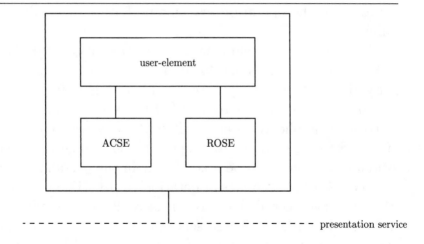

Figure 2.9: Application Entity not containing the RTSE

- ROSE uses RTSE services to transfer data which, in turn, use the presentation service.

In contrast, an alternative configuration might be like that shown in Figure 2.9 in which:

- the user-element uses ACSE services directly for association management; and,

- ROSE uses the presentation service for data transfer.

This is the configuration used by the OSI Directory.

Note that the same configuration must be present in both the application entities using an association. It is not possible for communication to occur if one AE contains an active RTSE and the other does not.

Remote Operations Service Element

The Remote Operations Service Element (ROSE) is responsible for request/reply *interactions*. An operation is *invoked* by an application process. In response, its peer returns one of three outcomes: a *result*, if the operation succeeded; an *error*, if the operation failed; or, a *rejection*, if the operation was not performed (e.g., due to network failure).

A surprising large number of applications use ROSE. For example, ROSE is used by message handling systems, directory services, and network management. The reason for this is that ROSE can easily support a *remote procedure call* (RPC) facility, which is what many distributed applications are built on. Many feel that the generality of ROSE and its ability to support a wide range of loosely coupled systems may very well be a key factor in the overall success of OSI.

Because of the "service orientation" of ROSE, a special set of conventions have been defined to concisely describe application services which utilize ROSE. These services are accessed through *ports*, in which a consumer makes use of a service offered by a provider.

It should be noted that the current OSI method for providing remote operations is based on a connection-oriented (CO-mode) model, whilst currently deployed non-OSI systems have successfully demonstrated the usefulness of a connectionless (CL-mode) approach. Fortunately, work on the CL-mode OSI upper-layers has been completed. Unfortunately, as of this writing, work on CL-mode support for the ROSE is stalled for, of all things, lack of interest!

For Further Reading

Each of the commonly used service elements are defined in two parts: a service definition and a protocol specification. ISO and CCITT have produced parallel sets of standards, which are technically aligned, and contain only small, audience-specific, variations. The ISO numbers are:

ASE	service	protocol
ACSE	8649	8650
RTSE	9066-1	9066-2
ROSE	9072-1	9072-2

and the CCITT numbers are:

ASE	service	protocol
ACSE	X.217	X.227
RTSE	X.218	X.228
ROSE	X.219	X.229

For information on application service elements specific to a particular application, consult the standards which define that application. For example, the OSI Directory defines two other application service elements (along with the corresponding application contexts). These are defined in the OSI Directory standard.

For general information on the OSI application layer structure, see [20]. Unfortunately, this document is unreadable, or at least not-understandable. Fortunately, its contents bear little, if any, relationship to standardized OSI applications. To make matters worse, in an "extensions" amendment to this standard [21], an entirely new direction is taken, of an even more obscure nature. A telling realization, noted by one expert, can be found by intersecting the ALS and the extended-ALS and then comparing the results with the description of the application layer in the OSI model: in brief, there are very few additions to the original description, other than a nonsensical discussion on "universal discourses" and "conceptual schemas." It is beyond the scope of *The Little Black Book* to speculate why the standards community is able to standardize applications but is unable to standardize the model used for describing applications. However, it is within the scope of a soapbox to observe that the construction, deconstruction, and reconstruction of the OSI ALS has likely cost the international economy several millions of dollars in travel, accommodations and many fine lunches and dinners.

That completes our whirlwind tour of OSI. Now, onto the de facto technology for Open Systems, the Internet suite of protocols.

soap...

...soap

2.2 The Internet Suite

The Internet suite of protocols grew out of early research into surviv-able multi-media packet networking sponsored by the US Defense Advanced Research Projects Agency (DARPA). In the beginning, there was only one network, called the ARPANET, which connected a few dozen computer systems around the country. With the advent of different networking technologies, such as Ethernet, Packet Radio, and Satellite, a method was needed for reliable transmission of information over media that do not guarantee reliable, error free delivery. (Information transmitted using these technologies can be lost or corrupted as the result, e.g., of radio propagation or packet collision.) Thus, the Internet suite of protocols was born.

Although, the Internet suite might be thought of as the property of the US military, this is an entirely pedantic view. The protocol suite is administered not by the US military, but by researchers sponsored by many areas of the US government. All computer users, regardless of nationality or profession, have benefited tremendously from the Internet suite.

The best term to use when describing the Internet suite of protocols is *focused*. There was a problem to solve, that of allowing a collection of heterogeneous computers and networks to communicate. Solving the internetworking communications gap required a good deal of cutting edge research. The Internet researchers made open systems a reality by limiting the problem, gauging the technology, and, by and large, making a set of well thought out engineering decisions. In the discussion that follows, the term *Internet Community* refers to all parties, world-wide, that use the Internet suite of protocols, regardless of whether they are connected. The largest internet in existence is termed the Internet (note the capital-I). Of course, one can be a member of the Internet community without actually having Internet connectivity, by virtue of using the Internet suite of protocols.

The Internet suite of protocols is, in the author's opinion, much more tractable than its OSI counterpart. Even so, it would be foolhardy to consider a full treatment of the Internet suite here. Instead, we begin with a brief introduction, condensed from *The Simple Book*. Following this, we'll focus on the application-layer portion of the Internet suite of protocols. In particular, we'll focus on the client-server model, and the presentation mechanisms used by many of the Internet application protocols.

2.2.1 Architectural Model

Like the OSI suite of protocols, there is an architectural model for the Internet suite of protocols, defined in [22]. For our purposes, it is useful to view the Internet suite of protocols as having four layers:

- the *interface* layer, which describes physical and data-link technologies used to realize transmission at the hardware (media) level;

- the *internet* layer, which describes the internetworking technologies used to realize the internetworking abstraction;

- the *transport* layer, which describes the end-to-end technologies used to realize reliable communications between hosts; and,

- the *application* layer, which describes the technologies used to provide end-user services.

It should be noted that other descriptions of the Internet suite of protocols use similar (or slightly different) terminology to describe the architecture. The author feels that this organization strikes a useful balance between historical perspective (from the original Internet research) and "modern" terminology (from the OSI Reference Model).

2.2.2 Services and Protocols

The current generation of protocols is *primarily* based on:

- a connection-oriented transport service, provided by the Transmission Control Protocol (TCP); and,

- a connectionless-mode network service, provided by the Internet Protocol (IP).

The major emphasis of the Internet suite is on the connection of diverse network technologies. To this day, excellent research continues on these issues.

There are several application protocols available for production use in the Internet suite:

- the Simple Mail Transfer Protocol (SMTP) [23,24], which provides store-and-forward service for textual electronic mail messages, and RFC822 [25], which defines the format of those messages;

- the File Transfer Protocol (FTP) [26], which provides file transfer services;

- TELNET [27], which provides virtual terminal services;

- the Domain Name System (DNS) [28], which primarily provides mappings between host names and network addresses; and,

- the Simple Network Management Protocol (SNMP) [29], which provides network management services.

The relationship between the application protocols and the end-to-end services is shown in Figure 2.10. This figure, which emphasizes simplicity over detail, also shows a protocol called the User Datagram Protocol (UDP), which is a connectionless-mode transport protocol that is little more than a simple pass-through to IP, and a protocol called the Internet Control Message Protocol (ICMP) which is used to report on the "health" of the internet layer.

2.2.3   The Application Layer Structure

Most of the applications in the Internet suite are based on a client-server model. In brief: a server process listens on a well-known TCP or UDP port,[2] and then performs actions based on the requests of a client process.

---

[2]A "port" is roughly analogous to OSI's concept of a *service access point* for the transport layer.

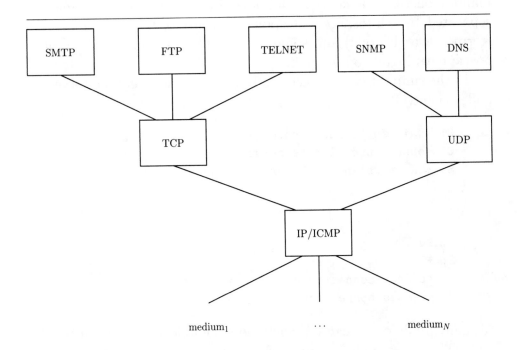

Figure 2.10: Brief Overview of Internet Protocols

In the case of most connection-oriented applications, once a TCP
connection is established, the server sends an initialization response
and then awaits commands. When the service is to be released, the
client sends a termination message, awaits a response, and then closes
the TCP connection.

Usually, both the commands and the responses are textual, terminated by a carriage-return/line-feed pair. This repertoire is termed
the NVT ASCII character set (defined in Pages 10–11 of [27]). Commands consist of a keyword followed by zero or more arguments,
separated by whitespace. Responses consist of a success-indicator
(termed a reply-code) and some textual information, usually a diagnostic meaningful to a human.

In the simplest case, consider a brief interaction between server(S)
and a client(C):

```
S: <wait for connection on TCP port 109>
C: <open connection to server>
S: +OK wp.psi.net POP server ready


...


C: QUIT
S: +OK
C: <closes connection>
S: <closes connection>
```

Actually, reply codes can be much more complicated. In both SMTP
and FTP, for example, a reply code is a three digit number indicating
not only the level of success or failure, but also operation-specific
information.

If the argument to a command is multi-line (such as the body of
the message), then a data-stuffing algorithm is used, e.g.,

```
S: <wait for connection on TCP port 25>
C: <open connection to server>
S: 220 wp.psi.net SMTP ready
C: MAIL FROM:<mrose@cheetah.ca.psi.com>
S: 250 sender ok
C: RCPT TO:<ole@interop.com>
```

```
S: 250 address ok
C: DATA
S: 354 Enter mail, end with "." on a line by itself
C: <<sends message>>
C: .
S: 250 message sent
C: QUIT
S: 221 wp.psi.net closing connection
C: <closes connection>
S: <closes connection>
```

The data-stuffing algorithm is simple: since the message is expressed in NVT ASCII, the message is sent line-by-line. If the beginning of a line begins with a period ('.'), then the client inserts a dot before sending the line. Whenever the server receives a line beginning with a dot, it strips it. If there are characters there besides the CR-LF pair, then the line is appended to the message buffer. Otherwise, the server knows that it has received the last line of the message.

Of course, this strategy works only if the object being transmitted is inherently ASCII. This works fine for Internet mail, which is used to exchange text-based, memo-oriented messages. But, for FTP, which is required to exchange arbitrary files in addition to textual ones, this is a problem. For that reason (and to support third-party transfers), FTP uses a second TCP connection solely for transmitting data.

Of course, if these Internet applications used a self-delimiting transfer syntax, then all of this would be unnecessary. However, in fairness to the Internet suite, it should be noted that the majority of these applications were designed, developed, implemented, and fielded long before OSI began serious work on abstract and transfer syntaxes. Further, in spite of not having the benefit of ASN.1 and the BER, the Internet applications are relatively straight-forward to implement (certainly in comparison to their OSI counterparts). And, as of this writing, unlike their OSI counterparts, the Internet applications are widespread, delivering useful service to a world-wide community.

Chapter 3

Introduction to the Directory

The need for directory services in networks has long existed. As noted earlier in Chapter 1, addresses form a fundamental component of the infrastructure in a network, and users — be they people or programs — need to take names and map them into corresponding addresses. This is the need which mandates a directory capability. Typically, this need has been solved by techniques that are specific to a given application or limited class of applications. Of course,

> any problem can be solved if you make the problem small enough.

As a result, many technologies have been successfully fielded for specific problems. Indeed, this is not intended as a criticism of these working systems, quite the reverse:

> projects with focus tend towards success, and those without focus tend towards failure.

Thus, focus is often the greatest virtue in any undertaking.

For the remainder of *The Little Black Book*, we focus on one particular technology used to provide directory services for computer-based systems. That technology is the OSI Directory, commonly referred to as X.500, or simply *The Directory*. What distinguishes The Directory from its worthy predecessors, is that it is intended as a global solution

for most (if not all) computer-communications systems which require
directory services.

soap...   This of course leads to an obligatory soapbox! As with all of
OSI, the OSI Directory strives for generality, regardless of the conse-
quences. When fully deployed, the Directory is meant to provide for
the distribution and retrieval of information about any and all real-
world objects of interest. The unfortunate part of such a philosophy is
that large problem domains rarely have solutions which are universally
good (a corollary of the "focus principle" above). In fact, it is not even
clear how well understood the current systems are, all of which have a
much narrower focus! The author believes that a working Directory is
a necessary condition for OSI to grow beyond the pilot stage. But the
author also suspects that the world would be better served by a more
focused approach. Throughout *The Little Black Book* we shall see how
generality is a curse, not a blessing. It introduces complexity and un-
certainty, and degrades performance. Further, given the historically
minimalist attitude taken by many implementors of standards-based
computer-communications software, it's not clear how many of the
...soap   "bells and whistles" will ever see substantive use.

Although the Internet suite of protocols is the de facto open systems technology, *The Little Black Book* examines only the OSI approach towards directory services. The reason for this is that there
is no truly corresponding technology in the Internet suite of protocols. The closest technology is the *Domain Name System* (DNS) [28],
which, in its present usage, is primarily used to provide mappings
between hosts and network addresses. This is a critical task, and the
DNS performs quite well in this capability.

A second task, also heavily used, is to provide *mail exchange* (MX)
mappings. An MX-record designates a mail-relay for a site or host.
This obviates the need for mail-routing tables, along with ad hoc
(and error-prone) mechanisms for updating them. The disadvantage
is that most routes are naturally relative to the source, and, if there
are multiple MX-records, there is no way to indicating which route is
optimal for a given sending site. However, this is the sole relationship
of the DNS to electronic mail (there are other mail-related records,
but they are infrequently used).

In order to retain some level of focus, the discussion opts to omit any further discussion of the DNS and to concentrate on the much more ambitious (perhaps ambitious to the point of folly) OSI approach.

However, no discussion of the DNS, however terse, is complete without a commentary on the state of software implementation for computer-communications.

> soap...

The success of DNS is somewhat amazing given the apparently poor state of some implementations of it. In particular, consider the *Berkeley Internet Name Domain server* (BIND) implementation of the DNS, which is a part of the Berkeley Standard Distribution (BSD) variant of the UNIX operating system. In the Internet, BSD UNIX is the most common platform, and the DNS is one of the most used applications. As a consequence, one might reasonably expect that the BIND implementation is well-written software. Given the numerous problems with DNS operations in the Internet since the introduction of BIND, this is most likely not the case. Indeed, one Internet wag has noted that BIND is really an abbreviation for *Bind Is Not Done*. Maintenance of BIND has become so problematic that there are now several variant versions, each incorporating a unique set of fixes and enhancements (and each having its own set of bugs).

It is difficult to assign blame in this regard. Parts of BIND were originally written in parallel by three separate graduate projects at U.C. Berkeley. For reasons shrouded in obscurity, these were then pieced together and an early version was placed into immediate production use with little, if any, maintenance support available. As might be expected, problems abounded, and only piecemeal solutions were applied on a case-by-case basis. This practice has continued for close to a decade, during which time many sites have developed their own variants of the software.

The most disturbing aspect of this situation are the actions taken by many vendors with BIND. Since BSD UNIX is the basis for many vendor platforms, BIND is usually shipped in one of its many incarnations, with its own set of particular bugs. Here is the true disadvantage of the reference implementation: because BSD UNIX is heavily used as the reference implementation of the TCP/IP suite of protocols, the DNS implementation is also heavily used — despite numerous problems with the implementation. The disturbing part is that some vendors, as evidenced by their "shrink-wrap-and-ship-it" attitude towards BIND, seem unwilling or unable to ship a solid DNS product.

In fairness to BIND, it continues in the tradition of *Sendmail*, the Internet message transfer agent, which is a part of BSD UNIX. As with BIND, Sendmail provides a cautionary tale as to how a reference implementation can be cursed with bad code: in addition to having a long history of bugs, security holes, and the like, Sendmail is amazingly difficult to configure. In many ways, Sendmail set the stage for BIND, by establishing the precedent of piecemeal solutions, multiple versions, and general lack of reliability. Further, the famous Internet "worm" incident of 1989, illustrated the "shrink-wrap-and-ship-it" attitude of many vendors, who were caught distributing versions of Sendmail with a gaping security hole.

It is not clear to the author which, either Sendmail or BIND, is the lesser of the two evils. What is clear is that computer-communications software, as evidenced by the lack of solid, high-quality implementations, is in a despicable state. What a joy it would be to change the name associated with the BIND abbreviation to *Bind Is Now (finally) Done*. Sadly, the author does not believe this joyful event will occur within his lifetime (particularly because he enjoys unhealthful foods and does not exercise very much).

| ...soap |

The discussion now considers the four models which comprise the OSI Directory Service.

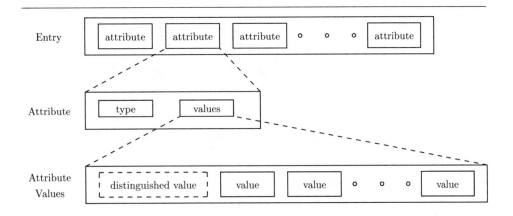

Figure 3.1: An Entry in the DIB

3.1 Information Model

The Directory manages *information objects*, which contain information about "interesting" objects in the "real-world."

These objects are modeled as *entries* in an information base, termed the *Directory Information Base* (DIB).

3.1.1 Entries

As shown in Figure 3.1, an entry consists of one or more *attributes*. An attribute consists of a *type*, and at least one *value*. Some of these values are termed *distinguished* attribute values, since they contribute towards the object's name in the DIB. (This will be more fully explained a little later on in Section 3.1.3 on page 57).

The attribute's type defines the characteristics of the attribute. In addition to explaining the meaning of the attribute in the real-world (the semantics, e.g., a telephone number), the type also defines:

- the syntax of the attribute (i.e., the corresponding ASN.1 data type);

- comparison characteristics (e.g., whether two attribute values can be compared for equality, or substring matching); and,

- if more than one attribute value is allowed.

In the Directory, there is a concise notation to capture these relationships. This is described in Section 4.1 starting on page 76.

3.1.2 Schema

One attribute of an entry, its `objectClass`, determines what kind of object this entry corresponds to (e.g., a person). The value of this attribute implies what types of attributes the entry *must* and *may* contain. For example, if the value of `objectClass` indicates that the entry corresponds to a person, then it would make sense for that entry to have a `surName` attribute. On the other hand, if the value of `objectClass` indicates that the entry corresponds to an organization, then a `surName` attribute would be inappropriate.

Object definition is based on the notion of *class inheritance*. This means that an object class can be defined as a "subclass" of a previously defined object class with additional refinements. As a subclass, the newly defined object "inherits" all the semantics of its superclass, along with its additional semantics. Thus, if `residentialPerson` is a subclass of `person`, then an instance of the `residentialPerson` object class has all the properties of a `person` object with some things which are particular to those people identified by their residence (such as a home address).

The `objectClass` attribute is multi-valued. This permits an entry to inherit the properties of many classes. The only hard-wired requirement in the Directory is that all objects must belong to the `top` class, which, not surprisingly, mandates an `objectClass` attribute for the object.

The OSI Directory is extensible in that it defines several common types of objects and attributes, and allows the definition of new objects and attributes. This extensibility will become an important factor as new OSI applications are developed that make use of the Directory.

3.1.3 Structuring

Entries are named using a hierarchical structure termed the *Directory Information Tree* (DIT). It is this structure which is used to uniquely name entries.

The name of an entry is termed its *Distinguished Name* (DN). It is formed by taking the DN of the parent's entry (which is considered empty if the parent is the root of the DIT), and adding the *Relative Distinguished Name* (RDN) of the entry. Each entry has one or more attribute values which are termed "distinguished." The unordered collection of values for these distinguished attributes forms the entry's RDN, which must distinguish an entry from all of its siblings.

So, given the rules above, a DN for an entry is built by tracing a path from the root of the DIT to that entry. Along the way, the RDNs are collected, each naming an arc in the path. There is said to be no entry at the root, so the root is unnamed and does not contribute an RDN.

Looking at the simple DIT shown in Figure 3.2, the name of the leftmost leaf would be:

```
countryName is "US"
organizationName is "PSI"
organizationalUnitName is "Operations"
commonName is "Manager"
```

Of course, this figure shows only a very simple example. The actual DIT is under multiple administrations and each is likely to apply different structuring policies to its portion of the DIT. Naming is discussed in much greater detail in Section 4.4 starting on page 122.

Finally, some entries in the DIT are called *aliases*. An alias entry contains a pointer to another entry (i.e., it has an attribute with a single-value containing the DN of another entry). Aliases provide a convenient mechanism to add additional alternate names to the DIT.

As might be imagined, the Directory is only useful if there is a single DIT. Unfortunately, the generality of the structuring rules for the DIT introduce several administrative difficulties. This is discussed in greater detail in Section 4.4 starting on page 122.

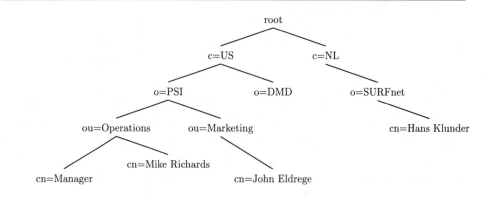

Figure 3.2: A Simple DIT

3.1.4   Naming and User-Friendliness

The Directory is intended to provide *user-friendly naming*. This permits a user of the Directory (not necessarily a person) to specify an object's name and retrieve additional addressing information. For the purposes of *The Little Black Book*, the discussion will focus on name to address mapping for use with electronic mail.

The idea of user-friendly naming is simple: both people and programs are very good at remembering "shorthand" information about things that they're interested in. The goal of the Directory is to take that specification and provide the detailed information actually required for correct operation of the system. Considering the complexity of such things as electronic mail addresses under OSI, the Directory is a truly essential part of a workable OSI mail system.

An important aspect of the naming architecture used by the Directory is to achieve user-friendliness. The "official" rationale is interesting.

Simply put, names should be deducible by people using incomplete information. In cases where the information available does not uniquely identify an object's entry, then additional information is required to provide uniqueness.

For example, if two objects have the same surname, then something else besides a surname must be provided to distinguish between the two objects, e.g., a first name.

Further, the Directory should not require that one or both of the objects have their surname modified in order to prevent such ambiguities.

In order to make effective use of this architecture, names should be chosen to exploit, rather than hide, the inherent ambiguity of the names used in the real-world. The Directory is designed to allow a user to provide incomplete information and then refine the search based on the matches that occur. When searching, different spellings, orderings, and so on should be appropriately matched (this is termed *approximate matching*).

Finally, aliases may be used to provide further direction. In short, the domain of search and deduction is purposely much larger than the range of entries to which those searches ultimately map.

Later on, in Section 4.4.4, the relationship between naming and user-friendliness will be re-examined, with some controversial results! The reader is urged not to skip directly to this section, but rather read all of Section 4.4 starting on page 122 to gain a full appreciation for the problems which lead to the position taken.

3.2   Functional Model

A *directory user* is a person or application process that accesses the Directory. This access is achieved through a *Directory User Agent* (DUA). The DUA communicates with the Directory on behalf of the user, so that a 1:1 relationship exists between the two. The internal composition of the Directory is completely invisible to the user. As the discussion will detail, very little of the internal composition need be known to the DUA.

The *functional model* of the Directory describes the interactions inside the Directory. The DIB is composed of DIB fragments, which are held by *Directory System Agents* (DSAs). These DSAs cooperate to provide the Directory Service.

To access the Directory, the directory user agent communicates with one or more DSAs.

In the simplest case, the DUA establishes an association to the DSA, asks for information, and the DSA responds with that information. This is a simple request/reply interaction:

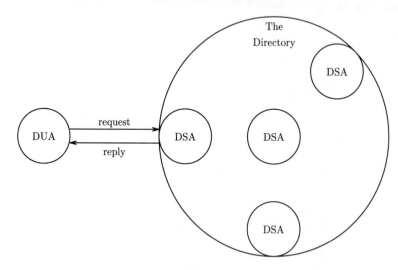

However, information in the Directory is distributed, and it is entirely possible that the DSA doesn't have the information needed to answer the request. In this case, the DSA must be able to identify another DSA which is somehow "closer" to the information.

The original DSA might return a *referral* to the DUA:

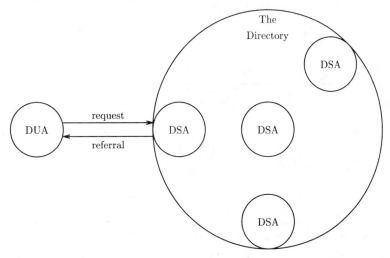

The referral contains the name and address of another DSA that either has the desired information or is closer to the information. The DUA then establishes an association to the second DSA, and the usual request/reply interaction occurs:

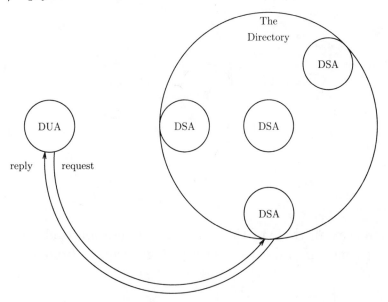

Alternatively, if the original DSA doesn't have the information, it might contact the second DSA directly. This is called *chaining*:

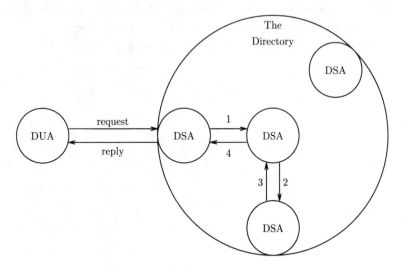

Of course, the original DSA might have to contact several DSAs to find the desired information. This may be done in parallel using a technique known as multicasting. The original DSA establishes an association to multiple DSAs and asks the same question of each:

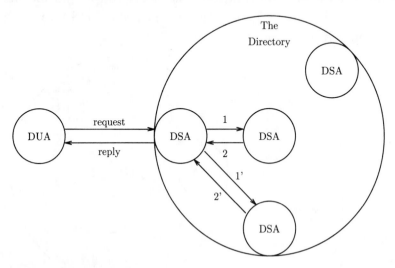

Note that all three of these modes of operation could be used, at different times, in order to answer a single request from a DUA.

There are two very complex problems that have to be solved in order for a distributed Directory to operate correctly:

- a DSA needs to know if it has all of the information needed to perform the operation resident; and,

- if not, a DSA must identify DSAs which are "closer" to the information, then decide if chaining or referral is the best way of proceeding.

These issues will be looked at in greater detail in Sections 6.1 and 6.3.6.

It is important to understand, however, that the Directory is not intended to be a general purpose database. In particular, it has three simplifying assumptions:

- queries (reads from the Directory) will be much more frequent than updates (writes to the Directory);

- transient conditions, in which the information in the Directory is not entirely consistent, may be commonplace; and,

- a hierarchical, rather than relational, architecture is used for naming.

In other words, the Directory does not purport to offer a fully distributed, fully reliable, and fully consistent database. Rather, it provides mechanisms for manipulation of information that is distributed. This is an important distinction.

Readers familiar with the long history of excellent research in distributed databases might wonder if this kind of technology could be appropriate as the underpinnings for the Directory. After all, recent work in distributed databases have led to important advances in the rapid access of arbitrary structures in a distributed environment. Of course, distributed database technology would be a perfect candidate for this application. However, for both historical and political reasons, the OSI Directory is not based on distributed database technology: the Directory has weak consistency properties and uses a relatively simplistic model of distributed operations.

soap...

It is far beyond the scope of *The Little Black Book* to debate the merits of this approach or its divergence from database technology, rather, this difference is merely noted.

...soap

Of course, the Directory must eventually correct transient inconsistencies, so that they are not long-lived. Nevertheless, it cannot guarantee consistency at any given instant.

If we ignore transient conditions, an important aspect of the Directory is that the answers it returns are independent of either the identity or the location of the application entity that is asking the questions: if the same question is asked by two different entities, then any answers returned should be the same. (Of course, access control might prevent an answer from being given.)

3.3 Organizational Model

The *organizational model* of the Directory describes the service in terms of the policy defining interactions between entities and the information they hold. That is, this model describes how portions of the Directory tree map onto the DSAs. This includes issues of replication (shadowing and caching) and access control. A *Directory Management Domain* (DMD) defines a portion of the Directory Tree and how it is managed.

A DMD consists of:

- one or more DSAs, which collectively hold a portion of the DIT on behalf of that administration;

- zero or more DUAs; and,

- a definition of the external behavior of the DMD, stating how the multiple DSAs in a DMD might be viewed from outside the DMD.

DMDs are further sub-divided into two categories:

- *administrative DMDs* (ADDMDs), which are run by a public service provider; and,

- *private DMDs* (PRDMDs), which are run by organizations not offering public services.

The architecture of the Directory might lead one to believe that this distinction is necessary. In fact, this division is used solely for political reasons. (The CCITT, a joint-author of the Directory standard, by some strange coincidence, is composed of PTTs.) Fortunately, the Directory standard does not really make use of the distinction between ADDMDs and PRDMDs.[1] Thus, one can use the term Directory Management Domain without a technical loss of generality.

---

[1] The distinction is relevant in the context of the International Telecommunications Union (ITU). ADDMDs are subject to the ITU's multi-lateral treaties, whilst PRDMDs are not.

soap...

Historically this artificial distinction has proven burdensome with OSI Message Handling (X.400), in which there are *administrative management domains* (ADMDs), which are operated by a PTT authority, and *private management domains* (PRMDs), which aren't. In theory, a given PRMD is subordinate to a particular ADMD. In practice, this works only when there is a single ADMD within a country. In countries with multiple PTTs, there are multiple ADMDs, and larger organizations with their own PRMDs often find it attractive to subscribe to several ADMDs. As such, the one-to-one mapping of PRMDs to ADMDs is lost, causing many problems when trying to route mail. In contrast, in countries with a single ADMD, this component is entirely superfluous, since knowledge of the country yields knowledge of the ADMD. Hence, the distinction between PTT-operated and non-PTT-operated management domains is unnatural.

...soap

3.4 Security Model

The *security model* of the Directory describes the service in terms of authentication and authorization.

An *authentication* policy is used to identify both DSAs and users of the Directory. The purpose of such a policy is to define the mechanisms by which an application entity is identified to the system. In the Directory, there are three kinds of authentication: *none, simple,* and *strong.* Simple authentication is based on password protection. When an entity wishes to be authenticated as acting on behalf of a particular entry in the Directory, it supplies a password, optionally protected by applying a one-way hashing function. This value is then compared to the `userPassword` attribute of the appropriate entry. (Obviously, the value of this attribute should not be readable from the Directory!) Strong authentication is based on public key encryption.

In all cases, whether simple (clear or protected) or strong authentication, the DSA may need to chain to another DSA in order to determine the validity of the binding requested by DUA. However, due to esoteric reasons of protocol, there are some limitations to the usefulness and security of the system if chaining is involved in order to perform authentication.

An *authorization* policy specifies, enforces, and maintains access rights. One way of doing this might be with an attribute defining an *access control list* describing the actions that a particular application entity may perform on a given object. However, no such attribute is defined as a part of the Directory.

The Directory standard does not actually define a security policy. This is considered a local matter. However, the standard does give guidelines on how access rights for the Directory might be specified.

3.5   Directory Standards

The base series of International standards on the Directory is defined
in [30]. These are technically aligned with the corresponding 1988
CCITT recommendations [31]. The differences between the International standard definition and the CCITT definition are quite small,
and, to the knowledge of the author and several others, there are no
technical differences between the two documents.

As of this writing, work continues towards the 1992 agreements on
the OSI Directory. However, stability cannot be assured until the end
of that year. Therefore, the *The Little Black Book* will purposefully
focus only on the 1988 work. If, for clarity's sake, a concept from the
ongoing work is introduced, then this will be clearly noted.

3.6 Implementation Focus

The Little Black Book will draw heavily on experiences gained with a particular implementation of the Directory and a White Pages service.

Although the 1988 work was an impressive undertaking, it is noticeably incomplete in several areas. For example, the Directory standard is silent on critical issues such as replication (shadowing and caching) and access control. These are things which must be considered when offering a real service. The implementation described here contains refinements to the 1988 work to address these issues. It must be emphasized that these refinements are in the spirit of the Directory standard, and a system which implements these refinements will interwork, albeit with less functionality, with conformant X.500 implementations that do not implement these refinements. Of course, in the discussion which follows, we must be careful to delineate where the Directory standard ends and a refinement begins.

Observant readers might ask why the Directory was made a stan- | soap... |
dard, when it was incomplete in so many ways. The answer lies in the four-year work cycle (termed a *Study Period*) of the CCITT, which jointly created the Directory standard. About two-years into the Study Period, it became clear that consensus could not be reached on all the issues. So, the remaining issues were placed into three categories: "must solve," "might solve," and "won't solve." Issues in the first category were finalized prior to the end of the Study Period, as were some of the issues in the second category. The remainder of the issues were left for examination after the Study Period. The criterion for categorization was whether the issue had to be solved in order to provide for interrogation of a read-only Directory. If the issue was critical to this, it was placed in the first category; otherwise, it was placed in one of the other two categories. And here, we find one of the greatest curses of generality: the incomplete system syndrome. Had the group which produced the Directory standard focused itself on a smaller problem, they could have solved it in four years. As a consequence, the Directory standard would already be widely implemented and in solid use today! Instead, because of the incompleteness, many are hesitant to implement any of it, not wishing to invest resources in development which may subsequently have to be changed. This

amazing turn of events has relegated OSI implementation to more of
a "research project" than a production undertaking.

...soap

The Directory implementation considered in *The Little Black Book*
is called QUIPU, and was developed at University College London.
QUIPU was originally developed as a part of the INCA (Integrated
Network Architecture) project under the auspices of the ESPRIT ini-
tiative of the EEC. The Inca of Peru did not have writing as a part
of their culture. Instead, they stored information on strings, carefully
knotted in a specific manner with colored thread, and attached to a
larger rope. Such a device was known as a *Quipu* (pronounced *kwip-
ooo*). The encoding was obscure, and could only be read by selected
trained people: the *Quipucamayocs*. The Quipu was a key component of Inca society, as it contained information about property and
locations throughout the extensive Inca empire.

QUIPU is a complete implementation of the OSI Directory, based
on the international work finalized in 1988. QUIPU has seen extensive pilot usage throughout North America, Europe, and the Pacific
Rim. Throughout *The Little Black Book*, QUIPU release 6.8 is described. As of this writing, this is the latest stable version of QUIPU
available. QUIPU release 6.8 is available as a part of the ISODE 6.8
Interim distribution, which was released on 11 March, 1991. Extensive documentation for QUIPU is part of the ISODE release. The
documentation is also available in book form, [32], which, in addition
to containing a manual on QUIPU, also contains a manual on a powerful X.400 system (Postie Pat), along with some introductory notes
by Stephen E. Kille of University College London, who is the principal
designer of both systems.

Of course, study of an implementation is greatly enhanced if it is
presented in a usage context. For our purposes, the discussion draws
on the PSI White Pages Pilot Project, an effort to provide a White
Pages service in the Internet, based on X.500 technology.

To implement a White Pages service using the OSI Directory, three
things are needed:

- an OSI infrastructure, this is provided by ISODE (discussed in
  some detail in Appendix C starting on page 337);

- an implementation of the OSI Directory, this is provided by QUIPU (discussed throughout the remaining chapters of *The Little Black Book*); and,

- a White Pages abstraction, provided by an administrative discipline (discussed throughout Section 5.1 starting on page 142), along with at least one user-interface through which the service is accessed (discussed in Section 5.4 starting on page 215).

It is important to distinguish between the White Pages *service* and the OSI Directory *technology* as defined in the international agreements. The White Pages abstraction is provided both by a focused use of the underlying OSI Directory technology (the administrative discipline) and by special user interfaces.

3.6.1   Writing Distinguished Names

The Directory standard defines how DNs are exchanged between OSI systems. This is done using an ASN.1 definition (shown later on page 90). Therefore, OSI systems can unambiguously transmit DNs across the network. Although the textual notation used to write DNs should be unimportant, for expository (and local) purposes it is important to have a concise notation.[2]

This leads us to our first refinement: namely the textual notations used for user type-in and when a DN is presented to the administrator or user. In QUIPU, a Distinguished Name is written as a left-to-right ordered series of RDNs separated by an '@'-sign with the most significant RDN appearing at the left; e.g.,

    c=FI@o=Microkonsultit Oy

refers to an entry with an RDN of

    organizationName is "Microkonsultit Oy"

whose parent is immediately below the root and has an RDN of

    countryName is "FI"

---

[2]Indeed, see [33] for an example of an amazingly good argument on naming, based on what some say is a total lack of understanding of the DNS.

The string to the left of the equals sign refers to the attribute type of the corresponding distinguished attribute value. QUIPU maintains a table mapping the `OBJECT IDENTIFIER` values used to denote an attribute type, and one or two strings. For example, the `commonName` attribute is officially known as the `OBJECT IDENTIFIER` value

> `2.5.4.3`

The mapping table for QUIPU tells it to accept type-in of either "`commonName`" or "`cn`" or even "`2.5.4.3`" to refer to this attribute type. (Because this particular attribute is typed so often, it is given an abbreviation.) If QUIPU comes across an attribute type not in its table, it simply prints the OID in dot notation.

Looking ahead, Table 4.1 on page 80 lists some of the official attribute types from the Directory standard, along with any abbreviations allowed by QUIPU, and the syntax associated with each attribute's value. Table 5.1 on page 143 lists the same information for additional attributes used in the PSI White Pages Pilot Project.

To avoid any potential ambiguity, one usually prefixes an '`@`'-sign to a string when referring to a fully qualified Distinguished Name; e.g.,

> `@c=GB@o=University College London`

always refers to the same entry regardless of context. This allows some user-interfaces to support the notion of a "current position" in the DIT. Users may then shorten their type-in by specifying partial DNs, e.g., if the current position is

> `@c=GB`

then specifying

> `o=University College London`

refers to an entry under `c=GB`, whilst specifying

> `..@c=IT`

refers to some entry under the root (the `..` tells the user-interface to move up a level in the DIT).

If an RDN consists of multiple attribute values, then these are separated by a '`%`'-sign; e.g.,

```
@l=North America@o=Anterior Technology%l=US
```

Thus far, we have considered only attributes whose values are printable strings. Using the QUIPU textual notation for writing DNs, a distinguished attribute value which uses the T.61 repertoire is written as:

```
@c=FI@o=FUNET@cn={T.61}Juha Hein\c4anen
```

The characters "\c4a" are used to represent the two-octet T.61 sequence denoting the character ä.

To date, these two conventions cover virtually all distinguished attribute values encountered. However, as the last resort, the raw BER encoding can be used. This is usually the case when the attribute type is not recognized (not present in the local mapping tables used by QUIPU), and the syntax can not be determined. e.g.,

```
@c=FI@o=FUNET@1.2.246.258.1.1.1={ASN}13065069726b6b6100
```

Chapter 4

Accessing the Directory

Discussion now turns to how the Directory is accessed. First, consideration is given to the informational infrastructure provided by the Directory. Following this, the service abstraction and protocol used to manipulate information objects are explored. Finally, the problematic area of naming is presented. These discussions will illustrate a central theme of this part of *The Little Black Book*, namely that the Directory offers a rich service, but without focus it is difficult to build useful systems with the technology.

4.1   Information Infrastructure

In the previous chapter it was observed that the Directory standard
uses concise notation to relate the characteristics of an attribute. In
fact, the Directory standard goes much further, it uses a concise notation to describe object classes, attributes, and sets of attributes.

It is instructive to consider this notation, as it captures much of
the "flavor" of the information infrastructure in the Directory. The
concise notation is based on the ASN.1 macro facility. It would be
foolhardy to attempt a complete explanation of this facility (see Chapter 8 of *The Open Book* for a substantive treatment). Instead, we'll
use some representative examples.

4.1.1   Object Class

An *object class* is defined using the **OBJECT-CLASS** macro, e.g.,

```
country OBJECT-CLASS
    SUBCLASS OF top
    MUST CONTAIN { countryName }
    MAY CONTAIN  { description,
                    searchGuide }
    ::= { objectClass 2 }
```

which defines an object class called `country`, with these properties:

- objects of this class inherit the properties of the object class
  called `top`;

- an entry corresponding to an object of this class must contain
  an attribute value of type `countryName`; and,

- an entry corresponding to an object of this class may contain attribute values of type `description` and/or of type
  `searchGuide`.

Finally, the **OBJECT IDENTIFIER** `{ objectClass 2 }` is used to authoritatively refer to this object class. This is a globally unique value.

To paraphrase, the `OBJECT-CLASS` macro defines an object class in terms of its superclasses (permitting a multiple-inheritance capability), along with the attributes which must or may be present in an instance of the object. Then object class is named using an `OBJECT IDENTIFIER`. As might be expected, the definition of the `OBJECT-CLASS` macro is much more precise. For our purposes, it is useful to note only that all three of the clauses, i.e.,

```
SUBCLASS OF
MUST CONTAIN
MAY CONTAIN
```

are optional. Further, it should be noted that object classes contain no prescriptions as to naming. Naming, or more generally, the structure of the DIT, is independent from the schema used to describe objects.

There are two special object classes in the Directory, `top`, which is the superclass of all object classes; and `alias` which contains a name pointer to another entry. The definitions of these two object classes are straight-forward:

```
top OBJECT-CLASS
    MUST CONTAIN { objectClass }
    ::= { objectClass 0 }

alias OBJECT-CLASS
    SUBCLASS OF top
    MUST CONTAIN { aliasedObjectName }
    ::= { objectClass 1 }
```

The Directory defines nearly 20 "selected" object classes, which includes `top`, `alias`, and `country`. The Directory standard purposefully makes it easy to define new object classes in order to achieve a degree of extensibility in the information infrastructure. As the discussion continues, other object classes, used in either QUIPU or the PSI White Pages Pilot Project, will be introduced. Exposition of the remainder of the "selected" object classes is postponed until Section 4.1.4 on page 82.

4.1.2   Attribute Syntaxes and Types

An *attribute syntax* is defined using the **ATTRIBUTE-SYNTAX** macro, e.g.,

```
caseIgnoreStringSyntax ATTRIBUTE-SYNTAX
    CHOICE { T61String, PrintableString }
    -- string comparisons are case-insensitive
    MATCHES FOR EQUALITY SUBSTRINGS
    ::= { attributeSyntax 4 }
```

which defines an attribute syntax with these properties:

- values are strings, taken from either the T.61 or Printable string repertoires; and,

- when matching two attribute values of this syntax, both equality and substring comparison have meaning.

Finally, the **OBJECT IDENTIFIER** { **attributeSyntax 4** } is used to authoritatively refer to this attribute syntax.

An *attribute type* is defined using the **ATTRIBUTE** macro, e.g.,

```
commonName ATTRIBUTE
    WITH ATTRIBUTE-SYNTAX
        caseIgnoreStringSyntax (SIZE (1..ub-common-name))
    ::= { attributeType 3 }
```

which defines an attribute type called **commonName**, authoritatively referred to by the **OBJECT IDENTIFIER** { **attributeType 3** }, whose values take the syntax described by **caseIgnoreStringSyntax**. Further, the length in octets of the attribute values are between 1 and some upper-bound.

Both of these macros are considerably more complicated than this example illustrates, so it's necessary to explain a bit more of each.

The **ATTRIBUTE** macro "sandwiches" two clauses between the

```
attributeName ATTRIBUTE
```

part and the

```
::= { -- object identifier assignment -- }
```

part. These are:

WITH ATTRIBUTE-SYNTAX: this contains either
the name of an attribute syntax, followed by a constraint
(e.g., the length restriction exemplified earlier), or an
ASN.1 type, possibly followed by some matching information.

SINGLE VALUE: this is an optional clause, that, if present,
indicates than an entry can contain at most one value of
this attribute type. If the clause does not appear, or if the
MULTI VALUE clause appears instead, then there is no
a priori limitations to the number of attribute values which
might be present.

The `ATTRIBUTE-SYNTAX` macro has an ASN.1 data type (possibly
with constraints) and one optional clause between the

```
syntaxName ATTRIBUTE-SYNTAX
    <<ASN.1 data type>>
```

part and the

```
::= { -- object identifier assignment -- }
```

part. This optional clause is:

MATCHES FOR: gives matching information. One or more
of these three keywords may appear:

EQUALITY: if present, then it makes sense to ask if two
values with this syntax are "equal";

SUBSTRING: if present, then it makes sense to ask if
one value with the syntax is contained within another
value of the same syntax; and,

ORDERING: if present, then it makes sense to compare
two values with this syntax and ask if one is "less than"
the other.

Attribute Name	Abbrev.	Syntax
aliasedObjectName		Distinguished Name
businessCategory		string
commonName	cn	string
countryName	c	ISO3166 code
description		string
facsimileTelephoneNumber		special
localityName	l	string
objectClass		Object Class
organizationName	o	string
organizationalUnitName	ou	string
physicalDeliveryOfficeName		string
postOfficeBox		string
postalAddress		special
postalCode		string
presentationAddress		special
registeredAddress		special
roleOccupant		Distinguished Name
seeAlso		Distinguished Name
stateOrProvinceName	st	string
streetAddress		string
surname	sn	string
telephoneNumber		special
telexNumber		special
title		string
userPassword		string

Table 4.1: Some Selected Attribute Types

The Directory standard defines over 40 "selected" attribute types, some of which are shown in Table 4.1. This table also shows the QUIPU abbreviation for the attribute type. If the **Syntax** column indicates **string**, then a variant of the case-ignore string syntax is used. If the column indicates **special**, then a special ASN.1 type is defined for the syntax.

4.1.3 Attribute Sets

It is often useful to group collections of related attributes into sets. This allows an object class definition to be more concise. An *attribute set* is defined using the **ATTRIBUTE-SET** macro, e.g.,

```
localeAttributeSet ATTRIBUTE-SET
    CONTAINS { localityName,
               stateOrProvinceName,
               streetAddress }
    ::= { attributeSet 2 }
```

which defines a set of attributes called `localeAttributeSet` containing the named attributes and authoritatively known by the OBJECT IDENTIFIER { attributeSet 2 }. The values in the CONTAINS clause may be attribute types or other attribute sets.

The Directory standard defines 4 "useful" attribute sets as part of its definition of "selected" object classes: one for organizations, one for locales, one for postal addressing, and one for telecommunications addressing.

4.1.4   Selected Object Classes

Having described how the components which make up object classes
are defined, it is now possible to discuss some of the "selected" object
classes defined in the Directory standard. Again, it must be emphasized that these object classes are only a starting point: even the early
Directory-based applications in use today make use of many more!

For our purposes, it is useful to divide the object classes into three
groups, arbitrarily termed organizational, locational, and application.
(These divisions are not part of the standard, they have been selected
to modularize the text which follows.)

Before doing so, consider the generic view of a person, as taken by
the Directory:

```
person  OBJECT-CLASS
    SUBCLASS OF top
    MUST CONTAIN { commonName,
                   surName }
    MAY CONTAIN  { description,
                   seeAlso,
                   telephoneNumber,
                   userPassword }
    ::= { objectClass 6 }
```

Organizational Object Classes

As shown in Figure 4.1, the organizational object classes are those
which describe the components of an organization. The `organization`
object class describes the organization itself, while departments within
the organization are described by the `organizationalUnit` object
class. Finally, the `organizationalPerson` and `organizationRole`
object classes describe people and roles which operate within the context of the organization.

---

organization **OBJECT–CLASS**
    SUBCLASS OF top
    MUST CONTAIN { organizationName }
    MAY CONTAIN { organizationalAttributeSet }
    ::= { objectClass 4 }

organizationalUnit **OBJECT–CLASS**
    SUBCLASS OF top
    MUST CONTAIN { organizationalUnitName }
    MAY CONTAIN { organizationalAttributeSet }   10
    ::= { objectClass 5 }

organizationalPerson **OBJECT–CLASS**
    SUBCLASS OF person
    MAY CONTAIN { localeAttributeSet,
                organizationalUnitName,
                postalAttributeSet,
                telecommunicationAttributeSet,
                title }
    ::= { objectClass 7 }   20

organizationalRole **OBJECT–CLASS**
    SUBCLASS OF top
    MUST CONTAIN { commonName }
    MAY CONTAIN { description,
                localeAttributeSet,
                organizationalUnitName,
                postalAttributeSet,
                roleOccupant,
                seeAlso,   30
                telecommunicationAttributeSet }
    ::= { objectClass 8 }

organizationalAttributeSet **ATTRIBUTE–SET**
    CONTAINS { description,
                localeAttributeSet,
                postalAttributeSet,
                telecommunicationAttributeSet,
                businessCategory,
                seeAlso,   40
                searchGuide,
                userPassword }
    ::= { attributeSet 3 }

Figure 4.1: Organizational Object Classes

Locational Object Classes

As shown in Figure 4.2 on page 85, the locality object classes are those
which loosely relate to locations. The `locality` object class describes
a locality itself, whilst the `residentialPerson` object class describes
a person in a residential context. Note that the `streetAddress` attribute type occurs in two attribute sets, and that both attribute sets
are present in the `MAY CONTAIN` clause of the `residentialPerson` object class. This does not imply that two values of the `streetAddress`
attribute type should be present — it's simply an artifact of an attribute type being useful in two contexts, a postal context and a locale
context.

locality **OBJECT–CLASS**
      SUBCLASS OF top
      MAY CONTAIN { description,
                localeAttributeSet,
                searchGuide,
                seeAlso }
      ::= { objectClass 3 }

residentialPerson **OBJECT–CLASS**
      SUBCLASS OF person   10
      MUST CONTAIN { localityName }
      MAY CONTAIN { localeAttributeSet,
                postalAttributeSet,
                telecommunicationAttributeSet,
                businessCategory }
      ::= { objectClass 10 }

telecommunicationAttributeSet **ATTRIBUTE–SET**
      CONTAINS { facsimileTelephoneNumber,
                internationalISDNNumber,   20
                telephoneNumber,
                teletexTerminalIdentifier,
                telexNumber,
                preferredDeliveryMethod,
                destinationIndicator,
                registeredAddress,
                x121Address }
      ::= { attributeSet 0 }

postalAttributeSet **ATTRIBUTE–SET**   30
      CONTAINS { physicalDeliveryOfficeName,
                postalAddress,
                postalCode,
                postOfficeBox,
                streetAddress }
      ::= { attributeSet 1 }

localeAttributeSet **ATTRIBUTE–SET**
      CONTAINS { localityName,
                stateOrProviceName,   40
                streetAddress }
      ::= { attributeSet 2 }

Figure 4.2: Locational Object Classes

Application Object Classes

As shown in Figure 4.3 on page 87, the application object classes are those which describe things used by applications. The `groupOfNames` object class describes a group of related objects. This can be used for distribution lists, committee structures, and the like. For example, the group named

> `o=Cosine@ou=Paradise@cn=Funded Partners`

might contain these four **member** attribute values:

> `c=NL@o=PTT Netherlands`
>
> `c=GB@o=X-Tel Services Ltd`
>
> `c=GB@o=University of London Computer Centre@ou=ULCC Cluster`
>
> `c=GB@o=University College London@ou=Computer Science`

Note that a **member** attribute value might actually refer to another `groupOfNames` entry in the Directory! OSI application processes and entities are described by the `applicationProcess` object class and the `applicationEntity` object class (respectively). Finally, the `dSA` object class is a refinement of an OSI application entity.

---

groupOfNames **OBJECT–CLASS**
    SUBCLASS OF top
    MUST CONTAIN { commonName,
          member }
    MAY CONTAIN { description,
          organizationName,
          organizationalUnitName,
          owner,
          seeAlso,
          businessCategory }   10
    ::= { objectClass 9 }

applicationProcess **OBJECT–CLASS**
    SUBCLASS OF top
    MUST CONTAIN { commonName }
    MAY CONTAIN { description,
          localityname,
          organizationalUnitName,
          seeAlso }   20
    ::= { objectClass 11 }

applicationEntity **OBJECT–CLASS**
    SUBCLASS OF top
    MUST CONTAIN { commonName,
          presentationAddress }
    MAY CONTAIN { description,
          localityName,
          organizationName,
          organizationalUnitName,
          seeAlso,   30
          supportedApplicationContext }
    ::= { objectClass 12 }

dSA **OBJECT–CLASS**
    SUBCLASS OF applicationEntity
    MAY CONTAIN { knowledgeInformation }
    ::= { objectClass 13 }

Figure 4.3: Application Object Classes

4.1.5   One Last Formalism for Attributes

Finally, consider one last formalism in ASN.1, which describes what an attribute looks like "inside" an entry:

```
Attribute ::=
    SEQUENCE {
        type
            AttributeType,

        value
            SET OF    -- at least one value is required
                AttributeValue
    }

AttributeType ::=
    OBJECT IDENTIFIER

AttributeValue ::=
    ANY
```

This pretty much summarizes what's been said about attributes all along: an attribute consists of a type named by an **OBJECT IDENT-IFIER** (which is given at the end of the **ATTRIBUTE** macro), and one or more values, which can be of any ASN.1 type. The **WITH ATTRIBUTE-SYNTAX** clause used when the attribute was defined describes exactly what kind of ASN.1 is used to generate the values.

4.1.6   The Directory Schema

The Directory standard has an interesting figure which summarizes all of the relationships we've seen thus far in the information infrastructure. This is shown in Figure 4.4.

4.1.7   Names

However, note that this figure doesn't say anything about how names are formed. In fact, we haven't really talked about names at all yet. It is important to appreciate that naming is outside the scope of the

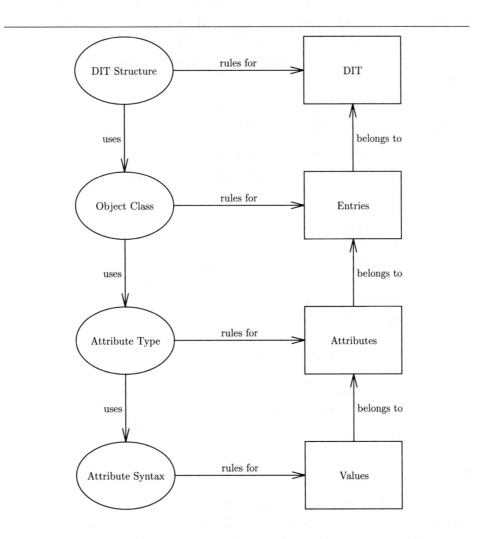

Figure 4.4: The Directory Schema

Directory schema. In fact, as we'll see later on, the Directory standard gives only guidelines, and no real rules, for how names should be assigned!

From the perspective of the information infrastructure, there are three kinds of things related to names: Relative Distinguished Names, Distinguished Names, and Alias Names. These have already been explained, so we need to introduce only a bit more formalism to complete the picture.

Relative Distinguished Names

A Relative Distinguished Name is simply the unordered collection of distinguished attribute values contained in an entry. Using the formalism of ASN.1:

```
RelativeDistinguishedName ::=
    SET OF
        AttributeValueAssertion

AttributeValueAssertion ::=
    SEQUENCE {
        type
            AttributeType,

        value
            AttributeValue
    }
```

Names

Because the Directory is intended to eventually support several naming paradigms, a Directory Name is actually a CHOICE. At present, there is but a single alternative, a Distinguished Name, though others might appear in the future.[1] A DN is simply the ordered collection of RDNs found by tracing a path from the root to the entry in question. Using the formalism of ASN.1:

---

[1] One staggers at the thought of the potential for mischief that could be wrought in a future version of the Directory standard.

```
Name ::=
    CHOICE {
        RDNSequence

        -- may be others in the future let's hope not!
    }

DistinguishedName ::=
    RDNSequence

RDNSequence ::=
    SEQUENCE OF
        RelativeDistinguishedName
```

Note how the ASN.1 **SEQUENCE** type is used to denote ordering of RDNs within a DN, whilst the **SET** type is used to denote a lack of ordering amongst the components within an RDN.

Alias Names

Finally, an Alias Name refers to a DN in which one of the component RDNs belongs to an alias entry. During name resolution, the value of the `aliasedObjectName` attribute is followed and the traversal "cuts over" to a new path. As a consequence of this, it is easiest to think of all alias entries as being leaf entries. For example, suppose an entry with name

```
c=AT@o=Widget Inc.@ou=Marketing
```

is an alias containing an `aliasedObjectName` of

```
c=AT@o=Widget Inc.@ou=Sales
```

If a Directory read operation referred to

```
c=AT@o=Widget Inc.@ou=Marketing
```

then it would return information about either the alias or the target, depending on the service controls associated with the operation.

But, if a Directory read operation referred to

```
c=AT@o=Widget Inc.@ou=Marketing@cn=Manager
```

then it would always indicate that it is returning information about

```
c=AT@o=Widget Inc.@ou=Sales@cn=Manager
```

Hence, because the Directory service always "normalizes" names below alias entries, alias entries always appear as leaves.

4.1.8   Implementation Focus

As with the entire ISODE, QUIPU is coded in the C programming language[34] and runs on the UNIX operating system. Hence, when reading the sections on implementation, it will be helpful to be familiar with the basics of C and the UNIX operating system.

Throughout the sections on implementation, the reader should keep in mind that an *implementation* of the Directory is being discussed. The data structures and access mechanisms are part of the implementation, they are most certainly *not* part of the Directory definition.

Attribute Types and Object Classes

In QUIPU, there are three tables which are used to keep track of attribute types and object classes. These tables are initialized from text files in a system area.

A fragment of the first table, *oidtable.gen*, is shown in Figure 4.5. This table keeps track of generic OBJECT IDENTIFIERs, to allow for shorter type-in, either by the user or in other files. The definitions are recursive, so that a textual string ultimately resolves into an OBJECT IDENTIFIER. For example, the string "quipu" will resolve into

```
0.9.2342.19200300.99
```

As might be imagined, when QUIPU wishes to display an OBJECT IDENTIFIER to the user, it finds the longest match possible, in order to display as much text — and as few numbers — as possible.

```
ccitt:                          0
iso:                            1
joint:                          2

# ccitt branch
data:                           ccitt.9
pss:                            data.2342
ucl:                            pss.19200300

quipu:                          ucl.99
thorn:                          ucl.100

# iso branch
memberBody:                     iso.2

ansi:                           memberBody.840
psi:                            ansi.113552

# joint branch
ds:                             joint.5
mhs:                            joint.6

nadf:                           mhs.6.5.2

# categories of information object
module:                         ds.1
serviceEnvironment:             ds.2
applicationContext:             ds.3
attributeType:                  ds.4
attributeSyntax:                ds.5
standardObjectClass:            ds.6
attributeSet:                   ds.7
algorithm:                      ds.8
abstractSyntax:                 ds.9

X500DAP:                        2.5.3.1
X500DSP:                        2.5.3.2
```

Figure 4.5: Partial Listing of QUIPU's Generic OID File

```
objectClass:                      attributeType.0    :ObjectClass
aliasedObjectName:                attributeType.1    :DN
knowledgeInformation:             attributeType.2    :CaseIgnoreString
commonName,cn:                    attributeType.3    :CaseIgnoreString
surname,sn:                       attributeType.4    :CaseIgnoreString
serialNumber:                     attributeType.5    :PrintableString
countryName,c:                    attributeType.6    :CountryString
localityName,l:                   attributeType.7    :CaseIgnoreString
stateOrProvinceName,st:           attributeType.8    :CaseIgnoreString
streetAddress:                    attributeType.9    :CaseIgnoreString
organizationName,o:               attributeType.10   :CaseIgnoreString
organizationalUnitName,ou:        attributeType.11   :CaseIgnoreString
title:                            attributeType.12   :CaseIgnoreString
description:                      attributeType.13   :CaseIgnoreString
searchGuide:                      attributeType.14   :Guide
businessCategory:                 attributeType.15   :CaseIgnoreString
postalAddress:                    attributeType.16   :PostalAddress
postalCode:                       attributeType.17   :CaseIgnoreString
postOfficeBox:                    attributeType.18   :CaseIgnoreString
physicalDeliveryOfficeName:       attributeType.19   :CaseIgnoreString
telephoneNumber:                  attributeType.20   :TelephoneNumber
telexNumber:                      attributeType.21   :TelexNumber
```

Figure 4.6: Partial Listing of QUIPU's Attribute Type File

The second table, a fragment of which is shown in Figure 4.6, keeps track of all the attribute types known to QUIPU. Each entry consists of at least three columns: the textual name of the attribute type (along with an optional textual abbreviation), the OBJECT IDENT-IFIER assignment for the attribute type, and, the attribute syntax associated with the type. A fourth, optional, column is used to indicate special options (e.g., storage options for an attribute). These attribute syntaxes are compiled into QUIPU, in a manner described momentarily. It should be noted that this file does not capture the notion of single-valuedness for an attribute type. In QUIPU, DUA implementations are expected to behave accordingly.

Finally, Figure 4.7 on page 96 shows a fragment of the third table, *oidtable.oc*, which keeps track of all the object classes known to QUIPU. This file contains definitions of both attribute sets and object classes. An entry defining an object class consists of five columns: the textual name of the object class, the **OBJECT IDENTIFIER** assignment for the object class, any superclass(es), any mandatory attributes, and any optional attributes. Again, it should be noted that this is entry-level schema information only; DIT structuring information is not present, as this is not part of the Directory's object class concept.

The reader should appreciate the straight-forward mapping from the various ASN.1 macros described earlier and these formats. Although *The Little Black Book* focuses on QUIPU as the landmark implementation of the OSI Directory, even the most strident of QUIPU's supporters will admit that it has many shortcomings. For example, one might suspect that QUIPU contains a compiler which accepts ASN.1 macro invocations and produces these files. This is not the case! The files are created and maintained manually. In order to aid distribution however, a future release of QUIPU will have a means for automatically distributing new files. However, having a compiler would make things a great deal easier and more automatic.

soap...

...soap

```
-- an attribute set
telecommunicationAttributeSet = facsimileTelephoneNumber, \
      internationaliSDNNumber, telephoneNumber, \
      teletexTerminalIdentifier, telexNumber, \
      preferredDeliveryMethod, destinationIndicator, \
      registeredAddress, x121Address


...


-- some object classes

top:                   standardObjectClass.0 : : \
                             objectClass :

alias:                 standardObjectClass.1 : top : \
                             aliasedObjectName :

country:               standardObjectClass.2 : top : \
                             countryName : \
                             description, searchGuide

locality:              standardObjectClass.3 : top : : \
                             description, localityName, \
                             stateOrProvinceName, \
                             searchGuide, seeAlso, streetAddress

organization:          standardObjectClass.4 : top : \
                             organizationName : \
                             organizationalAttributeSet

organizationalUnit:    standardObjectClass.5 : top : \
                             organizationalUnitName : \
                             organizationalAttributeSet

person:                standardObjectClass.6 : top : \
                             commonName, surName : \
                             description, seeAlso, \
                             telephoneNumber, userPassword
```

Figure 4.7: Partial Listing of QUIPU's Object Class File

Defining a new Syntax

New syntaxes are added by defining a new C structure along with several routines which manipulate this structure. Let's consider how the `integerSyntax` is defined, as shown in Figure 4.8 starting on page 98.

The key routine is `add_attribute_syntax` which creates an attribute syntax object. As might be imagined, only the routines which implement the abstraction for an attribute syntax know anything about the internal C structure representation. All other access is done via one of these "methods."[2]

---

[2]Observant readers might notice that this technique looks a lot like a simple-minded object-oriented approach layered on C. This is not far from the truth.

```
PE        intenc (x)
int    *x;
{
   return int2prim (*x);
}

int    *intdec (pe)
PE        pe;
{
   int       *x;                                                             10

   if (!test_prim_pe (pe, PE_CLASS_UNIV, PE_PRIM_INT))
         return NULL;

   if (x = (int *) smalloc (sizeof *x))
         *x = prim2num (pe);

   return x;
}
                                                                            20
int        intprint (ps, x, format)
PS        ps;
int    *x,
         format;
{
   ps_printf (ps, "%d", *x);
}

int    *intdup (x)
int    *x;                                                                  30
{
   int    *y;

   if (y  = (int *) smalloc (sizeof *y))
         *y = *x;

   return y;
}

int        intcmp (x, y)                                                    40
int    *x,
      *y;
{
   return (*x == *y ? 0 : (*x > *y ? 1 : −1));
}

int        intfree (x)
int    *x;
{
   free ((char *) x);                                                       50
}
```

Figure 4.8: Realizing the INTEGER attribute syntax

```
int    *intparse (str)
char   *str;
{
   int   i,
           *x = NULL;

   if (sscanf (str, "%ld", &i) == 1
           && (x = (int *) smalloc (sizeof *x)))
       *x = i;
                                                              10
   return x;
}

...

   (void) add_attribute_syntax ("Integer", (IFP) intenc, (IFP) intdec, (IFP) intparse,
                           intprint, (IFP) intdup, intcmp, intfree, NULLCP,
                           NULLIFP, FALSE);
```

Figure 4.8: Realizing the INTEGER attribute syntax (cont.)

The arguments to `add_attribute_syntax` are:

- the textual name of the attribute syntax (this is how the attribute type file, *oidtable.at*, gets linkage to the attribute syntax);

- the address of a routine which encodes an instance of the internal structure (henceforth abbreviated as "a value") as a PE (a data structure discussed momentarily);

- the address of a routine which decodes a PE into a value;

- the address of a routine which takes a textual representation of a value and allocates memory and initializes it with the corresponding value;

- the address of a routine which prints the value as text;

- the address of a routine which allocates a copy of a value;

- the address of a routine which compares two values, for equality and ordering (substring matching is implemented directly in the QUIPU DSA);

- the address of a routine which de-allocates a value;

- the name of a program which can be called to display a value
  to a user (useful when displaying complicated attribute values
  e.g., if an attribute value is a facsimile image, then the program
  will vary depending on the display device being used);

- the address of a routine which performs approximate matching
  between two values; and,

- a flag indicating whether multiple values should be displayed to
  the user on a single line, or one value per line.

During start-up, the routine `add_attribute_syntax` is called
once, for each attribute syntax known to QUIPU. After this initialization, the object tables are read to create entries for the attribute
types and object classes.

As might be expected, QUIPU also initializes a special "unknown"
attribute syntax to use when it encounters attributes that it has no
knowledge of. Values of this type are treated simply as BER encodings
of ASN.1 values. This has two impacts on a DSA's ability to search:

- only matching for equality is possible; and,

- if the attribute's syntax contains `IMPLICIT SET`s, then two attribute values may be incorrectly declared as not being equal.

This latter restriction is due to a requirement in the BER that ordering
of the members of a `SET` is unimportant, and hence indeterminent.

Representing Types, Values, and Names

Finally, let's look at a few key data structures.

The *C* structure used to model an attribute type is:

```
typedef struct attrType {
    struct oid_table {
        char    *ot_name;
        char    *ot_stroid;
        OID     ot_oid;
        OID     ot_aliasoid;    /* for transition... */
    }               oa_at;

    short           oa_syntax;
}   *AttributeType;
#define NULLAttrT ((AttributeType) 0)
```

where the `oa_at` element contains the textual and `OBJECT IDENT-`
`IFIER` representations of the name of the attribute type, and the
`oa_syntax` element is an offset into a table of all the attribute syntaxes. The routine `AttrT_new` is used to translate the textual name
of an attribute type into the corresponding structure.

The *C* structure used to model an attribute value is:

```
typedef struct attrVal {
    short           av_syntax;

    caddr_t         av_struct;
}   *AttributeValue;
#define NULLAttrV ((AttributeValue) 0)
```

where the `av_syntax` element is an offset into the table of attribute
syntaxes and the `av_struct` element is a pointer to the memory location of the internal form used by the method which implements the
attribute syntax. There are a large number of routines which manipulate attribute values in QUIPU, and presenting an exhaustive list
here would be inappropriate. Suffice it to say, that AVs can be easily
transformed.

QUIPU also has a special syntax used when the actual attribute values are available in a disk file rather than in memory. This allows attributes which are not likely to be used for interrogation, such as a photograph image, to be efficiently managed.

Next, the *C* structures used to model an attribute (both type and one or more values) is:

```
typedef struct attr_Sequence {
    struct attrType attr_type;

    AV_Sequence      attr_value;

    struct attr_Sequence
                  *attr_link;
}   *Attr_Sequence;
#define NULLATTR ((Attr_Sequence) 0)

typedef struct av_Sequence {
    struct attrVal  avseq_av;

    struct AV_Sequence
                  *avseq_next;
}   *AV_Sequence;
#define NULLAV ((AV_Sequence) 0)
```

The first structure represents a list of attributes: for each of these, the `attr_type` element contains information about the attribute type, the `attr_value` element is a pointer to a linked-list of attribute values, and, the `attr_link` element is a pointer to the next attribute. The second structure represents a list of attribute values: for each of these, the `avseq_av` element contains a single attribute value, and, the `avseq_next` element is a pointer to the next value. Of course, there is a redundancy in that both attribute types and values have syntax information. This was put in to simplify the routines that deal with attribute values.

So, to traverse a list of attributes looking for a particular value, the code might be:

```
Attr_Sequence eptr;
AV_Sequence   avs;

for (eptr = list_of_attributes; eptr; eptr = eptr -> attr_link)
    if (AttrT_cmp (eptr -> attr_type, desired_type) == 0)
        for (avs = eptr -> attr_value; avs; avs = avs -> avseq_next)
            if (AttrV_cmp (&avs -> avseq_av, desired_value) == 0)
                do_something_here ();
```

Similarly to traverse a list of attributes looking for any values of a particular syntax, the code might be:

```
Attr_Sequence eptr;
AV_Sequence   avs;

for (eptr = list_of_attributes; eptr; eptr = eptr -> attr_link)
    if (eptr -> attr_type -> oa_syntax == desired_syntax)
        for (avs = eptr -> attr_value; avs; avs = avs -> avseq_next)
            do_something_here ();
```

Finally, the last structures to be considered represent DNs and RDNs:

```
typedef struct rDN {
    struct attrType rdn_at;

    struct attrVal  rdn_av;

    struct rDN      *rdn_next;
} *RDN;
#define NULLRDN ((RDN) 0)

typedef struct dN {
    RDN             dn_rdn;

    struct dN       *dn_parent;
} *DN;
#define NULLDN ((DN) 0)
```

The first structure represents the components of a Relative Distinguished Name: for each component, the `rdn_at` element contains information about the attribute type, the `rdn_av` element contains information about the distinguished attribute value, and, the `rdn_next` element is a pointer to the next component of the RDN. The second structure represents the components of a Distinguished Name: for each RDN, the `dn_rdn` element contains the RDN value, and, the `dn_parent` element is a pointer to the subordinate RDN. As such, this element has a confusing name: `dn_parent` points to an immediately subordinate entry in the DIT, not the superior entry!

So, to print a Distinguished Name, the code might be:

```
DN    dn;
RDN   rdn;

for (dn = dn_to_print; dn; dn = dn −> dn_parent) {
      for (rdn = dn −> dn_rdn; rdn; rdn = rdn −> rdn_next) {
          AttrT_print (ps, &rdn −> rdn_at, READOUT);
          ps_print (ps, "=");
          AttrV_print (ps, &rdn −> rdn_av, READOUT);

          if (rdn −> rdn_next)                                    10
                ps_print (ps, "%");
      }

      if (dn −> dn_parent)
          ps_print (ps, "@");
}
```

As might be imagined, QUIPU supplies a large number of routines which manipulate names, including a routine to print a name in one of several different formats.

4.2   The Directory Service

It is now time to see how information objects are manipulated by using the Directory. As noted earlier, the user accesses the Directory through a Directory User Agent (DUA). In turn, the DUA enters into a set of request/reply interactions with the Directory, as represented by one or more DSAs.

Before the interactions occur, a DUA initiates an association to a DSA. During the association establishment, authenticating information may be exchanged. In this case, the DUA identifies itself on the user's behalf using a Distinguished Name. If authentication is enabled at the DSA, then it consults the entry for the DN to validate the DUA's identity. As noted earlier, authentication may be performed by simple password or by techniques based on the use of public keys.

After an association is established, the DUA may initiate two kinds of interactions:

- *interrogation* requests, which return information about either the DIT or the DIB;

- *modification* requests, which change either the structure of the DIT or the contents of the DIB.

These interactions may be qualified:

- by *service controls*, e.g., to limit the depth of a search, or to disallow chaining; and,

- by *security parameters*, e.g., to use digital signatures;

The latter are beyond the scope of *The Little Black Book*, but the former will be re-introduced right after the Directory operations are presented.

The Directory will always generate a reply to each DUA request. The reply is either a result or an error indication. If a result is returned, then this reply is specific to the particular operation issued by the DUA. In contrast, if an error is returned, then this reply is one of several commonly defined exception conditions. That is, a different ASN.1 data type is used to represent the result of each kind of

Directory operation, whilst the same collection of ASN.1 data types is used to represent the possible errors that any Directory operation might encounter. One such reply might be a referral telling the DUA to contact a particular DSA and retry the request.

4.2.1 Interrogation Requests

The DIB and the DIT are simply different perspectives on the entries contained in the Directory. (The DIT imposes a hierarchical relationship on the entries through the use of Distinguished Names, whereas the DIB does not have the concept of relating entries via naming.) All operations manipulate entries: from the DIB perspective, this manipulation occurs by interrogating or modifying the attributes of an entry; from the DIT perspective, in order to find an entry, its name must be resolved and this involves traversing the DIT. Further, the structure of the DIT is changed if an operation changes the distinguished attribute values in an entry.

There are five kinds of requests to interrogate the DIT and DIB:

- *read*, which returns some or all of the attributes associated with an entry. If a DUA is interested in single or multiple attributes, then it specifies those attributes in the read request. The Directory will return the values of precisely those attributes. Otherwise, all attribute values are returned. In either case, the requestor can indicate that only the attribute types be returned, which may be useful in certain applications.

- *compare*, which compares a DUA-supplied attribute value to an attribute value for an entry. This allows the actual value to remain hidden in the Directory. (Simple authentication makes use of this.)

- *list*, which returns the Relative Distinguished Names of the immediate subordinates of an entry.

- *search*, which applies an arbitrary boolean filter to the attributes of the subtree starting at a particular entry, and returns the names of those entries satisfying the search criteria. The depth of the search may be limited to:

– only the specified entry;

– the immediate subordinates to the specified entry, but not including the entry itself; or,

– the whole-subtree starting at that entry, including the entry itself.

It's not clear why there are Directory list, read, and compare operations, since the Directory search operation can be invoked in such a way as to closely emulate the characteristics of these other operations. If one has already "signed-on" for implementing search, then having read, list, and compare operations adds only to the complexity of the protocol without adding real functionality. Alternately, it's not really clear how useful the Directory would be unless one does "sign-on" to implement search! (The search operation will be considered in greater detail later on in Section 5.2.1 starting on page 160.)

soap...

...soap

- *abandon*, which allows the DUA to cancel a previous request. If considerable searching is involved, spanning multiple DSAs (that might cross continents), then this can be a useful feature.

With the exception of abandon, the interrogation requests are performed relative to a named entry in the Directory. In most cases, the request affects only that object. In others (search and list), subordinate objects might also become involved. Regardless, it is possible for a DUA to have several requests pending over a single association with a DSA. It is up to the DSA to schedule execution of the requests based on their ordering and priority, and act accordingly.

4.2.2 Modification Requests

There are four kinds of requests to change the structure of the DIT or modify information in the DIB:

- *add*, which is used to add a new entry to the DIB. Arbitrary insertion into the DIT is not allowed: these entries must be placed beneath entries already containing immediate subordinates that are leaves. This ensures that the DSA responsible for that portion of the DIT is the DSA which performs the addition. Otherwise, confusion would result! For example, if an entry was inserted above another entry, then the names of all the subordinate entries would change!

- *remove*, which is used to remove an entry from the DIB. Only leaves in the DIT may be removed.

- *modify*, which is used to add, change, or delete, the attributes in an entry.

- *modify RDN*, which is used to change the Relative Distinguished Name of a leaf entry. Note that this is not a general "move" request, since the entry retains its position in the DIT. This ensures that the DSA responsible for that portion of the DIT is the DSA that actually performs the request. Of course, leaf entries may be moved by simple deletion and re-insertion.

The restrictions imposed on the modification requests are quite telling. These are due primarily to the distributed nature of the Directory. The protocol used between DSAs was not designed to provide the functionality necessary to provide general modification of the shape and content of the DIT.

Note that Directory management, per se, is noticeably missing. The Directory standard is conspicuously silent on matters such as:

- management of access control;

- management of replication (shadowing and caching);

- management of *schema*, which defines the shape and structure of portions of the DIT; and,

- management of *knowledge information*, which defines which DSAs contain what portions of the DIT.

Before re-focusing on implementation, it is useful to consider the actual service controls available on most Directory operations. There are five:

options: any of several straight-forward indications:

preferChaining
chainingProhibited
dontUseCopy
dontDereferenceAliases
localScope

except for the last one which is implementation-specific. If present, it indicates that the operation should be performed within a limited scope, presumably either within the DSA or the local DMD.

priority: one of three arbitrary settings, `low`, `medium` (the default), and `high`.

timeLimit: the maximum number of seconds in which the service should be provided, if absent, no explicit time limit is imposed. If this time limit expires for a list or search operation, partial results will be returned (and flagged as such).

sizeLimit: for the list and search operations, the maximum number of entries which should be returned by the operation. If this size limit expires, partial results will be returned (and flagged as such).

scopeOfReferral: one of two settings, either `dmd` or `country`, indicating what the requestor views as a relevant referral to a DSA.

4.2.3 Implementation Focus

QUIPU contains a DSA and several DUAs. In this section, we'll look almost exclusively at QUIPU's DUAs.

In QUIPU, the DUA interface can be used directly at the programmatic level, or exported from an interface process called `dish` — the DIrectory SHell. The present *C* language interface, termed `libdsap`, supports associations with multiple DSAs simultaneously, but is based

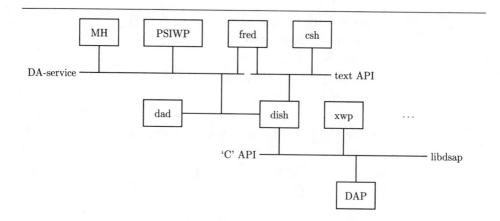

Figure 4.9: Programmatic Interfaces for the QUIPU DUAs

on a synchronous interface. An interrupt from the user, if not disabled, will automatically result in the abandon operation being invoked. Thus, depending on the implementation strategy of the program using **libdsap**, the abandon operation may be unavailable.

Figure 4.9 shows the various APIs which are available to a QUIPU DUA, along with some of the programs which make use of them. For now, we'll (briefly) consider only the **libdsap** API for *C*. Later on, in Section 5.4 starting on page 215, other parts of this figure will be explored.

The simplest interaction with **libdsap** consists of initializing the library, establishing an association with a DSA, performing one or more DAP operations, and then releasing the association. Rather than run through the entire API, let's consider just the highlights of each of these steps.

Initialization is achieved by calling two routines:

```
char  **argp;

quipu_syntaxes ();

argp = argv,
dsap_init (&argc, &argp);
```

The first routine, **quipu_syntaxes**, reads the object tables described earlier in Section 4.1.8 on page 92.

The second routine, `dsap_init`, reads the UNIX command line for interesting arguments, such as the name of the DSA to contact, and then consults a system configuration file. These arguments can either be taken directly from the command line (as shown in the example), or constructed by the program. The configuration file includes such information as:

- where the object tables are located;

- the "local" part of the DIT (i.e., the name of the entry in the DIT that represents the "local" site, such as an organizational entry); and,

- the address of the "local" DSA

As shown in Figure 4.10, binding to a DSA is somewhat more complicated. First, the bind arguments are set: the desired version of X.500 (of which there is presently only one, thank goodness!), the DN of the user (bound using simple authentication), and the password, if any, of the user. Then, the routine `ds_bind` is called. If an error occurs, then either the service is unavailable or there was a security error.

There are many interesting operations which might be performed, but in the interest of simplicity, Figure 4.11 on page 113 shows how to a read an entry. The library maintains a cache of previous results that a DUA may choose to employ. So, the code in this example first sees if the desired entry is in the cache. If not, or if the cached entry contains only partial information and the user desires full information, a Directory read is performed. First, the service controls are initialized: if the entry is an alias, the alias should be read instead of being followed; further, if the local DSA doesn't have the information, it is asked to chain the request to another DSA, rather than return a referral; the priority of this request is low, but no time nor size limit is placed on its execution (a read request returns exactly one entry on success, so the size limit is superfluous); and, no scope of referral should be applied to the request. Next, the desired attributes from the entry are selected: if the user didn't specify any attributes, all attributes in the entry are selected, otherwise, only the attributes listed are selected.

```
DN    userdn;
char *password;

...

struct ds_bind_arg ba;
struct ds_bind_arg br;
struct ds_bind_error be;

bzero ((char *) &ba, sizeof ba);                                        10
bzero ((char *) &br, sizeof br);
bzero ((char *) &be, sizeof be);

ba.dba_version = DBA_VERSION_V1988;
if (ba.dba_dn = userdn)
    ba.dba_auth_type = DBA_AUTH_SIMPLE;
if (ba.dba_passwd_len = strlen (passwd))
    (void) strcpy (ba.dba_passwd, passwd);
if (ds_bind (&ba, &be, &br) != DS_OK)
    error ("unable to bind to directory (%s)",                         20
        be.dbe_type == DBE_TYPE_SECURITY ? "security error"
                                    : "DSA unavailable");
```

Figure 4.10: Binding to a DSA

In either event, the DSA is asked to provide the types and values which are present in the entry. Finally, the read is performed. On success, the results are added to the cache.[3] The `cache_entry` routine will coalesce the result into an existing cache entry, as appropriate. Finally, memory allocated during the read operation is released, and the entry read from the cache.

Releasing the association is simple, the routine `ds_unbind` is called which takes no arguments.

---

[3]Observant readers might ask if this caching should be automatic. Because the motivation for DUA caching varies, depending on the purpose of the DUA, it was felt that this must be explicitly performed by the programmer.

```
DN    dn_of_interest;
Attr_Sequence attrs_of_interest;

register Entry newentry;
struct ds_read_arg ra;
struct ds_read_result rr;
struct DSError re;

bzero ((char *) &ra, sizeof ra);
if ((newentry = local_find_entry (ra.rda_object = dn_of_interest,            10
                          FALSE)) == NULLENTRY
        || !newentry -> e_lock    /* values present? */
        || (!attrs_of_interest && !newentry -> e_complete)) {
    ra.rda_common.ca_servicecontrol.svc_options =
                    SVC_OPT_DONTDEREFERENCEALIAS | SVC_OPT_PREFERCHAIN;
    ra.rda_common.ca_servicecontrol.svc_prio = SVC_PRIO_LOW;
    ra.rda_common.ca_servicecontrol.svc_timelimit = SVC_NOTIMELIMIT;
    ra.rda_common.ca_servicecontrol.svc_sizelimit = SVC_NOSIZELIMIT;
    ra.rda_common.ca_servicecontrol.svc_scopeofreferral =
                    SVC_REFSCOPE_NONE;                                        20

    if (!attrs_of_interest) {
        ra.rda_eis.eis_allattributes = TRUE;
        ra.rda_eis.eis_select = NULLATTR;
    }
    else {
        ra.rda_eis.eis_allattributes = FALSE;
        ra.rda_eis.eis_select = attrs_of_interest;
    }
    ra.rda_eis.eis_infotypes = EIS_ATTRIBUTESANDVALUES;                      30

    while (ds_read (&ra, &re, &rr) != DS_OK) {
        /* if not a referral, or if unable to bind to new DSA
                return an error
            otherwise...
        */

        ra -> rda_object =
                re -> ERR_REFERRAL.DSE_ref_candidates -> cr_name;
    }                                                                        40

    cache_entry (&rr.rdr_entry,
                    ra.rda_eis.eis_allattributes,
                    ra.rda_eis.eis_infotypes);

    entryinfo_comp_free (&rr.rdr_entry, 0);

    newentry = local_find_entry (adn, FALSE);
}
```

Figure 4.11: Reading an Entry

4.3   The Directory Access Protocol

The protocol used between the DUA and DSA, the Directory Access
Protocol (DAP), is largely uninteresting.

4.3.1   Application Layer Structure of a DUA

The DAP resides at the OSI application layer, using the ACSE to
establish and release an application layer association and remote operations to convey its interactions. The DUA always initiates the
association, and once an association is established, the DUA may
consume the services made available at three ports:

- a read port, which allows the invocation of the Directory read,
  compare, and abandon operations;

- a search port, which allows the invocation of the Directory
  search and list operations; and,

- a modify port, which allows the invocation of the Directory add
  entry, remove entry, modify entry, and modify RDN operations.

It should be noted that ports are little more than a notational con-
venience: they are always packaged together in a single service, and
an observer cannot determine that the service contains three distinct
ASEs. For example, although the abandon operation is supposed to
be realized through the read port, one can also abandon searches. Figure 4.12 shows the application layer structure of a DUA (or a DSA
which communicates with a DUA).

   All three service ports use the same abstract syntax (set of data
definitions), so only two abstract syntaxes are used on a DAP-association, one for the ACSE, and the other to access the Directory ports.
All of these characteristics of a DAP-association are summarized using
the ASN.1 notation shown in Figure 4.13. In this figure, the variables
starting with `id-` are `OBJECT IDENTIFIER`s defined in the Directory
standard.

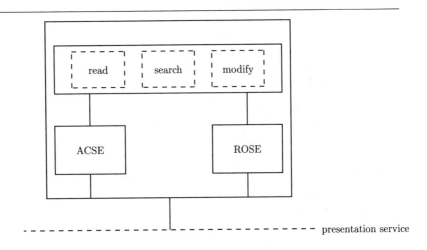

Figure 4.12: Application Layer Structure of a DUA

directoryAccessAC **APPLICATION–CONTEXT**
    APPLICATION SERVICE ELEMENTS { aCSE }
    BIND DirectoryBind
    UNBIND DirectoryUnbind
    REMOTE OPERATIONS { rOSE }
    INITIATOR CONSUMER OF { readASE, searchASE, modifyASE }
    ABSTRACT SYNTAXES { id–as–acse, is–as–directoryAccessAS }
    ::= id–ac–directoryAccessAC

readASE **APPLICATION–SERVICE–ELEMENT**   10
    CONSUMER INVOKES { read, compare, abandon }
    ::= id–ase–readASE

searchASE **APPLICATION–SERVICE–ELEMENT**
    CONSUMER INVOKES { search, list }
    ::= id–ase–searchASE

readASE **APPLICATION–SERVICE–ELEMENT**
    CONSUMER INVOKES { addEntry, removeEntry, modifyEntry, modifyRDN }
    ::= id–ase–modifyASE   20

Figure 4.13: Concise Description of DUA Application Context

```
ReadArgument ::=
    SET {
        object[0]
            Name,

        selection[1]
            EntryInformationSelection
            DEFAULT {},

        COMPONENTS OF                                          10
            CommonArguments
    }

EntryInformationSelection ::=
    SET {
        attributeTypes
            CHOICE {
                allAttributes[0]
                    NULL,
                select[1]                                      20
                    SET OF AttributeType
            }
            DEFAULT allAttributes,

        infoTypes[2]
            INTEGER {
                attributeTypesOnly(0),
                attributeTypesAndValues(1)
            }
            DEFAULT attributeTypesAndValues                    30
    }
```

Figure 4.14: Partial ASN.1 for Read Argument

4.3.2   Directory Interactions

Once a DAP-association is established, the DUA may invoke an operation from any of the three ports, using ROSE. A brief example, showing how a single attribute can be read for an entry, should present the basic flavor of a DAP-interaction.

The user wishes to examine any values associated with the attribute type `description` in the entry `c=US@cn=Manager`, with the service option that if this is an alias entry, then it should not be followed. The DUA uses the read port and invokes a read operation. A portion of the abstract syntax for the argument to this operation is shown in Figure 4.14.

```
{
    object[0]
        {
            {
                { { 2.5.4.6, "US" } },
                { { 2.5.4.3, "Manager" } }
            }
        },

    selection[1]
        {
            {
                select[1]
                    { { 2.5.4.13 } }
            }
        },

    [30]
        {
            {
                options[0]
                    { dontDereferenceAlias }
            }
        }
}
```

Figure 4.15: Example ASN.1 Value Notation of a Read Argument

In the context of the example, the argument given to ROSE might look something like the ASN.1 value shown in Figure 4.15.[4] Here we see three components: first, the DN of the entry to be read, consisting of two RDNs, each containing a single attribute value; second, the attribute that should be read, expressed as an **OBJECT IDENTIFIER**; and, third, a service control bit.

---

[4]Of course, the compact binary representation of the Basic Encoding Rules is used when this is carried on the wire — as with other figures throughout *The Little Black Book*, an extended form of ASN.1's value notation is used for the purposes of exposition.

```
ReadResult ::=
   SET {
          entry[0]
             EntryInformation,

             COMPONENTS OF
                CommonResults
   }

EntryInformation ::=                                                    10
   SEQUENCE {
          DistinguishedName,

       fromEntry
          BOOLEAN
          DEFAULT TRUE,

          SET OF
             CHOICE {
                AttributeType,                                          20
                Attribute
             }
             OPTIONAL
   }
```

Figure 4.16: Partial ASN.1 for Read Result

If the DSA is able to perform the operation, it returns a result. A portion of the abstract syntax for the result to this operation is shown in Figure 4.16.

```
{
    entry[0]
        {
            {
                {
                    { { 2.5.4.6, "US" } },
                    { { 2.5.4.3, "Manager" } }
                },

                fromEntry
                    FALSE,

                {
                    {
                        2.5.4.13,
                        { "(haggard) Manager of the US DMD" }
                    }
                }
            }
        }
}
```

Figure 4.17: Example ASN.1 Value Notation of a Read Result

In the context of the example, the result given to the ROSE might look something like the ASN.1 value shown in Figure 4.17. Here we see three components: first, the DN of the entry that was actually read; second, a flag indicating that the information is from a copy of the entry; and, third, the value associated with the desired attribute type (there is only one).

NameError ::=

 ...

  SET {
   problem[0]
    INTEGER {
     noSuchObject (1),
     aliasProblem (2),
     invalidAttributeSyntax (3),
     aliasDereferencingProblem (4)
    },   10

   matched[1]
    Name
  }

Figure 4.18: Partial ASN.1 for Name Errors

Instead, if an exception occurs and the DSA is unable to perform the operation, it returns a error. For the read operation, although there are several errors possible, let's consider just one, **NameError**. Associated with this error is a parameter having the abstract syntax shown in Figure 4.18.

```
{
    problem[0]
        {
            noSuchObject
        },

    matched[1]
        {
            { { { 2.5.4.6, "US" } } }
        }
}
```

Figure 4.19: Example ASN.1 Value Notation of a Read Error

In the context of the example, the parameter given to the ROSE
might look something like the ASN.1 value shown in Figure 4.19. Here
we see two components: first, an integer indicating which exception
occurred; and, an indication of how far name resolution got before
the exception was raised.

4.4   The Structure of the DIT

The Directory is intended for interrogation, and to be used effectively, interrogation algorithms must execute in DUAs to find information. (Such algorithms are described throughout Section 5.2 starting on page 159.) Skipping ahead slightly, an interrogation algorithm can not be designed in a vacuum, it requires some knowledge of the DIT structure.

Thus, the designer of an interrogation algorithm is left with a conundrum: either a piece of the DIT can be "carved off" for use with the algorithm, or the algorithm must be designed for suboptimal behavior as it stumbles around the DIT in a knowledge-poor fashion.

Unfortunately, there can be but a single DIT in the world! Although authority may be delegated for structuring different portions of the DIT, a consistent tree must result: a DN must refer to exactly one information object. An implication of this is that there must be universally agreed upon rules as to how the top-most level of the DIT is structured.

soap... Because the Directory standard describes a technology, and not a policy of usage, it does not define rules for forming names and structuring the DIT. Although understandable from the technology perspective, given the problems this causes in usage, the hands-off philosophy taken by the Directory standard is arguably reprehensible.

Because the remainder of this chapter deals with policy, and not technology, arguably this soapbox should extend to the chapter's end. However, the author has strived for balance and rationality in the text ...soap which follows. Therefore, the soapbox ends here.

4.4.1   Naming is Problematic

In fairness to the Directory standard,

in general, naming is a problem.

Let's look at just a few problems.

Lack of Naming Authorities

Although the Directory facilitates the exchange of infrastructural information, it neither creates the information, nor does it assign values to it. A duly recognized naming and numbering authority is responsible for this.

Throughout OSI, a heavy emphasis is placed on the ability to delegate authority. For example, OSI network numbers (as described in Section 4.1.1 of *The Open Book*) are structured for delegation, as are the ubiquitous **OBJECT IDENTIFIER**s. The standards community has taken the forward-thinking position of optimizing for delegation and this is half the problem.

However, to carry the day, it is necessary to have in place the procedural infrastructure to delegate numeric-prefixes so that others may make assignments. For some reason, at least in the author's native country, this just didn't happen in the '80s.

Consider the following: the standard on OSI network layer addressing has been finalized since early 1987, and until late 1990, there was no entity willing or able to assign network addresses within the US. One positive development was when the US General Services Administration was finally empowered to assign NSAP-prefixes to organizations within the US Federal Government. As of this writing, although there are plans (there are *always* plans), no one is handing out NSAP-prefixes to private organizations. It's not really clear how one is supposed to run a network without network numbers, but perhaps this is unimportant for "demo purposes." | soap... |

Next, the basic standard on Message Handling Systems has been finalized since 1984. Associated with an X.400 address are two components, an Administrative Management Domain (ADMD) and a Private Management Domain (PRMD). ADMD names are required to be unique within a country, and in some quarters, it is believed that PRMD names should also be unique within a country. Regardless, this implies a national registry of ADMD names in the US. As of this writing, although there are plans (there are *always* plans), no one is managing an ADMD registry in the US. It's not really clear how one is suppose to exchange mail without mail addresses, but perhaps this is also unimportant for "demo purposes."

In the US, the North American Directory Forum has emerged to look at the problem of how names will be assigned under c=US. Their efforts may very well be the turning point. However, as of this writing, it's just too early to tell.

The author sincerely hopes that things aren't so bad in other countries, but has this nagging suspicion that things are seriously *charlie-foxtrot* the world over as far as OSI registration is concerned. Needless to say, Internet proponents literally giggle themselves into seizures when they hear about things like this — they've always understood that registration must be fast, easy, and above all accessible. Perhaps this is due to having a single sponsor over a decade ago (the Internet registration process is now decentralized). Regardless, how one could expect anyone to seriously consider a protocol suite without having a mechanism for assigning names or addresses is a mystery.

> ...soap

Commercial ADDMDs

In a commercial environment, privacy is given the utmost consideration. Therefore, when several organizations offer competing directory services within a country, they will individually act to minimize the amount of information which outsiders can derive from the part of the DIT they manage. A likely policy is that an ADDMD may simply refuse to publish its internal schema, but will, of course, insist on a well-published schema for other parts of the DIT.

Rogue PRDMDs

On the other end of the spectrum, little control can be exerted over organizations running their own Directory service, they are free to structure their part of the DIT to their own liking. Thus, in the absence of government mandate, it is unlikely that a national decision would be able to reach into the organizational level, nor would we want it to!

Some multi-national organizations are even so bold as to suggest that they be placed directly under the root of the DIT! Egos aside, whilst it may be appropriate to place international organizations (such as The Red Cross) directly under the root, multi-nationals do not enjoy the universal standing accorded an international organization.

Further, this is likely to make it harder to find information within the organization since interrogation algorithms need to know about yet another place where something might be hiding. With some careful thinking, it should become obvious that entries (listings) should be placed (listed) where others are likely to look for them.

In brief, there are interests at cross-purposes and no mediating influences on the naming problem.

4.4.2 The Rosetta Stone of the Directory

The only guidance given by the Directory standard is Annex B, *Suggested Name Forms and DIT Structures*, in the document which defines the "selected" object classes (ISO9594-7/X.521). This is not part of the standard. The structuring aspects of the annex are briefly summarized in Figure 4.20 on page 126. The term *rosetta stone* was first applied to this structure by the group which developed the Directory standard.

It should be noted that the suggested DIT structure, although appearing to be quite general, is still insufficient to meet many real-world considerations. Consider two examples:

- It may be reasonable to establish localities directly under the root, to represent world regions. Under each locality, it would be useful to have the countries in that region. But, according to the suggested DIT structure, countries must appear directly under the root.

- It is not uncommon for organizations to be subordinate to other organizations, For example, the World Health Organization is an internationally-recognized organization that is a part of the the United Nations, another internationally-recognized organization. One would suspect that both should be represented as organizations in the Directory, with the former begin subordinate to the latter. But, according to the suggested DIT structure, organizations may not appear under other organizations.

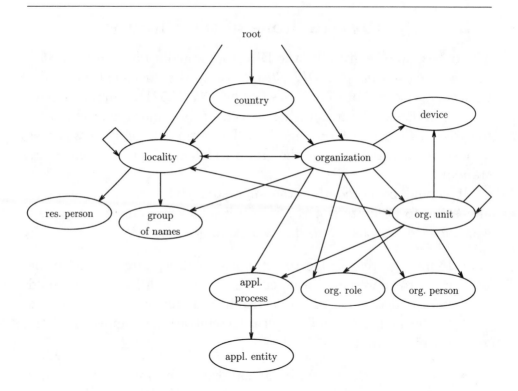

Figure 4.20: Suggested DIT Structure in the Directory standard

Fortunately there has been some progress within different organizations on developing a naming architecture:

- The *Cooperation for OSI Networking in Europe* (COSINE) and Internet communities are working on a joint architecture.

- The *European Workshop for Open Systems* (EWOS), an organization developing OSI profiles, is developing a structure for use within Europe.

- The *North American Directory Forum* (NADF), a collection of X.400 and X.500 service providers, is developing a structure for use within North America.

All three groups have been working since 1990, and are separately making progress towards different goals. In Appendix A starting on page 305, some thoughts are given as to how one might go about forming a national decision for c=US.

4.4.3 A Possible National Decision

To consider the difficulty in producing a naming architecture, let's consider how a hypothetical country might go about it. We'll call this country *Freedonia*, and say that its country code is FF. It must be emphasized that what follows is only an example.

To begin, it should be observed that there are several different naming universes that can be realized in the Directory Information Tree (DIT). For example, geographical naming, community naming, political naming, organizational naming, and so on. The choice of naming universe largely determines the difficulty in mapping a user's query into a series of Directory operations. Although it is possible to simultaneously support multiple naming universes with the DIT, this is likely to be unnatural. Thus, the national decision for Freedonia focuses on a single naming universe. That naming universe is based on *civil authority*. That is, it uses the existing civil naming infrastructure within Freedonia and suggests a (nearly) straight-forward mapping on the DIT.

Although the Freedonia decision focuses on a single naming universe, it should be observed that some other naming universes might be supported with some cooperation.

There are two aspects Freedonia's naming architecture: a DIT structure, as shown in Table 4.2 on page 135, and a set of related Schema definitions, as shown in Figure 4.21 starting on page 136.

Choice of RDN Names

The key aspect to appreciate for choice of RDNs is that they should provide a large name space to avoid collisions: the naming strategy must provide enough "real estate" to accommodate a large demand for entries. This is the *primary* requirement for RDNs. A *secondary* requirement is that RDNs should be meaningful (friendly to people) and should not impede searching.

However, it is important to understand that this second requirement can be achieved by using additional (non-distinguished) attribute values. For example, if the RDN of an entry is

```
organizationName=Ministry of Finance
```

then it is perfectly acceptable (and indeed desirable) to have other values for the `organizationName` attribute, e.g.,

```
organizationName=MOF
```

The use of these abbreviated names as non-distinguished attribute values greatly aids searching whilst avoiding unnecessary Distinguished Name conflicts.

In order to appreciate Freedonia's approach, it is important to understand that it leverages, wherever possible, existing naming infrastructure within Freedonia. That is, it relies heavily on non-OSI naming authorities which already exist.

Naming at the National Level

Freedonia consists of several provinces, has a thriving business environment, and several providers of commercial directory services. Thus, directly under `c=FF`, three kinds of names may be registered:

- Organizations (and other entities) with National Standing

- The Provinces

- ADDMD operators

Organizations with National Standing

Sadly, there is no authority in Freedonia which unambiguously registers the alphanumeric names of organizations with national standing. (Business entities register within provinces or a locality within a province.) This left the decision-makers in Freedonia with a choice: they could either disallow organizations being registered directly under `c=FF`, or they could empower the *Freedonian National Standards Institute* (FNSI), to maintain a registry. Freedonia's decision-makers decided on the latter course.

Thus, for each organization registering with the FNSI to achieve national standing in Freedonia, an instance of an `ffOrganization` object is used. The RDN is formed as

```
fnsiOrgNumericCode=<FNSI numeric org code>
```

e.g.,

```
fnsiOrgNumericCode=101
```

provides the RDN for the Federal Government of Freedonia. Of course, this entry would contain many other attributes such as

```
organizationName=Government of Freedonia
```

and

```
organizationName=Federal Government
```

The Provinces

The Government of Freedonia maintains a series of *Freedonian Information Processing Standards* (FIPS). One of these assigns both a two-digit alpha postal code and a two-digit numeric postal code to each province. Although the decision-makers in Freedonia would have preferred to use the alpha code, or even the full name of the province, as the distinguished attribute value, they opted to use the numeric code to be consistent with the decision on organizations with national standing.

Thus, for each province, an instance of an `ffProvince` object is used. The RDN is formed as

```
fipsProvNumericCode=<FIPS numeric province code>
```

e.g.,

```
fipsProvNumericCode=06
```

provides the RDN for the Province of Calafia. Of course, this entry would contain many other attributes such as

```
stateOrProvinceName=Calafia
```

and

```
fipsProvAlphaCode=CA
```

ADDMD Operators

There is no authority in Freedonia which unambiguously registers the names of ADDMD operators. So, the decision-makers in Freedonia told the service providers to get together and jointly manage the registry in the spirit of commercial cooperation. (Either that, or new regulatory legislation would have to be introduced into Freedonia's House of Representatives.)

Thus, for each ADDMD operator, an instance of a `ffADDMD` object is used. The RDN is formed as

```
addmdName=<full name of ADDMD>
```

e.g.,

```
addmdName=Teasdale Directory Services
```

Naming within a Province

At the regional level three kinds of names may be registered:

- The Regional Government

- Populated Places

- Organizations (and other entities) with Regional Standing

The Regional Government

For the Regional Government, an instance of an **organization** object is used. The RDN is formed as:

```
organizationName=Government of <regional entity>
```

e.g.,

```
organizationName=Government of the Province of Calafia
```

Populated Places

Another Freedonian Information Processing Standard maintains a registry of all populated places within Freedonia, on a per-province basis, and assigns a five-digit numeric code to each. (By combining the two-digit province code and the five-digit place code, any populated place in Freedonia is uniquely identified.)

Thus, for each populated place within a province, an instance of an **ffPlace** object is used. The RDN is formed as

```
fipsPlaceNumericCode=<FIPS numeric place code>
```

e.g.,

```
fipsPlaceNumericCode=37000
```

Of course, this entry would contain many other attributes such as

```
localityName=Freedonia City
```

Organizations with Regional Standing

An organization is said to have regional standing if it is registered with the "Provincial Secretary" of that region, as an entity doing business in the region.

For each organization with regional standing, an instance of an `organization` object is used. The RDN is formed as

```
organizationName=<registered name of organization>
```

e.g.,

```
organizationName=Streetside Lemonade
```

might provide the RDN for a business entity registered within one of Freedonia's provinces. In this case, the entry thus named would be immediately subordinate to the `ffProvince` entry for that province.

Note that other non-distinguished attributes, such as an FNSI numeric name form value, may be included in an entry.

Naming within Organizations (of any standing)

The internal structure of each `ffOrganization` or `organization` object is a matter for that organization to establish. The decision-makers in Freedonia *knew* they could not exert any control over either PRD-MDs nor organizations. However, they strongly recommended that `organizationalUnit` objects be used for structuring. (If an organization uses a locality-based organizational hierarchy, this information can still be represented using the `organizationalUnit` object.)

Naming within ADDMDs

The internal structure of each `ffADDMD` object is a matter for that service-provider to establish.

Naming within a Populated Place

At the local level three kinds of names may be registered:

- The Local Government

- Organizations (and other entities) with Local Standing

- Citizens

The Local Government

For the Local Government, if any, an instance of an `organization` object is used. The RDN is formed as:

```
organizationName=Government of <local entity>
```

e.g.,

```
organizationName=Government of Freedonia City
```

Organizations with Local Standing

An organization is said to have local standing if it is registered with the County or City Clerk or similar entity within that locality as an entity "doing business" in that place.

For each organization with local standing, an instance of an `organ- ization` object is used. The RDN is formed as

```
organizationName=<registered name of organization>
```

Note that other non-distinguished attributes, such as an FNSI numeric name form value, may be included in an entry.

Naming of Citizens

There is no centralized naming entity which registers the citizens of Freedonia. The decision-makers of Freedonia decided that entries for citizens should be subordinate to the `ffPlace` object which most accurately reflects their place of residence.

For each citizen (wishing to have an entry in the Directory), an instance of a `residentialperson` is used. The RDN is usually multi-valued, formed as

```
commonName=<person's full name>
streetAddress=<person's street address>
```

However, because `streetAddress` is often considered private information, based on agreement with the entity managing the DMD and
the person, some other, distinguishing attribute may be used, including a "serial number" (having no other purpose). It should be noted
however that this is non-helpful in regards to searching, unless other
attribute values containing meaningful information are added to the
entry and made available for public access. In brief, if an attribute is
available for interrogation, then obviously it isn't private information.

Naming of OSI Entities

Naming of OSI application processes and entities remains with the
scoping DMD. However, to foster interoperability, the decision-makers
of Freedonia insist that: first, application entity objects must be immediately subordinate to application process objects; and, second,
application entities are represented by the `ffApplicationEntity` object, which is identical to the `applicationEntity` object except that
an attribute value of `supportedApplicationContext` is mandatory.

Level	Element	objectClass	Superior	RDN
root	0			
international	1	country	0	countryName
national	2	ffProvince	1	fipsProvNumericCode
	3	ffOrganization	1	fnsiOrgNumericCode
	4	ffADDMD	1	addmdName
regional	5	organization	2	organizationName
	6	ffPlace	2	fipsPlaceNumericCode
local	7	organization	6	organizationName
	8	residentialPerson	6	commonName, other
organizational	9	organizationalUnit	3,5,7,9	organizationalUnitName
	10	organizationalRole	3,5,7,9	commonName
	11	organizationalPerson	3,5,7,9	commonName
application	12	applicationProcess	3,5,7,9	commonName
	13	ffApplicationEntity	12	commonName

Table 4.2: The DIT Structure for Freedonia

FF–SCHEMA { – – *ffModule schema(1)* – – }

DEFINITIONS ::= **BEGIN**

IMPORTS
   OBJECT–CLASS, **ATTRIBUTE**
        FROM InformationFramework
          { joint–iso–ccitt ds(5) module(1)
               informationFramework(1) }
   caseIgnoreStringSyntax   10
        FROM SelectedAttributeTypes
          { joint–iso–ccitt ds(5) module(1)
               selectedAttributeTypes(5) }
   locality, organization, applicationEntity, top
        FROM SelectedObjectClasses
          { joint–iso–ccitt ds(5) module(1)
               selectedObjectClasses(6) }
     ;

                                        20

ff **OBJECT IDENTIFIER** ::= { – – *TBD* – – }

ffModule   **OBJECT IDENTIFIER** ::= { ff 1 }
ffAttributeType **OBJECT IDENTIFIER** ::= { ff 4 }
ffObjectClass   **OBJECT IDENTIFIER** ::= { ff 6 }

– – *object classes*

ffProvince **OBJECT–CLASS**   30
   SUBCLASS OF locality
   MUST CONTAIN { fipsProvNumericCode,
              fipsProvAlphaCode,
              ProvOrProviceName }
   ::= { ffObjectClass 1 }

ffPlace **OBJECT–CLASS**
   SUBCLASS OF locality
   MUST CONTAIN { fipsPlaceNumericCode,
              localityName }   40
   ::= { ffObjectClass 2 }

ffOrganization **OBJECT–CLASS**
   SUBCLASS OF organization
   MUST CONTAIN { fnsiOrgNumericCode }
   ::= { ffObjectClass 3 }

ffApplicationEntity **OBJECT–CLASS**
   SUBCLASS OF applicationEntity
   MUST CONTAIN { supportedApplicationContext }   50
   ::= { ffObjectClass 4 }

ffADDMD **OBJECT–CLASS**
   SUBCLASS OF top
   MUST CONTAIN { addmdName }
   ::= { ffObjectClass 5 }

Figure 4.21: The Schema for Freedonia

−− attribute types

fipsProvNumericCode **ATTRIBUTE**
       −− semantics and values defined in FF FIPS PUB
   WITH ATTRIBUTE−SYNTAX
   NumericString (**SIZE** (2))   *−− leading zero is significant*
     MATCHES FOR EQUALITY
   SINGLE VALUE
   ::= { ffAttributeType 1 }

10

fipsProvAlphaCode **ATTRIBUTE**
       −− semantics and values defined in FF FIPS PUB
   WITH ATTRIBUTE−SYNTAX
   PrintableString (**SIZE** (2))
     MATCHES FOR EQUALITY   *−− case−insensitive*
   SINGLE VALUE
   ::= { ffAttributeType 2 }

fipsPlaceNumericCode **ATTRIBUTE**
       −− semantics and values defined in FF FIPS PUB   20
   WITH ATTRIBUTE−SYNTAX
   NumericString (**SIZE** (5))   *−− leading zeros are significant*
     MATCHES FOR EQUALITY
   SINGLE VALUE
   ::= { ffAttributeType 3 }

fnsiOrgNumericCode **ATTRIBUTE**
       −− semantics and values defined in FNSI registry
   WITH ATTRIBUTE−SYNTAX INTEGER
     MATCHES FOR EQUALITY   30
   ::= { ffAttributeType 4 }

addmdName **ATTRIBUTE**
       −− semantics and values defined in FF registry
   WITH ATTRIBUTE−SYNTAX caseIgnoreStringSyntax
   ::= { ffAttributeType 5 }

END

Figure 4.21: The Schema for Freedonia (cont.)

4.4.4   Reflections on the Freedonia Naming Architecture

Although the stated goal of using a hierarchical approach to naming is to achieve user-friendly names, the decision-makers of Freedonia discovered that the hierarchical approach was most useful in mapping the civilian infrastructure of Freedonia onto the DIT.

The lack of a Freedonian national registry for organizations is unfortunate, but it illustrates an important point: user-friendliness in names comes from the ability of the search operation to work on any attribute value in an entry, not just the entry's *distinguished* attribute values.

By using numbers, rather than names, the burden on Freedonia's lawyers was reduced since organizations were no longer inclined to make a fuss over who got to use which RDN at the Freedonian National Level.[5] More importantly, it's clear that one could just as easily use serial numbers for RDNs, because searching worked just fine.

The drawback, which caused much debate in the Freedonia's House of Representatives, is that users are unlikely to directly type-in DNs. Rather, the interrogation algorithms must derive the DN, based on user input, and then perform a read operation on the derived DN. The decision-makers of Freedonia decided that it was unlikely that names taken from Annex B of X.521 could be typed by a person, so requiring the interrogation algorithm to do a derivation, in the absence of existing configuration information, was deemed to be a reasonable approach.

Indeed, the more radical of the decision-makers of Freedonia desire to entirely hide the Directory from the end-user, since Freedonia's citizens (primarily honest tradesmen) have their own idea about what a friendly name is, and a DN doesn't even come close.

---

[5]This resulted in a surplus of available billable hours in Freedonian corporate law. In turn, a commensurate percentage of the lawyers in Freedonia moved into Freedonian personal injury law.

So, by using DNs such as

```
c=FF
    @fnsiOrgNumericCode=101
    @ou=Office of the Leader of Freedonia
    @cn=Rufus T. Firefly
```

the decision-makers of Freedonia feel they can be assured that the manufacturers of DUAs will take extra care in developing reasonable interrogation algorithms.

In brief, the *Freedonia Assertion* states:

> *hierarchical names are useful only for the purpose of delegation; user-friendly naming comes not from Distinguished Names, but rather from the search operation working over all attribute values.*

Decision-makers in other venues have much to learn from the Free- soap... donian national decision, in terms of its successes and failures as a naming scheme. In particular, deciding to use the existing civil infrastructure minimized the amount of registration infrastructure that had to be built and resulted in a DIT that closely mimiced Freedonian society. As one of Freedonia's most able statesmen put it:

> *It always makes good sense to make use of the good work of others.*

Further, Freedonian showed itself as being very pro-OSI, by actually tackling the problem and doing something, even if the motto of the Freedonian Civil Service is:

> *Doing anything is almost always worse than doing nothing.*

It was clear that OSI simply wasn't going to happen in Freedonia until the Directory was put in place, and the Directory couldn't be put in place until Freedonia resolved its national decision. No DIT naming scheme is perfect, nor even optimal, but Freedonia's decision-makers developed a scheme which was viable and then had the *chutzpah* to implement it!

Of course, the author doesn't believe that the Freedonia Assertion should be applied blindly: it's always preferable to use friendly alphanumeric name forms for RDNs, instead of numeric name forms, whenever possible! However, it is useful to study the Freedonian national decision as it presents an interesting insight on the relationship between RDNs and non-distinguished attribute values. For example, a browsing DUA for Freedonia shouldn't display RDNs, as they aren't meaningful to people. Rather, it should use the search operation and retrieve some of the more interesting attributes for display. However, the choice of what constitutes an "interesting" attribute value may be problematic — each DUA designer will likely have a different algorithm for determining this. Nonetheless, it is the job of the DUA to make the DIT appear friendly, regardless of the perversity of the native naming architecture.

⌊...soap⌋

Chapter 5

Applying the Directory

It is now time to discuss how the Directory may be used to build applications. Although the primary focus is on using the Directory to achieve a White Pages service, a few other related uses will be explored.

Discussion begins by presenting the administrative discipline for a White Pages service. Following this, interrogation algorithms which provide the means for traversing the DIT to find information are discussed. This leads to a consideration of interrogation algorithms for several applications. Finally, we return to focus on White Pages looking at some actual applications which have been fielded.

5.1   A White Pages Pilot

In July of 1989, NYSERNet, Inc., a not-for-profit company running a regional network in the Internet, started a pilot offering a White Pages service using OSI technology. Since that time, Performance Systems International (PSI) a provider of commercial Internet and OSI internetworking service, has been extending and evaluating the service in response to experience gained during the operation of the White Pages Pilot.

At its inception, the service was seen as promising in three respects:

- it hoped to provide a large, distributed information service involving administration by multiple organizations;

- it was the first production-quality field test of the OSI Directory; and,

- it was the first large scale production application of OSI technology on top of the popular Internet suite of protocols.

The choice of OSI Directory as the cornerstone technology was not made lightly: the richness of the service was evident, and early prototype work had demonstrated that the underlying technology could be realized. Further, it has often been noted that:

> *if one is going to crash and burn, then it's probably best to be at the front of the airplane.*

Given the magnitude of the white pages problem in the Internet, this analogy seemed quite apt!

5.1.1   White Pages Pilot Schema

The White Pages Pilot uses the THORN X.500 Naming Architecture, as described in [35], as the basis of its schema.[1]

---

[1]The THORN project was a significant ESPRIT project, which implemented directory services [36]. THORN is an abbreviation for *THe Obviously Required Nameservice.*

Attribute Name	Abbrev.	Syntax
accessControlList	acl	special
associatedDomain		string
eDBinfo		special
favouriteDrink	drink	string
friendlyCountryName	co	string
homePhone		string
homePostalAddress		special
info		string
lastModifiedBy		Distinguished Name
lastModifiedTime		Universal Time
manager		Distinguished Name
masterDSA		Distinguished Name
mobileTelephoneNumber	mobile	string
otherMailbox		special
pagerTelephoneNumber	pager	string
photo		G3 facsimile
quipuVersion		string
rfc822Mailbox	mail	string
roomNumber		string
secretary		Distinguished Name
slaveDSA		Distinguished Name
treeStructure		Object Class
userClass		string
userId	uid	string

Table 5.1: Some Additional Attribute Types

Object Classes

The THORN Naming Architecture defines several additional object classes that are useful in a White Pages service. Because of this there are several additional attribute types defined, some of which are shown in Table 5.1. As with Table 4.1 shown earlier on page 80, this table also shows the QUIPU abbreviation for the attribute type. If the **Syntax** column indicates **string**, then a variant of the case-ignore string syntax is used. If the column indicates **special**, then a special ASN.1 type is defined for the syntax.

friendlyCountry

In order to provide user-friendly identification of sovereign nations, a new object class, subordinate to the **country** class, is defined:

```
friendlyCountry OBJECT-CLASS
    SUBCLASS OF country
    MUST CONTAIN { friendlyCountryName }
    ::= { quipuObjectClass 3 }
```

```
friendlyCountryName ATTRIBUTE
    WITH ATTRIBUTE-SYNTAX caseIgnoreStringSyntax
    ::= { quipuAttributeType 8 }
```

Recall that **country** objects are identified by their two-letter ISO 3166 code, e.g., c=IS for Iceland. (A list of these, current as of this writing, is shown in Table 5.2). By including the **friendlyCountry** as a value of a country's **objectClass** attribute, more descriptive strings can be used for searching,[2] e.g., the entry for c=DK might have

```
friendlyCountryName= Denmark
friendlyCountryName= DK
friendlyCountryName= The Kingdom of Denmark
```

thornObject and thornPerson

In order to provide for some uniformity across object classes defined in the THORN schema, the **thornObject** object class is defined:

```
thornObject OBJECT-CLASS
    SUBCLASS OF top
    MAY CONTAIN { info,
                  photo,
                  lastModifiedTime,
                  lastModifiedBy,
                  audio }
    ::= { thornObjectClass 3 }
```

---

[2]The "friendly" in **friendlyCountryName** refers to user-friendliness in naming, and doesn't necessarily reflect the Directory's view of how friendly a country is. It is interesting to note that the use of relatively obscure 3166 codes for naming countries smacks of the logic behind the Freedonian national decision.

AD	Andorra	GI	Gibraltar	NT	Neutral Zone
AE	United Arab Emirates	GL	Greenland	NU	Niue
AF	Afghanistan	GM	Gambia	NZ	New Zealand
AG	Antigua and Barbuda	GN	Guinea	OM	Oman
AI	Anguilla	GP	Guadeloupe	PA	Panama
AL	Albania	GQ	Equatorial Guinea	PE	Peru
AN	Netherlands Antilles	GR	Greece	PF	French Polynesia
AO	Angola	GT	Guatemala	PG	Papua New Guinea
AQ	Antarctica	GU	Guam	PH	Philippines
AR	Argentina	GW	Guinea-Bissau	PK	Pakistan
AS	American Samoa	GY	Guyana	PL	Poland
AT	Austria	HK	Hong Kong	PM	St. Pierre and Miquelon
AU	Australia	HM	Heard & McDonald Islands	PN	Pitcairn
AW	Aruba	HN	Honduras	PR	Puerto Rico
BB	Barbados	HT	Haiti	PT	Portugal
BD	Bangladesh	HU	Hungary	PW	Palau
BE	Belgium	ID	Indonesia	PY	Paraguay
BF	Burkina Faso	IE	Ireland	QA	Qatar
BG	Bulgaria	IL	Israel	RE	Reunion
BH	Bahrain	IN	India	RO	Romania
BI	Burundi	IO	British Indian Ocean Terr.	RW	Rwanda
BJ	Benin	IQ	Iraq	SA	Saudi Arabia
BM	Bermuda	IR	Islamic Republic of Iran	SB	Solomon Islands
BN	Brunei Darussalam	IS	Iceland	SC	Seychelles
BO	Bolivia	IT	Italy	SD	Sudan
BR	Brazil	JM	Jamaica	SE	Sweden
BS	Bahamas	JO	Jordan	SG	Singapore
BT	Bhutan	JP	Japan	SH	St. Helena
BU	Burma	KE	Kenya	SJ	Svalbard & Jan Mayen Islands
BV	Bouvet Island	KH	Democratic Kampuchea	SL	Sierra Leone
BW	Botswana	KI	Kiribati	SM	San Marino
BY	Byelorussian SSR	KM	Comoros	SN	Senegal
BZ	Belize	KN	Saint Kitts and Nevis	SO	Somalia
CA	Canada	KP	Dem. People's Rep. of Korea	SR	Suriname
CC	Cocos (Keeling) Islands	KR	Republic of Korea	ST	Sao Tome and Principe
CF	Central African Republic	KW	Kuwait	SU	USSR
CG	Congo	KY	Cayman Islands	SV	El Salvador
CH	Switzerland	LA	Lao People's Democratic Rep.	SY	Syrian Arab Republc
CI	Cote d'Ivoire	LB	Lebanon	SZ	Swaziland
CK	Cook Islands	LC	Saint Lucia	TC	Turks and Caicos Islands
CL	Chile	LI	Liechtenstein	TD	Chad
CM	Cameroon	LK	Sri Lanka	TF	French Southern Territories
CN	China	LR	Liberia	TG	Togo
CO	Colombia	LS	Lesotho	TH	Thailand
CR	Costa Rica	LU	Luxembourg	TK	Tokelau
CS	Czechoslovakia	LY	Libyan Arab Jamahiriya	TN	Tunisia
CU	Cuba	MA	Morocco	TO	Tonga
CV	Cape Verde	MC	Monaco	TP	East Timor
CX	Christmas Island	MG	Madagascar	TR	Turkey
CY	Cyprus	MH	Marshall Islands	TT	Trinidad and Tobago
DD	German Democratic Rep.	ML	Mali	TV	Tuvalu
DE	Federal Rep. of Germany	MN	Mongolia	TW	Province of China Taiwan
DJ	Djibouti	MO	Macau	TZ	United Republic of Tanzania
DK	Denmark	MP	Northern Mariana Islands	UA	Ukrainian SSR
DM	Dominica	MQ	Martinique	UG	Uganda
DO	Dominican Republic	MR	Mauritania	UM	US Minor Outlying Islands
DZ	Algeria	MS	Montserrat	US	United States
EC	Ecuador	MT	Malta	UY	Uruguay
EG	Egypt	MU	Mauritius	VA	Vatican City State
EH	Western Sahara	MV	Maldives	VC	St. Vincent & the Grenadines
ES	Spain	MW	Malawi	VE	Venezuela
ET	Ethiopia	MX	Mexico	VG	British Virgin Islands
FI	Finland	MY	Malaysia	VI	US Virgin Islands
FJ	Fiji	MZ	Mozambique	VN	Viet Nam
FK	Falkland Islands	NA	Namibia	VU	Vanuatu
FM	Micronesia	NC	New Caledonia	WF	Wallis and Futuna Islands
FO	Faroe Islands	NE	Niger	WS	Samoa
FR	France	NF	Norfolk Island	YD	Democratic Yemen
GA	Gabon	NG	Nigeria	YE	Yemen
GB	United Kingdom	NI	Nicaragua	YU	Yugoslavia
GD	Grenada	NL	Netherlands	ZA	South Africa
GF	French Guiana	NO	Norway	ZM	Zambia
GH	Ghana	NP	Nepal	ZR	Zaire
		NR	Nauru		

Table 5.2: ISO 3166 Alphabetic Country Codes

Using the **thornObject** as a superclass, several other object classes are defined to model THORN objects.

For our purposes, the most relevant is:

```
thornPerson OBJECT-CLASS
    SUBCLASS OF thornObject, person
    MAY CONTAIN { userid
                  textEncodedORAddress,
                  rfc822Mailbox,
                  favouriteDrink,
                  roomNumber,
                  userClass,
                  homePhone,
                  homePostalAddress,
                  secretary,
                  personalTitle }
    ::= { thornObjectClass 4 }
```

pilotPerson

Even with all these additional attributes, the administrators of the White Pages Pilot decided that a few more were necessary to capture information about persons in the Internet:

```
pilotPerson OBJECT-CLASS
    SUBCLASS OF thornPerson
    MAY CONTAIN { localeAttributeSet,
                  postalAttributeSet,
                  telecommunicationAttributeSet,
                  businessCategory,
                  title,
                  otherMailbox,
                  mobileTelephoneNumber,
                  pagerTelephoneNumber }
    ::= { psiObjectClass 1 }
```

This progression:

- from **thornObject**, which captures information about a class of objects;

- to `thornPerson`, which merges that information with generic personal information; and finally,

- to `pilotPerson`, which merges all of that with additional information specific to people in the pilot

shows how the extensibility facilities in the Directory's Information Framework can easily be put to (ab)use.

An entry belonging to the `pilotPerson` class may have any of several attributes which aren't found in an instance of the `person` object class. Here are just a few!

favouriteDrink: which is a string describing the user's favorite drink.

homePhone: which is a string describing the phone number of the object using the international notation; e.g.,

```
+1 518-555-5555
```

homePostalAddress: which describes how physical mail is addressed to the person's home.

info: which is additional, textual, information about the person.

mobileTelephoneNumber: which is a string describing the user's mobile number (e.g., for a cellular phone).

otherMailbox: which is the user's computer mail address in various domains. The string syntax of this attribute's value is special:

```
<domain> $ <mailbox>
```

e.g.,

```
internet $ mrose@psi.com
```

The current list of mail domains are: applelink, bitnet, compuserve, genie, internet, mcimail, nasamail, preferred, and uucp.

pagerTelephoneNumber: which is a string describing the user's pager number.

photo: which is a facsimile bitmap of the user's face.

rfc822Mailbox: which is the user's computer mail address in the Internet.

roomNumber: which is a string describing where the person resides at the location.

secretary: which is the Distinguished Name of the user's administrative support.

userClass: which describe's the user's classification; e.g.,

```
staff
```

userid: which is the user's login name; e.g.,

```
mrose
```

documentSeries and document

In order to experiment with document identification and retrieval with the Directory, the THORN Naming Architecture defines two object classes:

```
documentSeries OBJECT-CLASS
    SUBCLASS OF top
    MUST CONTAIN { commonName }
    MAY CONTAIN  { description,
                   seeAlso,
                   telephoneNumber,
                   localityName,
                   organizationName
                   organizationalUnitName }
    ::= { thornObjectClass 9 }
```

```
document OBJECT-CLASS
    SUBCLASS OF thornObject
    MUST CONTAIN { documentIdentifier }
    MAY CONTAIN { commonName,
                  description,
                  seeAlso,
                  localityname,
                  organizationName,
                  ourganizationalUnitName,
                  documentTitle,
                  documentVersion,
                  documentAuthor,
                  documentLocation,
                  obsoletesDocument,
                  obsoletedByDocument,
                  updatesDocument,
                  updatedByDocument,
                  keywords,
                  subject,
                  abstract,
                  authorCN,
                  authorSN,
                  documentStore }
      ::= { thornObjectClass 6 }
```

This first describes a series of documents under a common administration, whilst the second describes an individual document.

domainRelatedObject

Finally, since the White Pages Pilot is being deployed in the Internet, there is a need to map between objects defined in terms of the Internet Domain Name System (such as an Internet mailbox) and portions of the DIT. Accordingly, several new object classes are defined. For our purposes, only one is of interest:

```
domainRelatedObject OBJECT-CLASS
    SUBCLASS OF top
    MUST CONTAIN { associatedDomain }
    ::= { thornObjectClass 17 }

associatedDomain ATTRIBUTE
    WITH ATTRIBUTE-SYNTAX ia5StringSyntax
    ::= { thornAttributeType 37 }
```

Skipping ahead a bit, Section 5.2.5 starting on page 199 presents an interrogation algorithm for mapping between a Internet mailbox and a Distinguished Name.

Country	DSAs	Organizations	Entries
Australia	14	15	16536
Canada	10	10	21300
Denmark	1	1	16
Finland	10	13	10316
Great Britain	38	33	67345
Germany	9	85	9026
Iceland	1	1	185
Netherlands	2	69	2132
Norway	3	40	3714
Spain	2	3	141
Switzerland	5	9	4554
Sweden	6	17	3035
United States	66	74	167577
Total	177	370	296440

Table 5.3: International Participation in QUIPU Pilot

5.1.2   White Pages Pilot DIT Structure

The White Pages Pilot maintains three portions of the DIT:

    c=US

    l=North America

    o=Internet

all directly under the DIT root.

Other national and regional Directory pilots interact with the White Pages Pilot to provide coverage in many European countries and also in the Pacific Rim. Table 5.3 gives a basic idea as to the scope of International Pilot participation as of January, 1991.

DMD for @c=US

This is the primary focal point for the White Pages Pilot. As shown in Figure 5.1 on page 152, a two-level naming scheme is used for organizations (i.e., organizations are placed directly under c=US). Obviously, such an approach will not scale, but in the absence of the ever-elusive national decision discussed in Section 4.4.1, it is the most straight-forward direction to follow in the short-term.

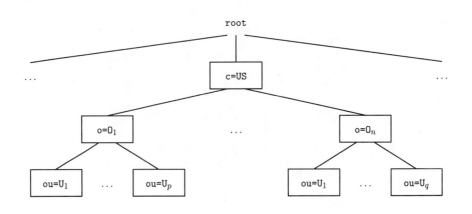

Figure 5.1: DMD for @c=US

As of January, 1991, some 70 sites were participating in the White Pages Pilot, and all but 6 were running their own DSAs and acting as a PRDMD:

Type	Number	
University	27	
Corporate	18	
Government	10	
Non-profit	9	
Remote	6	
70	**total**	

The DIT under c=US, at that time, contained approximately 225,000 entries.[3]

---

[3]These figures differ from those shown in Table 5.3 on page 151. The figures in the table were automatically generated by repeated sweeps through the Directory, in which only national and organizational DSAs were contacted, and the number of entries they mastered was tallied. Thus, if an organization employs multiple DSAs, only a part of the organization's entries are counted. In contrast, the 225K figure is determined periodically by hand, and includes all entries mastered throughout the US.

DMD for @l=North America

As a part of an experiment, this portion of the DIT was created. It contains entries for organizations both in the United States and Canada (there is no pilot currently running, to the author's knowledge, in Mexico). This allows a simple DUA to search for a top-level organization in either country. Because there are more effective algorithms which achieve the same results, this portion of the DIT is likely to be retired soon.

DMD for @o=Internet

Three subtrees are maintained under this portion of the DIT: two document series, the Internet Request For Comments (RFCs), and the FYI series; and site contact information.

A typical entry in a document series might contain these attributes:

```
objectClass        - document
documentIdentifier - RFC1216
documentTitle      - Gigabit network economics and paradigm shifts
documentVersion    - April 1, 1991
authorCN           - P. Richard
authorSN           - Richard
authorCN           - P. Kynikos
authorSN           - Kynikos
```

Hence, one might imagine that a bibliographic retrieval tool, which used the Directory could find an RFC of interest, and, if the document's author had an entry in the DIT, a **documentAuthor** link could be followed for additional contact information.

A typical entry for a **siteContact** object, which is a subclass of the **pilotPerson** object, might contain these attributes:

```
objectClass        - siteContact
commonName         - Schoffstall, Martin
commonName         - PSINET
ipNetworkNumber    - 128.145.0.0
ipNetworkNumber    - 128.145
surName            - Schoffstall
whoisIdent         - MS9
ipNetworkName      - PSINET
telephoneNumber    - (703) 620-6651
rfc822Mailbox      - SCHOFF@PSI.COM
seeAlso            - c=US
                     @o=Performance Systems International
```

```
@ou=Administration
@ou=Reston
@cn=Martin Schoffstall
```

Hence, one might imagine that a network management system, upon detecting a fault with the IP network 128.145, could access the Directory to retrieve pertinent information so that the operator could contact an entity responsible for that network.

5.1.3   White Pages Pilot Guidelines

In addition to providing the Directory software, the White Pages Pilot provides an Administrator's Guide containing detailed information on establishing and maintaining a PRDMD. Among other things, the document provides a set of guidelines to PRDMD operators within the pilot as to how these object classes should be used. These guidelines are summarized in Tables 5.4 through 5.7, starting on page 155. The tables are hopefully straight-forward:

- Each is divided into two parts: "primary class" attributes, which are those attributes found because of the entry's most subordinate object class; and, "superclass" attributes, which are those attributes found in an entry because of multiple-inheritance.

  For example, if the entry corresponds to a `pilotPerson` object, then the primary class attributes are those found with person, whilst the superclass attributes are those required because of class inheritance. Usually, two different entries of the same class will have similar values used for those attributes required by the superclass, whilst different values are used for the primary class attributes. Of course, for two sibling entries, the attribute values corresponding to the RDN will always be different.

- Sometimes the attributes are multi-valued, in this case, an '&'-sign is used to indicate that the union of the values listed in the table is present.

Note that these tables refer to two object classes which have not yet been introduced, namely `quipuObject` and `quipuNonLeafObject`. These are described in Section 6.3.3.

Superclass Attributes		
Attribute Name	**Status**	**Value**
objectClass	M	top & quipuObject
		& quipuNonLeafObject
		& domainRelatedObject
acl	M	
masterDSA	M	
slaveDSA	O	
Primary Class Attributes		
Attribute Name	**Status**	**Value**
objectClass	M	organization
organizationName	RDN	
associatedDomain	O	
postalAddress	O	
registeredAddress	O	
streetAddress	O	
physicalDeliveryOfficeName	O	
stateOrProvinceName	O	
postalCode	O	
localityName	O	
telephoneNumber	O	
facsimileTelephoneNumber	O	
telexNumber	O	
description	O	

Legend

M: mandatory

O: optional, but recommended

RDN: mandatory, must form the RDN for object

Table 5.4: WPP Guidelines for Organization Entries

Superclass Attributes		
Attribute Name	**Status**	**Value**
objectClass	M	top & quipuObject
		& quipuNonLeafObject
	O	& domainRelatedObject
acl	M	
masterDSA	M	
slaveDSA	O	
Primary Class Attributes		
Attribute Name	**Status**	**Value**
objectClass	M	organizationalUnit
organizationalUnitName	RDN	
associatedDomain	O	
postalAddress	O	
registeredAddress	O	
streetAddress	O	
physicalDeliveryOfficeName	O	
stateOrProvinceName	O	
postalCode	O	
localityName	O	
telephoneNumber	O	
facsimileTelephoneNumber	O	
telexNumber	O	
description	O	

Legend

M: mandatory

O: optional, but recommended

RDN: mandatory, must form the RDN for object

Table 5.5: WPP Guidelines for Organizational Unit Entries

Superclass Attributes		
Attribute Name	**Status**	**Value**
objectClass	M	top & quipuObject
acl	M	
Primary Class Attributes		
Attribute Name	**Status**	**Value**
objectClass	M	organizationalRole
commonName	RDN	
postalAddress	O	
registeredAddress	O	
streetAddress	N	
physicalDeliveryOfficeName	N	
stateOrProvinceName	N	
postalCode	N	
localityName	O	
telephoneNumber	O	
facsimileTelephoneNumber	O	
telexNumber	O	
description	O	
roleOccupant	O	

Legend

M: mandatory

O: optional, but recommended

N: optional, not recommended

RDN: mandatory, must form the RDN for object

Table 5.6: WPP Guidelines for Organizational Role Entries

Superclass Attributes		
Attribute Name	**Status**	**Value**
objectClass	M	top & quipuObject
acl	M	
Primary Class Attributes		
Attribute Name	**Status**	**Value**
objectClass	M	person & thornPerson & pilotPerson
commonName	RDN	
surName	M	
postalAddress	O	
registeredAddress	O	
roomNumber	O	
streetAddress	L	
telephoneNumber	O	
facsimileTelephoneNumber	L	
telexNumber	L	
rfc822Mailbox	O	
otherMailbox	X	
userid	O	
userClass	O	
description	O	
info	O	
businessCategory	O	
title	O	
userPassword	O	
mobileTelephoneNumber	X	
pagerTelephoneNumber	X	
favouriteDrink	O	
secretary	X	
seeAlso	X	
photo	X	
homePostalAddress	O	
homePhone	O	

Legend

M: mandatory

O: optional, but recommended

L: optional, use if value different than immediate superior

X: optional, use only if applicable

RDN: mandatory, must form the RDN for object

Table 5.7: WPP Guidelines for Pilot Person Entries

5.2 Interrogation Algorithms

Now that we have explained the Information Framework used within the White Pages Pilot, let's consider how interrogation algorithms are built.

The goal of an *interrogation algorithm* is to provide the user-friendly characteristic of guessability: based on identifying information supplied by the user, an interrogation algorithm will identify one or more Distinguished Names which are likely to be of interest.

An interrogation algorithm starts with some knowledge of the DIT structure (or at least knowledge of the portion of the DIT that is of interest). The user supplies identifying criteria, and the algorithm then executes in an environment containing user options. One can imagine that the manager of the local DMD initializes the user options, and individual users can customize their environment if need be.

Once the algorithm begins execution it invokes Directory operations, primarily search and read. In between the invocation of these operations, the algorithm may interact with the user, as appropriate, in order to focus the invocation of subsequent operations during the algorithm's execution.

The challenge of designing an interrogation algorithm is two-fold, as the algorithm should require the least possible knowledge of the DIT-structure, whilst still executing efficiently. The Directory standard is silent in the area of interrogation algorithms, so the remainder of this section can be viewed as describing refinements. These refinements are not specific to QUIPU, they are merely outside the scope of the Directory standard.

As noted with the lack of guidance in DIT structuring, the Directory standard describes a technology, and not a policy of use. Therefore, it does not define any interrogation algorithms (indeed, it hardly alludes to their existence). Although understandable from the technology perspective, this hands-off philosophy taken by the Directory standard causes problems in usage and is thus rather unfortunate.

soap...

The usual comment made by Directory "experts" is:

> *when searching for someone, you don't want to start at the*
> *root of the DIT, it would take too long and be too expensive;*
> *the search should be a bit more focused.*

In terms of thinking through the problems of designing interrogation algorithms, this seems to be the level of detail achieved by most of the so-called "experts." The author finds this attitude amazingly naive. Without a carefully designed DIT structure and associated interrogation algorithms, the notion of a "public directory service" is simply unachievable.

`...soap`

5.2.1 Directory Search Revisited

Because interrogation algorithms make heavy use of the Directory search operation, it is worthwhile to consider this operation in a little more than the cursory detail provided earlier in Section 4.2.1. The search operation takes six kinds of arguments:

baseobject: a DN naming the entry at the base of the subtree where searching is to begin.

subset: an indication as to which entries should be searched, one of: `baseobject`, `oneLevel`, or `wholeSubtree`.

filter: an arbitrarily complex boolean expression which is applied to each entry to be searched.

The operands are the attribute values of the entry, and the operators are:

operator	abbrev.
logical-and	∧
logical-or	∨
logical-not	¬
equality	=
substring-containment	∈
greater-than or equal	≥
less-than or equal	≤
value is present	∃
approximately equal	≈

The symbols appearing in the right column will be used in *The Little Black Book* to express these operators. (Fortunately, only a few of these symbols will be needed!)

The expressions in the filter may be arbitrarily grouped, and there may be zero or more sub-expressions given to the logical-and (∧) and logical-or (∨) operators. Because of this, it is useful to think of an ∧-expression as being initialized to value **TRUE**, and then each operand being evaluated. As soon as one returns **FALSE**, evaluation of the ∧-expression ceases. Similarly, think of an ∨-expression as being initialized to value **FALSE**, and then each operand being evaluated. As soon as one returns **TRUE**, evaluation of the ∨-expression ceases.

searchaliases: a flag indicating how aliases encountered during the evaluation of the search should be dealt with. If **TRUE**, then the alias will be dereferenced and the filter will be applied to the corresponding entry; otherwise, the filter will be applied to the attributes in the alias entry. Note that the `dontDereferenceAliases` service control determines how each entry is selected as the base-object for the search,

whilst the `searchAliases` flag determines the entries which
are actually searched.

entryInformationSelection: this indicates what kind of information should be returned about any entries which satisfy
the filter. All the attributes can be returned, or a subset. In the latter case, the DUA indicates exactly which
attribute values it is interested in. In either case, this parameter also indicates whether the attribute types should
be returned, or the attribute types and all values. Regardless of these settings, the Distinguished Name is always
returned to indicate which entries were matched. (Figure 4.14 back on page 116 has a more formal description
of `entryInformationSelection`).

service controls: these were discussed earlier on page 108.

For the purposes of exposition, the interrogation algorithms we look
at will make minimal use of service controls. However, sophisticated
implementations of these algorithms will most likely use service controls at the request of the user (i.e., in order to limit the expected
cost of a query).

To begin our exploration of interrogation algorithms, we'll look at
a simple one.

5.2.2 Simple Naming

The philosophy of the *Simple Naming* algorithm is that people are
identified by name/place pairs, not unlike the listing services found
in the telephone system. Before you can search for someone's phone
number, you need to know the area in which the person is listed.[4]
The algorithm will make minimum use of non-naming attributes, but
will ask for user-assistance when multiple matches are encountered.

---

[4]It turns out that the actual algorithms used for listing services are extraordi-
narily sophisticated. Use of this analogy should not imply that the Simple Naming
algorithm is intended as a replacement. Quite the contrary, the author finds it unlikely that the Directory will be able to compete with the telephone system's listing
services for quite some time!

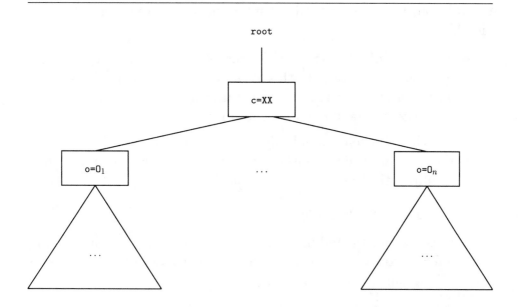

Figure 5.2: Two-level Naming Architecture

Knowledge

The Simple Naming algorithm has knowledge of a two-level naming architecture. Locations (organizations or localities) to be searched all share the same superior entry in the DIT, whilst persons within a given location are contained somewhere in an arbitrarily structured subtree. Figure 5.2 presents such a structure, which looks remarkably similar to Figure 5.1 presented earlier. It should be noted that this figure shows locations as being subordinate to a country. The Simple Naming algorithm does not mandate this, instead it assumes that all locations are immediately subordinate to a single entry in the DIT.

User Input

The Simple Naming algorithm requires one mandatory input, a simple string containing some naming information about the target, e.g.,

```
geoffrey goodfellow
```

In addition, three other kinds of information can optionally be provided:

- The kind of object: If the user is able to provide a classification of the target, this can be used to focus the search. The choices are: `person`, `organization`, `organizationalUnit`, `organizationalRole`, and `locality`.

  As with all the optional information, the user-interface can derive this information either explicitly (the user fills-in a form), or implicitly from context, e.g., if the user says

    find the chairman

  then a sophisticated interface would determine that the naming information was "chairman" and that use of "the" indicated a role within the organization.

- Qualifying Information: If the user is able to provide some non-naming information, which would help to distinguish between possible choices, then this too can be used to focus the search. For the Simple Algorithm, this is a textual string. For example, if looking for an organization, this information might indicate the type of business.

- Locational Information: If the user has a good idea of where the target is located, then this too can be used to focus the search.

User Environment

The Simple Naming algorithm has one item in the user's environment, a *locational table* indicating where it should look for different kinds of targets, e.g.,

What	Base
default	`@c=US@o=Performance Systems International`
organization	`@l=North America`
unit	`@c=US@o=Performance Systems International`
role	`@c=US@o=Performance Systems International`
locality	`@c=US`
person	`@c=US@o=Performance Systems International`

This table would likely be initialized by the local DMD manager, and would not be modified by, or even known to, the typical user.

Algorithm

To formally describe an interrogation algorithm, it's necessary to have some kind of notation. ASN.1 is a data description language and does not really provide a means for capturing the notion of a "code fragment." So, we'll have to augment ASN.1 accordingly. The particular set of augmentations used in *The Little Black Book* was developed by Stephen E. Kille of University College London, as a part of the work on his User-Friendly Naming Scheme (discussed in Section 5.2.3 on page 176). The augmentations are not formally defined, it's really just a smattering of *C* and *Pascal* constructs with ASN.1. In the future it might be useful to define a "real" language for describing execution in terms of ASN.1, but for now, we'll use Kille's pseudo-code.

To begin, we'll need to define a few data structures. These are shown in Figure 5.3 on page 166.

Table ::=
  SET OF
      SEQUENCE {
          kind
                ObjectClass,
          base
                DN
      }

DN ::=   10
  SEQUENCE OF
      RDN

RDN ::=
  SET OF
      DAV

DAV ::=
  SEQUENCE {
      type   20
        OBJECT IDENTIFIER,

      value
        ANY DEFINED BY type
  }

Figure 5.3: Data Structures for the Simple Algorithm

Figure 5.4 on page 168 shows the top-level of the Simple Naming algorithm. The routine `twoLevelMatch` takes inputs of:

kind: the kind of object, if unspecified by the user, the special value `default` is passed;

name: the naming information;

qual: the qualifying information, if unspecified by the user, an empty string is passed;

location: the locational information, if unspecified by the user, an empty string is passed; and,

bases: the locational table from the user-environment.

If the user specified a location, the routine `simpleMatch` is called to find an organization with the specified name. The parameters given to `simpleMatch` indicate that no qualifying information should be used in searching, and the place to look for the organization is found in the locational table. The `simpleMatch` routine returns a list of zero or more DNs.

If `simpleMatch` found any DNs likely to be of interest, the algorithm checks to see if more than one DN was found. If so, for each of the locations found by the search, the user is asked if searching should continue there. For each so indicated, `simpleMatch` is called accordingly. Otherwise, if only one DN of interest is found, then `simpleMatch` is called directly (the DN is extracted from the sequence by using the **head** function) without asking the user. Either way, the results, a list of zero or more DNs is returned.

If the user did not specify a location, the user-environment is consulted, and a single call to `simpleMatch` is made.

Figure 5.5 starting on page 169 shows the `simpleMatch` routine, which is straight-forward but tedious. First, a list of attributes types is collected into `alist`, based on the kind of object to look for. Second, `qlist` is set to the attribute type meaningful for qualifying information, again based on the kind of object to look for. Third, a determination is made as to whether the Directory search should be a whole-subtree search or a single-level search.

```
twoLevelMatch (kind: ObjectClass; name, qual, location: String;
              bases: Table): SET OF DN
{
  x: DN;
  dlist, matches: SET OF DN;

  matches = NULL;
  IF (location) THEN
      IF (dlist = simpleMatch ("organization", location, NULL,
                       findTable ("organization", bases))) THEN              10
          IF (length (dlist) > 1) THEN
              FOR x IN dlist DO
                  IF (userSaysSo (x)) THEN
                      matches += simpleMatch (kind, name, qual, x);
              RETURN matches;
          ELSE
              RETURN simpleMatch (kind, name, qual, head (dlist));
      ELSE
          -- tell user nowhere to look
          RETURN NULL;                                                       20
  ELSE
      RETURN simpleMatch (kind, name, qual, findTable (kind, bases));
}
```

Figure 5.4: Top-Level for the Simple Algorithm

Finally, the Directory Search is performed. The filter for the search consists of two parts. The first part is constructed by applying the **approximateMatch** operator over the search string and the attribute types which convey naming information for the kind of object, and using a logical-OR of each term. Thus, if looking for a person, and the search string is "**goodfellow**," the first part of the filter would look like:

$$surName \approx \text{"goodfellow"}$$
$$\lor \quad rfc822Mailbox \approx \text{"goodfellow"}$$

The second part of the filter is constructed if the qualifying information is non-empty. It is constructed by applying the **equality** operator over the qualifying information and the attribute type which conveys qualifying information for the kind of object. Thus, if looking for a person, and the qualifying information is **president**, the second part of the filter would look like:

$$title \approx \text{"president"}$$

```
simpleMatch (kind: ObjectClass; name, qual: String; base: DN): SET OF DN
{
    x: DN;
    alist, qlist: SET OF AttributeType;
    subsettype: SubsetType;

    IF (kind == person) THEN
        alist = { surName, rfc822Mailbox };
    ELSE
        IF (kind == organization) THEN                                        10
            alist = { organizationName };
        ELSE
            IF (kind == organizationalUnit) THEN
                alist = { organizationalUnitName };
            ELSE
                IF (kind == organizationalRole) THEN
                    alist = { commonName };
                ELSE
                    IF (kind == locality) THEN
                        alist = { localityName };                            20
                    ELSE
                        alist = { commonName, surName, rfc822Mailbox };

    IF (kind == person) THEN
        qlist = { title };
    ELSE
        IF (kind == organization) THEN
            qlist = { businessCategory };
        ELSE
            IF (kind == organizationalUnit) THEN                             30
                qlist = { businessCategory };
            ELSE
                IF (kind == organizationalRole) THEN
                    qlist = { title };
                ELSE
                    IF (kind != locality) THEN
                        qlist = { title };

    IF (kind == organization OR kind == locality) THEN
        subsettype = oneLevel;                                               40
    ELSE
        subsettype = wholeSubtree;

    ...
```

Figure 5.5: Search Operation for the Simple Algorithm

...

```
-- map onto Directory Search
-- baseObject: 'base'
-- subset: 'subsetType'
-- filter:
--     build OR-conjuction of 's' using approximateMatch over 'alist'
--     if 'qual' isn't empty:
--         build filter-item of 'qual' using equality over 'qlist'
--         AND with original filter                                   10
-- selection: attributes and values of
--     telephoneNumber, rfc822Mailbox

-- cache returned entries and associated attributes/values

RETURN search-results;
}
```

Figure 5.5: Search Operation for the Simple Algorithm (cont.)

The actual search filter is the logical-AND of both parts, e.g.,

$$(\text{surName} \approx \text{"goodfellow"}$$
$$\lor \ \text{rfc822Mailbox} \approx \text{"goodfellow"})$$
$$\land \ \text{title} \approx \text{"president"}$$

If there was no qualifying-information, the first item by itself is used as the search filter. As a part of the policy of this algorithm, the Directory is asked to supply the attribute types and values for two different attribute types (we'll find out why later). The results of the search, if any, are then cached. The `simpleMatch` then returns the list of DNs (possibly empty) that resulted from the Directory search.

Finally, let's take a step back and look at a complete example. The user supplies the input

> *find some person named "goodfellow" at some company named "anterior"*

The routine `twoLevelMatch` is invoked with the arguments shown in Figure 5.6.

Since a `location` argument (`anterior`) is present, the routine `simpleMatch` is called with the arguments:

```
kind:    organization
name:    "anterior"
qual:    NULL
base:    {
             { { localityName, "North America" } }
         }
```

The Directory search operation is invoked with:

```
baseObject:     {
                    { { localityName, "North America" } }
                }
subsetType:     oneLevel
selection:      {
                    { telephoneNumber },
                    { rfc822Mailbox },
                }
```

and a filter of:

$$\text{organizationName} \approx \text{"anterior"}$$

The Directory search returns a single entry:

```
l=North America@o=Anterior Technology%l=US
```

(Recall that the %-sign indicates that the second RDN is multi-valued.) The entry, along with the associated attributes, is cached, and the DN of the entry is returned.

```
kind:          person
name:          "goodfellow"
qual:          NULL
location:      "anterior"
bases:         {
                 { default,
                   {
                     { { countryName, "US" } },
                     { { organizationName,
                         "Performance Systems International" } }
                   }
                 },
                 { organization,
                   {
                     { { localityName, "North America" } }
                   }
                 },
                 { organizationalUnit,
                   {
                     { { countryName, "US" } },
                     { { organizationName,
                         "Performance Systems International" } }
                   }
                 },
                 { organizationalRole,
                   {
                     { { countryName, "US" } },
                     { { organizationName,
                         "Performance Systems International" } }
                   }
                 },
                 { locality,
                   {
                     { { countryName, "US" } }
                   }
                 },
                 { person,
                   {
                     { { countryName, "US" } },
                     { { organizationName,
                         "Performance Systems International" } }
                   }
                 }
               }
```

Figure 5.6: Example Arguments to twoLevelMatch

The routine `twoLevelMatch` sees that a single DN was returned, and invokes `simpleMatch` once again, but with these arguments:

```
kind:     person
name:     "goodfellow"
qual:     NULL
base:     {
              { { localityName, "North America" } },
              {
                  { organizationName, "Anterior Technology" },
                  { localityName, "US" }
              }
          }
```

The Directory search operation is invoked with:

```
baseObject:     {
                    { { localityName, "North America" } },
                    {
                        { organizationName,
                          "Anterior Technology" },
                        { localityName, "US" }
                    }
                }
subsetType:     wholeSubtree
selection:      {
                    { telephoneNumber },
                    { rfc822Mailbox },
                }
```

and a filter of:

$$\text{surName} \approx \text{"goodfellow"}$$
$$\lor \ \text{rfc822Mailbox} \approx \text{"goodfellow"}$$

It turns out that the `baseObject` of the search is an alias pointing to a different part of the DIT, e.g.,

```
c=US@o=Anterior Technology
```

so the search operation dereferences the alias prior to applying the filter. The results of the Directory search are cached, and the corresponding list of DNs are returned, which in turn are returned by `twoLevelMatch`.

So why is the Directory search operation asked to return any `telephoneNumber` or `rfc822Mailbox` values? Recall that the user might be asked to select from the matches which have been made. In this case, it is useful to present some minimal information as to the choices. By asking for a few key attributes, other than naming information, the user can be presented with a little extra information when making a choice. For example, if asked to choose between several organizations, a phone number (containing an area code) might help; similarly, if asked to choose between several people, a mailbox might be useful. Of course, the Directory search operation could have been directed to return all attributes, but this is wasteful of network bandwidth.

5.2.3 White Pages Lookup

Although the Simple Naming algorithm is good for exposition, it is probably inadequate for a generic White Pages service. It appears to need strengthening in two areas:

- The assumption of a two-level naming architecture leads to inefficiency when the user has a more detailed understanding of where the object is located.

- Use of a single base object for searching is too restrictive. Clever readers have probably deduced that the DMD for

    l=North America

was created to circumvent this restriction in the Simple Naming algorithm. This portion of the DIT contains aliases to those organizations with national standing in both the United States and Canada. Thus, a user interested in finding an organization in either country can search in just one place. A better means, outside of micro-structuring the DIT for particular applications, is needed. For example, in the Internet, the DNS has used the concept of a *search-list* to great advantage.

Kille's User-Friendly Naming Scheme

In an effort to develop a more general interrogation algorithm, Steve Kille has developed a "user-friendly naming scheme" [37]. Kille's scheme avoids the limitations of the Simple Naming algorithm, and is of use in several applications of the Directory.

The philosophy of the User Friendly Naming (UFN) scheme is that objects are identified by ordered, but untyped, bits of naming information, e.g.,

```
marshall rose, psi
```

These are termed *purported names*. Although it is up to the user to order the naming information, this information needn't be complete. For example, the two purported names

```
kille, ucl, gb
kille, cs, ucl, gb
```

might both resolve to the same entry in the Directory.

As with the Simple Naming algorithm, the UFN algorithm will ask for user-assistance, when appropriate. In an improvement over the Simple Naming algorithm however, the UFN algorithm has a notion of the "goodness" of a match. This allows the algorithm to proceed in a somewhat more autonomous fashion and still achieve good results.

Knowledge

The UFN algorithm has knowledge of a multi-level naming architecture:

- Directly under the root of the DIT, countries, organizations, and localities, might be found.

- In the intermediate levels of the DIT, organizations, organizational units, and localities, might be found, and interrogation is guided on the basis of the RDNs encountered.

In addition, special treatment is given to the ISO 3166 country codes.

User Input

The UFN algorithm requires one mandatory input, a purported name. This is treated as a sequence of strings, termed *naming components*, read from left to right, in which the leftmost component represents naming information for the object's RDN. Naming components are separated by commas, and if a component contains a comma, then double-quotes are used according, e.g.,

```
L. Eagle, "Sue, Grabbit, and Run", Oxford
```

is a purported name containing three naming components, the second component is:

```
Sue, Grabbit, and Run
```

To focus the search, a knowledgeable user might include some typing information in the naming information, e.g.,

```
James Hacker, l=Oxford, Widget Inc.
```

in which the second component indicates that it refers to something having a `localityName` value of "Oxford."

User Environment

The UFN algorithm has one item in the user-environment, a search-list. In a public DUA for North America, the list might be:

Range	Bases
1,2:	c=US
	c=CA
	–
3,+:	–
	c=US
	c=CA

This is read as:

> *if the purported name contains one or two naming components, first look under* c=US, *then look under* c=CA,[5] *and then look under the root;*
>
> *otherwise, if three or more components are present, look under the root, then look under* c=US, *and then look under* c=CA.

In an organizational DUA, the list might be somewhat different:

Range	Bases
1:	c=US@o=Performance Systems International@ou=Sales
	c=US@o=Performance Systems International
	c=US
	–
2:	c=US
	c=US@o=Performance Systems International
	–
3,+:	–
	c=US
	c=US@o=Performance Systems International

As with the Simple Naming algorithm, these search-lists are configured by the local DMD manager, and are probably never seen by the users.

---

[5]For the benefit of US-centric readers, CA refers to the country of Canada, not the state of California in the US.

Algorithm

The data structures used in the UFN algorithm are shown in Figure 5.7. The only tricky part is the representation of a purported name. Although it is a sequence of strings, the sequence is inverted. Thus, the purported name

```
kille, cs, ucl, gb
```

would be represented as:

```
{ "gb", "ucl", "cs", "kille" }
```

If one asked for the **head** of this sequence, then the string "gb" would be returned. The **tail** of this sequence is not a string, but the sequence:

```
{ "ucl", "cs", "kille" }
```

which does not contain the **head** of the original sequence.

```
PurportedName ::=        -- inverted, e.g., { "us", "psi", "rose" }
    SEQUENCE OF
        String

RDN ::=
    DAV
    -- simplification, as potentially multi-value

DAV ::=
    SEQUENCE {                                                        10
        type
            OBJECT IDENTIFIER,
        value
            ANY DEFINED BY type
    }
EnvironmentList ::=
    SEQUENCE OF
        EnvironmentItem

EnvironmentItem ::=
    SEQUENCE {                                                        20
        lower-bound
            INTEGER,
        upper-bound
            INTEGER,
        environment
            Environment
    }

Environment ::=
    SEQUENCE OF                                                       30
        DN

DN ::=
    SEQUENCE OF
        RDN
```

Figure 5.7: Data Structures for the UFN Algorithm

```
friendlyMatch (p: PurportedName; el: EnvironmentList): SET OF DN
{
    e: EnvironmentItem;

    FOR (e = head (el); e; e = head (el = tail (el)))
        IF (length (p) <= e.upper−bound
                && length (p) >= e.lower−bound) THEN
            RETURN envMatch (p, e.environment);

    RETURN NULL;                                                        10
}


envMatch (p: PurportedName; e: Environment): SET OF DN
{
    x: DN;
    matches: SET OF DN;

    FOR (x = head (e); x; x = head (e = tail (e)))
        IF (matches = purportedMatch (x, p)) THEN                       20
            RETURN matches;
}
```

Figure 5.8: Top-Level for the UFN Algorithm

Figure 5.8 shows the top-level of the algorithm. The routine
`friendlyMatch` is given the purported name supplied by the user
and the search-list. This routine finds the first entry in the search-
list which bounds the number of components given in the purported
name. This entry is passed, along with the purported name, to the
routine `envMatch`. This routine simply traverses the list of starting
places, and for each, invokes the routine `purportedMatch`. The first
time a non-empty list of DNs is derived, this is returned. An alternate
policy would be to go through all the starting places and collect all
the matches, rather than returning the first set of matches found.

Figure 5.9 on page 183 shows how matches are found from a particular starting place. This is a rather complicated procedure, so we'll proceed slowly. This procedure makes use of several routines which do the real searching:

keyedSearch: used when a naming component of the form

      `type=value`

is being examined;

rootSearch: used when a naming component refers to something subordinate to the root of the DIT;

leafSearch: used when the final naming component (the leftmost string supplied by the user) is encountered; and,

intermediateSearch: used otherwise.

The routine begins by checking if the length of the purported name is one. If so, this was the leftmost string provided by the user, and contains naming information about the object's RDN. The routine `purportedMatch` goes through an amusing decision tree:

- If the string contains typing information, e.g.,

      `surName=Kille`

  then a keyed search is performed, starting at the base object given to `purportedMatch`.

- Otherwise, if the place to start searching is the root, then the routine `rootSearch` is invoked (this has knowledge of the DIT structure immediately subordinate to the root). If anything is found, it's returned; otherwise, a more general search routine, `leafSearch`, is invoked, and the results, if any, are returned.

purportedMatch (base: DN; p: PurportedName): **SET OF** DN
{
   s = head (p): String;
   dlist, matches: **SET OF** DN;

  IF (length (p) == 1) **THEN**
    IF (containsType (s)) **THEN**
      RETURN keyedSearch (base, lhs (s), rhs (s));
    ELSE
      IF (length (base) == 0) **THEN**   10
        IF (matches = rootSearch (s)) **THEN**
          RETURN matches;
        ELSE
          RETURN leafSearch (base, s, oneLevel);
      ELSE
        IF (length (base) == 1
                OR NOT present (base, OrganizationName)) **THEN**
          IF (matches = intermediateSearch (base, s)) **THEN**
            RETURN matches;
          ELSE   20
            RETURN leafSearch (base, s, length (base) > 1
                          ? wholeSubtree : oneLevel);
        ELSE
          IF (matches = leafSearch (base, s, wholeSubtree)) **THEN**
            RETURN matches;
          ELSE
            RETURN intermediateSearch (base, s);

  IF (containsType (s)) **THEN**
    dlist = keyedSearch (base, lhs (s), rhs (s));   30
  ELSE
    IF (length (base) == 0) **THEN**
      dlist = rootSearch (s);
    ELSE
      dlist = intermediateSearch (base, s);

  matches = **NULL**;
  FOR x **IN** dlist **DO**
    matches += purportedMatch (x, tail (p));

                                                      40
  RETURN matches;
}

Figure 5.9: Purported Match for the UFN Algorithm

- Otherwise, if the place to start searching is immediately subordinate to the root (such as a country), or is geographical (not yet within an organization), then the routine known as `intermediateSearch` is invoked (this has knowledge of the DIT structure immediately subordinate to objects such as countries and highly-placed organizations and localities). If anything is found, this is returned; otherwise, `leafSearch` is invoked, and the results, if any, are returned.

- Otherwise, the routine `leafSearch` is invoked (this has knowledge of the DIT structure at the lowest levels of the DIT). If anything is found, this is returned; otherwise, `intermediateSearch` is invoked, and the results, if any, are returned.

If the length of the purported name passed to `purportedMatch` contains more than one string, the head of this purported name represents naming information about the RDN of an object which is higher in the DIT than the target. Now, the decision tree is much simpler:

- If the string contains typing information, then `keyedSearch` is performed.

- Otherwise, if the place to start searching is the root, the routine `rootSearch` is invoked.

- Otherwise, the routine `intermediateSearch` is invoked.

- Regardless, for each of the DNs (if any) found by one of these routines, `purportedMatch` will recurse, saying that a match should be attempted using the tail of the purported name, starting at one of the DNs previously found. These are collected and returned.

```
rootSearch (s: String): SET OF DN
{
   IF (is3166 (s)) THEN
      RETURN search (NULL, oneLevel, s,
                  { countryName, friendlyCountryName, organizationName },
                  { equality },
                  NULL);
   ELSE
      RETURN search (NULL, oneLevel, s,
                  { friendlyCountryName, organizationName, localityName },      10
                  { substrings, approximateMatch },
                  NULL);
}
```

Figure 5.10: Root Search for the UFN Algorithm

The routine for searching from the root, `rootSearch` is shown in Figure 5.10. If the string corresponds to an ISO 3166 code, the routine `search` is invoked, to look for objects immediately subordinate to the root with an attribute, found in either a country or an organization, that exactly matches the search string. (Apparently, locality objects are to be named with strings with length greater than two.) Otherwise, the search is for objects immediately subordinate to the root with an attribute, found in either a country, organization, or locality, that is either contained within or approximately matched by the string.

The routine for searching below the root, `intermediateSearch`, is shown in Figure 5.11. The decision algorithm for this routine is rather clever: it looks at the DN corresponding to the base of the search, and tries to determine what kind of structuring is being used.[6]

---

[6]Note that if the Freedonian Naming Architecture had been used, this strategy would not always work properly since organizations with national standing have an RDN using the `fnsiOrgNumericCode` attribute instead of using the `organizationName` attribute. This suggests that either: the decision-makers of Freedonia should probably continue to use the FNSI numeric name form value, and use the `organizationName` attribute instead of creating a new one; or, that the algorithm needs more generalization. In the latter case, an alternate strategy would be for the algorithm to retrieve the `objectClass` attribute (as part of a prior search) and then examine the values therein, rather than making guesses on the basis of the RDNs encountered. Alternately, the Directory standard provides a `searchGuide` attribute which might be helpful.

```
intermediateSearch (base: DN; s: String): SET OF DN
{
    IF (present (base, organizationalUnitName)) THEN
        RETURN search (base, oneLevel, s,
                { organizationalUnitName },
                { substrings, approximateMatch },
                { organizationalUnit });
    ELSE
      IF (present (base, OrganizationName)) THEN
        RETURN search (base, oneLevel, s,                              10
                { organizationalUnitName, localityName },
                { substrings, approximateMatch },
                { organizationalUnit, locality });
      ELSE
        IF (present (base, localityName)) THEN
          RETURN search (base, oneLevel, s,
                  { organizationName },
                  { substrings, approximateMatch },
                  { organization });
        ELSE                                                          20
          RETURN search (base, oneLevel, s,
                  { organizationName, localityName },
                  { substrings, approximateMatch },
                  { organization, locality });
}

present (d: DN; t: AttributeType): BOOLEAN
{
    x: RDN;
                                                                      30
    FOR x IN d DO
      IF (x.type == t) THEN
        RETURN TRUE;

    RETURN FALSE;
}
```

Figure 5.11: Intermediate Search for the UFN Algorithm

leafSearch (base: DN; s: String; subsettype: SubsetType): **SET OF** DN
{
   RETURN search (base, subsettype, s,
               { commonName, surName, userId},
               { substrings, approximateMatch },
               NULL);
}

keyedSearch (base: DN; type, value: String): **SET OF** DN   10
{
   RETURN search (base,
               length (base) > 1 ? wholeSubtree : oneLevel,
               value,
               { str2Attr (type) },
               { substrings, approximateMatch },
               NULL);
}

Figure 5.12: Leaf/Key Searches for the UFN Algorithm

Based on that determination, it calls the routine **search** to perform a single-level search looking for attributes, likely to be found in a subordinate object existing in such a structure, which either contain or approximately match the search string. For example, if the place to start searching has an `organizationaUnit1Name` attribute as a part of its name, then the algorithm believes it should look for a subordinate organizational unit to match the search string.

The routine for searching the bottom-most levels of the DIT, `leafSearch`, is shown in Figure 5.12. It simply calls the **search** routine looking for attributes, likely to be found in a leaf object, which either contain or approximately match the search string. The `keyedSearch` routine is also shown in this figure. It also does a simple search, but looking for the user-supplied attribute type (the routine `str2Attr` converts a string into the desired attribute type). If the place to start looking is below the country-level, then a whole-subtree search is performed. Otherwise the search is single-level.

Finally, the routine **search** is shown in Figure 5.13 on page 188.

```
search (base: DN; subsettype: SubsetType; s: string;
    alist: SET OF AttributeType;
    matchtypes: SET OF MatchType;
    objectClasses: SET OF ObjectClass): SET OF DN
{
  x: DN;
  dlist, exact, good: SET OF DN;

  −− map onto Directory Search
  −− baseObject: 'base'                                             10
  −− subset: 'subsetType'
  −− filter:
  −−      build OR−conjuction of 's' using 'matchtypes' over 'alist'
  −−      if 'objectClasses' isn't empty:
  −−          build OR−conjuction of 'objectClasses' using equality
  −−                over objectClass
  −−          AND with original filter
  −− selection: attributes and values of
  −−      countryName, friendlyCountryName, organizationName
  −−      organizationalUnitName, localityName,                      20
  −−      commonName, surName, userId

  −− cache returned entries and associated attributes/values
  dlist = search−results;

  exact = NULL, good = NULL;
  FOR x IN dlist DO
    IF (last (DN).value == s) THEN
      exact += x;
    ELSE                                                            30
      FOR y IN cache (x, alist) DO
        IF (y.value == s) THEN
          good += x;

  IF (exact) THEN
    RETURN exact;
  IF (good) THEN
    RETURN good;

  −− present dlist to user                                          40
  −− return only those that are of interest
}
```

Figure 5.13: Search Operation for the UFN Algorithm

Virtually all of the parameters to the Directory search operation are supplied by the routine which invokes `search`. What remains is for `search` to build the filter, and then invoke the Directory search operation. The filter for the search consists of two parts. The first part is constructed by applying the supplied operators over the search string and the attribute types, using a logical-OR of each term. Thus, if `search` was invoked with

```
base:               {
                      { { countryName, "US" } }
                    }
subsettype:         oneLevel
s:                  "PSI"
alist:              { organizationName, localityName }
matchTypes:         { substrings, approximateMatch }
objectClasses:      { organization, locality }
```

the first part of the filter would look like:

$$\text{organizationName} = \texttt{"*PSI*"}$$
$$\lor \quad \text{organizationName} \approx \texttt{"PSI"}$$
$$\lor \quad \text{localityName} = \texttt{"*PSI*"}$$
$$\lor \quad \text{localityName} \approx \texttt{"PSI"}$$

The second part of the filter is constructed if the set of object classes supplied in `objectClasses` is non-empty. It is constructed by applying the `equality` operator over the object classes and the attribute type `objectClass`, using a logical-OR of each term. Thus, continuing with the set of arguments above, the second part of the filter would look like:

$$\text{objectClass} = \texttt{"organization"}$$
$$\lor \quad \text{objectClass} = \texttt{"locality"}$$

The actual search filter is the logical-AND of both parts, e.g.,

$$(\text{organizationName} = \texttt{"*PSI*"}$$
$$\lor \quad \text{organizationName} \approx \texttt{"PSI"}$$
$$\lor \quad \text{localityName} = \texttt{"*PSI*"}$$
$$\lor \quad \text{localityName} \approx \texttt{"PSI"})$$
$$\land \quad (\text{objectClass} = \text{organization}$$
$$\lor \quad \text{objectClass} = \text{locality})$$

If the set of desired object classes was empty, the first item by itself is used as the search filter. The results, if any, of the Directory search are cached. For each entry returned, its name is categorized as:

exact: if the RDN of this entry is exactly equal to the search string;

good: if this entry contains an attribute whose value is exactly equal to the search string; or,

bad: otherwise.

If there is at least one match which is exact, the list of exact matches is returned; otherwise, if there is at least one good match, the list of good matches is returned. Otherwise, the list of bad matches is presented to user, who is asked to select zero or more of them. Only those selected by the user are returned.

Although the UFN algorithm appears complicated, experience with it in the White Pages Pilot has been quite positive. Let's consider a brief example to put things in perspective.

Suppose that `friendlyMatch` is invoked with the arguments shown in Figure 5.14. (Note that the sequence "{ }" refers to the root of the DIT.)

The routine traverses through the search-list, and finds that the first item bounds the length of the purported name, which is two. So, `envMatch` is invoked. In turn, the DNs in the item are traversed. The first to be tried is `c=US`, and `purportedMatch` is invoked as:

```
base:       {
                { { countryName, "US" } }
            }
p:          { "psi", "rose" }
```

Since the length of the supplied purported name is not one, the first decision tree is skipped, and the second one applied. This results in a call to `intermediateSearch` with these arguments:

```
base:       {
                { { countryName, "US" } }
            }
s:          "psi"
```

Since the base for searching does not contain any of the attributes that `intermediateSearch` checks for, the last branch in its decision tree is taken. This results in a call to **search** with these arguments:

```
base:               {
                        { { countryName, "US" } }
                    }
subsettype:         oneLevel
s:                  "psi"
alist:              { organizationName, localityName }
matchTypes:         { substrings, approximateMatch }
objectClasses:      { organization, locality }
```

```
p:      { "psi", "rose" }
el:     {
          { 1, 2,
            {
              {
                { { countryName, "US" } }
              },
              {
                { { countryName, "CA" } }
              },
              { }
            }
          }
          { 3, 32767,
            {
              { },
              {
                { { countryName, "US" } }
              },
              {
                { { countryName, "CA" } }
              }
            }
          }
        }
```

Figure 5.14: Example Arguments to friendlyMatch

As a result of the previously explained behavior of **search**, a Directory search operation is invoked accordingly, and, for the purposes of this example, the Directory returns one match:

```
c=US@o=Performance Systems International
```

The **search** routine determines that the search string "psi" is not contained in the RDN of this entry, but that the entry does have a non-distinguished **organizationName** attribute which exactly matches the search string. So, this DN is assigned to the **good** list, which is subsequently returned to **intermediateSearch**, which returns it to **purportedMatch** (back on page 183). At this point, **purportedMatch** invokes itself with these arguments:

```
base:      {
                { { countryName, "US" } },
                { { organizationName,
                     "Performance Systems International" } }
           }
p:         { "rose" }
```

Since the length of the supplied purported name is one, the first decision tree is taken. As the search string does not contain typing information, and the length of the base object is two, the routine **leafSearch** is called with these arguments:

```
base:      {
                { { countryName, "US" } },
                { { organizationName,
                     "Performance Systems International" }
                }
           }
s:         "rose"
subsettype:    wholeSubtree
```

This in turn results in a call to **search** with:

```
base:               {
                        { { countryName, "US" } },
                        { { organizationName,
                             "Performance Systems International" } }
                    }
subsettype:         wholeSubtree
s:                  "rose"
alist:              { commonName, surName, userId }
matchTypes:         { substrings, approximateMatch }
objectClasses:      NULL
```

This results in a Directory search operation being invoked with this filter:

$$commonName = \texttt{"*rose*"}$$
$$\lor \quad commonName \approx \texttt{"rose"}$$
$$\lor \quad surName = \texttt{"*rose*"}$$
$$\lor \quad surName \approx \texttt{"rose"}$$
$$\lor \quad userID = \texttt{"*rose*"}$$
$$\lor \quad userID \approx \texttt{"rose"}$$

for the purposes of this example, the Directory returns one match:

```
c=US
    @o=Performance Systems International
    @ou=Research and Development
    @ou=Santa Clara
    @cn=Marshall Rose
```

The **search** routine determines that the search string "**rose**" is not contained in the RDN of this entry, but that the entry does have a non-distinguished **surName** attribute which exactly matches the search string. So, this DN is assigned to the **good** list, which is subsequently returned to **leafSearch**, which returns it to **purportedMatch** (back on the bottom of page 183). This routine now returns (back to itself), and a list of DNs, containing this one DN, is ultimately passed back up as the stack unwinds!

5.2.4 Application Entity Lookup

Although a White Pages service is a fine application for the Directory, the Directory should also provide support for other applications. For example, OSI application-layer entities need to be able to derive the application entity titles (AETs) of their peers, in order to map these into the corresponding presentation address. Although, the derivation of the AET is outside the scope of OSI, it seems natural to use the Directory to aid this process — especially when one considers that it is the Directory that will be asked to perform the mapping from AET to presentation address. In *The Open Book*, the portion of an OSI application entity that performs this resolution (AET derivation and then presentation address mapping) is termed the DASE. Of course, as noted in *The Open Book*, this functionality whilst necessary, is left as a local matter by the Application-Layer standard.

One approach towards application entity lookup is to use the UFN algorithm with an additional outer-layer. Let's pursue this strategy. The user, a computer program, will supply a purported name for its peer entity, along with the name of the application context that its entity should support, termed the *supported application context*. For example, if the local program wishes to find an FTAM responder for the purposes of generic file transfer, it would supply a application context of

```
iso-ftam OBJECT IDENTIFIER ::=
    { iso standard 8571 application-context(1) iso-ftam(1) }
```

We'll use the UFN to find the `applicationProcess` object in the Directory which corresponds to the peer entity, and then we'll look below this object to find the desired `applicationEntity`. We'll call this approach the AE-lookup algorithm.

Knowledge

In addition to the knowledge aspects of the UFN algorithm, the AE-lookup algorithm expects that the desired `applicationEntity` object is subordinate to an `applicationProcess`. Further, immediate subordinates are to be favored over distant subordinates.

User Input

The AE-lookup algorithm requires two mandatory inputs, a purported name, and an **OBJECT IDENTIFIER** corresponding to the desired application context. Examples of the former might be:

```
sc, psi, us
hubris, cs, ucl, gb
```

whilst an example of the latter might be:

```
1.0.8571.1.1
```

User Environment

The AE-lookup algorithm requires a search list, for use with the UFN-algorithm.

```
aeLookup (p: PurportedName; sac: OBJECT IDENTIFIER;
        el: EnvironmentList): SET OF DN
{
   x: DN;
   dlist, matches: SET OF DN;

   IF ((dlist = friendlyMatch (p, el)) == NULL) THEN
      RETURN NULL;

   matches = NULL;                                          10
   FOR x IN dlist DO
      matches += aeSearch (x, sac, oneLevel);

   IF (matches == NULL) THEN
      FOR x IN dlist DO
         IF (length (x) >= 2)
            matches += aeSearch (x, sac, wholeSubtree);

   RETURN matches;
}                                                           20
```

Figure 5.15: Top-Level for the AE-lookup Algorithm

Algorithm

Figure 5.15 shows the top-level of the algorithm, which starts with a call to **friendlyMatch** (shown way back on page 181) to resolve the purported name into a list of DNs. If this fails, the empty-list is returned. Otherwise, for each DN found, the routine **aeSearch** is invoked, to perform a single-level search starting at the DN. The results are collected, and if anything at all was found, the collected list is returned. Otherwise, the list of DNs returned by **friendlyMatch** is again traversed and applied to **aeSearch**, which this time is asked to perform a whole-subtree search.

Figure 5.16 shows the routine **aeSearch**. This invokes a simple Directory search operation, looking for entries which have the desired application context, and asking that all attribute values found in the entry be returned. The results, if any, are cached, and then returned.

Let's look at an example. Suppose that **aeLookup** is invoked with:

```
p: { "us", "psi", "sc" }
sac:    1.0.8571.1.1
```

along with the usual user-environment (which is shown on the bottom

aeSearch (base: DN; sac: **OBJECT IDENTIFIER**;
     subtreeType: SubtreeType): **SET OF** DN
{
   -- map onto Directory Search
   -- baseObject: 'base'
   -- subset: 'subtreeType'
   -- filter:
   --   build filter–item of 'sac' using equality over
   --   supportedApplicationContext
   -- selection: all attributes and values   10

   -- cache returned entries and associated attributes/values
   RETURN search–results;
}

Figure 5.16: Search Operation for the AE-lookup Algorithm

---

of page 192), and that the subsequent call to `friendlyMatch` returns a single DN, namely:

```
c=US
    @o=Performance Systems International
    @ou=Research and Development
    @ou=Santa Clara
```

(Observant readers might ask why the RDN of this entry isn't a `commonName`. The answer is that this entry has several `objectClass` values, one is `organizationalUnit`, another is `applicationProcess`. It's left as an exercise to the reader as to what attribute values are likely to be in this entry as a result.) The routine `aeSearch` is now invoked to perform a single-level search starting at this DN looking for an object with the desired application context. One such entry is found and returned:

```
c=US
    @o=Performance Systems International
    @ou=Research and Development
    @ou=Santa Clara
    @cn=filestore
```

5.2.5   Internet Mailbox Lookup

For the final interrogation algorithm to be considered, let's examine how one might map between an Internet mailbox or domain-name, such as

    `jpo@xtel.co.uk`

or

    `xtel.co.uk`

using an entry in the Directory.

    This may be useful for several applications. For example, the user's mail-reader could, upon delivery of a message, examine the `From:` field, apply this interrogation algorithm, retrieve a picture of the sender from the Directory, and then display this for the user.

    One approach is to populate the DIT with a special attribute type that can be searched for. For those non-leaf objects in the DIT which have a correspondence to an Internet domain, we add the value `domainRelatedObject` to the object class, and then one or more `associatedDomain` values. For example, the entry for `c=US` might contain

    `associatedDomain= us & bitnet & com & edu & gov & mil & net`

whilst the entry for `c=GB` might contain

    `associatedDomain= uk & gb`

Entries lower in the DIT would have more qualified domain-names, e.g., the entry for

    `c=GB`
        `@o=X-Tel Services Ltd.`

might contain

    `associatedDomain= xtel.co.uk`

This approach, which we'll call the DNS-mapping algorithm, will use single-level searching to identify the lowest entry in the DIT which contains a suffix of the desired domain-name.

Knowledge

The DNS-mapping algorithm has knowledge of a multi-level naming architecture, in which `associatedDomain` values are used as road-signs.

User Input

The DNS-mapping algorithm requires one mandatory input, a domain-name.

User Environment

There is no user-environment associated with the DNS-mapping algorithm.

DNS-mapping Algorithm

First, let's see how mappings of domain-names to the DIT can be accomplished. Once this is done, we'll see how mailbox-mapping can be layered on top of this.

There is a single data structure used by the two algorithms:

```
Domain ::=    -- e.g., { "xtel", "co", "uk" }
    SEQUENCE OF
        String
```

Figure 5.17 on page 202 shows the DNS-mapping algorithm. There is a global variable called `dnsLevel` which will keep track of the maximum number of domain-name components successfully matched. The routine `dnsMapping` first sets `dnsLevel` to zero, and then calls `dnsMatch` asking it to return a list of DNs which match (or come close to matching) the indicated domain. The second argument tells `dnsMatch` where to start looking (the root), and the third argument indicates what matches have been found thus far (none).

`dnsMatch` places a copy of the domain-name argument into `dp`, and then enters a boundless loop. For each iteration, it checks if the number of components in the current value of `dp` is less than `dnsLevel`. If so, any results previously collected are returned. Otherwise, a single-level Directory search operation is invoked. The filter for the search is simple: `dp` is coalesced into a textual string, and the `equality` operator is applied over this string and the attribute type `associatedDomain`. Hence, if the value of `dp` was

{ "xtel", "co", "uk" }

then the search filter would be

associatedDomain = "xtel.co.uk"

If the search operation didn't find anything, `dp` is set to its tail, and the next iteration is taken. Otherwise, a check is made to see if this match found a deeper domain-name than previous searches. If so, this fact is remembered, and any previous matches are discarded. The routine now loops through the matches just found. For each of these, any previous results are saved, and the routine `dnsMatch` recurses by

```
dnsLevel: INTEGER;

dnsMapping (dns: Domain): SET OF DN
{
   dnsLevel = 0;
   RETURN dnsMatch (dns, NULL, NULL);
}


dnsMatch (dns: Domain; base: DN; matches: SET OF DN): SET OF DN          10
{
   i: INTEGER;
   x: DN;
   dlist, dprev: SET OF DN;
   dp: Domain;

   dp = dns;

   FOR (; TRUE; )
      IF ((i = length (dp)) < dnsLevel)                                  20
         RETURN matches;

      −− map onto Directory Search
      −− baseObject: 'base'
      −− subset: oneLevel
      −− filter:
      −−      build filter−item of 'dp' using equality over associatedDomain

      if (dlist = search−results) THEN
         IF (i > dnsLevel) THEN                                          30
            dnsLevel = i, matches = NULL;
         FOR x IN dlist DO
            dprev = matches;
            matches = dnsMatch (dns, x, matches);
            IF (dprev == matches) THEN
               matches += x;
            ELSE
               IF (i < dnsLevel) THEN
                  BREAK;
         DONE                                                            40
      ELSE
         IF (!(dp = tail (dp)))
            RETURN matches;
   DONE
}
```

Figure 5.17: DNS-mapping Algorithm

looking in one of these new matches. If no new matches were found by the recursion, then the new match is added to the list of previous results. Otherwise a check is made to see if the new matches were deeper than before. If so, the inner-loop terminates.

This use of recursion is confusing at best. Let's look at a simple example. Suppose that dnsMatch is invoked with

```
dns:     { "xtel", "co", "uk" }
base:    NULL
matches: NULL
```

The first search performed is at the root with a filter of:

$$\texttt{associatedDomain} = \texttt{"xtel.co.uk"}$$

This returns nothing, so the next search is performed at the root with a filter of:

$$\texttt{associatedDomain} = \texttt{"co.uk"}$$

This returns nothing, so the next search is performed at the root with a filter of:

$$\texttt{associatedDomain} = \texttt{"uk"}$$

This returns c=GB, the variable dnsLevel is set to one, and dnsMatch recurses. The first search performed is at c=GB with a filter of:

$$\texttt{associatedDomain} = \texttt{"xtel.co.uk"}$$

This returns

```
c=GB
    @o=X-Tel Services Ltd.
```

the variable dnsLevel is set to three, and dnsMatch recurses. The first search performed with a filter of:

$$\texttt{associatedDomain} = \texttt{"xtel.co.uk"}$$

This returns nothing, and dnsMatch now returns since the depth of dp is less-than dnsLevel. The next time the outer-loop is iterated (in the second call to dnsMatch), dp is { "co", "uk" }, and the

matches found thus far are immediately returned. The stack unwinds
again, dp contains the empty sequence, and the matches found thus
far are immediately returned to dnsMapping.

It took five single-level Directory searches to perform this mapping.
An obvious optimization is to use a more complicated filter for each
search, e.g.,

$$\text{associatedDomain} = \text{"xtel.co.uk"}$$
$$\vee \;\; \text{associatedDomain} = \text{"co.uk"}$$
$$\vee \;\; \text{associatedDomain} = \text{"uk"}$$

and then selecting the entries which had the longest match. This
would reduce the number of searches from nine to three. There
are many possible optimization strategies, for example, [38] suggests
building a separate tree of domain names.

```
mboxMapping (local: String; domain: Domain): SET OF DN
{
    x: DN;
    dlist, matches: SET OF DN;

    if ((dlist = dnsMapping (domain)) == NULL) THEN
        RETURN NULL;

    matches = NULL;
    FOR x IN dlist DO                                              10
        IF (length (x) >= 2) THEN
                −− map onto Directory Search
                −− baseObject: 'x'
                −− subset: wholeSubtree
                −− filter:
                −−    build filter−item of 'local@' using initial−substring over rfc822Mailbox
            matches += search−results;
        ELSE
            −− warn user that domain did not resolve below country−level
            ;                                                     20

    RETURN matches;
}
```

Figure 5.18: Mailbox-mapping Algorithm

Mailbox-mapping Algorithm

Figure 5.18 shows the Mailbox-mapping algorithm, which, considering the complexity DNS-mapping algorithm, is thankfully simple. First, the routine **dnsMapping** is called to resolve the domain-name into likely DNs for searching. For each, if the DN is at least two levels deep, a whole-subtee search is performed, looking for entries with the desired mailbox. Instead, if the DN is subordinate to the root, a warning is printed that the domain-name could not be resolved below the country-level. This occurs for domain-names which do not have signposts in the DIT. The results of the mailbox searches are collected together and this collection is returned.

Let's look at a simple example. Suppose that `mboxMapping` is invoked with

```
local:    jpo
dns:      { "xtel", "co", "uk" }
```

and that the subsequent call to **dnsMapping** returns a single DN, namely:

```
c=GB@o=X-Tel Services Ltd.
```

A whole-subtree search is now performed with this filter:

$$\texttt{rfc822Mailbox} = \texttt{"jpo@*"}$$

which returns one match:

```
c=GB@o=X-Tel Services Ltd.@cn=Julian Onions
```

5.3 Implementation Focus

Having become exhausted while examining interrogation algorithms, it's time to look at a few implementation-specific aspects.

5.3.1 The Split-DASE

Because of the complexity of implementing the DAP, it may be difficult to embed the AE-lookup algorithm in each OSI application entity. One solution, the one taken by ISODE, is to split the DASE (that portion of the AE which executes the AE-lookup algorithm) into two parts and then connect those parts with a smaller, gentler, protocol. This is termed a split-DASE architecture. *The Open Book* described the original approach used by ISODE, but things have improved considerably since that writing. So, here is the new protocol, as shown in Figure 5.19 starting on page 208. The protocol is layered on the OSI connection-oriented transport service, because, unlike its predecessor, the new split-DASE protocol allows callbacks, and there is little point in re-inventing the re-transmission algorithms of the transport layer for this class of application. (Of course, there is also little point in making this new split-DASE an application-layer protocol, as there would be no gain in useful functionality.)

Readers who are familiar with the AE-lookup algorithm presented back in Section 5.2.4, will see how these ASN.1 data structures capture linkages in the algorithm:

- An ISODE application establishes an OSI transport connection to the local DASE-server, called *dased*.

- For each AE-title which must be derived, an instance of the `Query-REQ` data structure is serialized and sent to the DASE-server. In order to minimize the amount of Directory-related code loaded into the application, most of the arguments are textual-strings using the QUIPU conventions. The DASE-server will map these into internal data structures for manipulation, and ultimately into the Directory ASN for transmission to the DSA.

```
Query−REQ ::=
    [0] IMPLICIT
        SEQUENCE {
            name                    -- e.g., { "cs", "ucl", "gb" }
                SEQUENCE OF
                    IA5String,

            interactive             -- true IFF allow callbacks
                BOOLEAN,
                                                                        10
            envlist                 -- search list
                SEQUENCE OF         --    (defined in UFN)
                    Environment,

            context                 -- e.g., "iso ftam"
                IA5String,

            userdn                  -- DN for binding
                IA5String
                OPTIONAL,
                                                                        20
            passwd                  -- for simple authentication
                IA5String
                OPTIONAL
        }

Query−RSP ::=
    [3] IMPLICIT
        SEQUENCE {
            friendly[0]             -- friendly name                    30
                IA5String
                OPTIONAL,

            name[1]                 -- a DN in Directory ASN
                ANY
                OPTIONAL,

            value[2]                -- a PSAPaddr in Directory ASN
                ANY
                OPTIONAL,                                               40

            diagnostic[3]           -- in case of error
                IA5String
                OPTIONAL
        }

    ...
```

Figure 5.19: Split-DASE Protocol

...

```
Callback−REQ ::=
    [1] IMPLICIT
        SEQUENCE {
            string              −− e.g., "smith"
                IA5String,

            choices              −− list of possible matches
                SEQUENCE OF
                    SEQUENCE {
                        friendly
                            IA5String,
                        complete
                            IA5String
                        }
        }

Callback−RSP ::=
    [2] IMPLICIT
        SEQUENCE OF
            IA5String
```

Figure 5.19: **Split-DASE Protocol (cont.)**

Some sites might wish to make their application-entities available only for local use. One possible strategy for this is to protect the corresponding entry in the Directory with an access-control-list. In this case, an ISODE application must supply a DN and a password for use with simple authentication in order to bind to the Directory and be authorized to read the desired entry. The last two optional elements of the `Query−REQ` data structure are used in this circumstance.

- When the DASE-server has finished executing the AE-lookup algorithm, it returns an instance of the `Query−RSP` data structure. Included in this is a textual representation of the selected AE, suitable for display to a human user, along with a diagnostic string which is present if the algorithm failed to find any suitable entries in the Directory. (The `name` and `value` elements will not be present in this case.)

- If the ISODE application indicated that it was running interactively (as flagged in the query-request), then when the AE-lookup algorithm needs to interact with the user, the DASE-server will send an instance of the `Callback-REQ` data structure. This consists of a search-string (the string the algorithm was trying to match), and one or more pairs of possible matches. The first string in each pair is a string suitable for display to a human-user, the second string is the corresponding DN of the match.

The ISODE application presents the search string and possible matches to the user, collects those selected by the user, and then sends an instance of the `Callback-RSP` data structure containing the appropriate DNs.

5.3.2   Transport Listener

Now let's consider the other half of the problem, namely, how does an ISODE end-system determine which services it should offer. In the current release of ISODE, most services are started by a transport-listener, called *iaed*. When UNIX goes multi-user, *iaed* is started. It connects to the Directory and begins a search in a "local portion" of the DIT, looking for entries whose `objectClass` attribute contains the value:

```
iSODEApplicationEntity OBJECT-CLASS
    SUBCLASS OF applicationEntity
    MUST CONTAIN { execVector }
    ::= { quipuObjectClass 8 }
```

An example of such an entry might be:

```
objectClass                  - iSODEApplicationEntity
commonName                   - file service
presentationAddress          - ...
supportedApplicationContext - 1.0.8571.1.1
execVector                   - iso.ftam
```

For each entry found, the *iaed* listens on the transport address contained within the corresponding presentation address — it is impractical with *iaed* to listen on a presentation address, and there is little benefit to be gained either! When an incoming call is received for one of these, *iaed* forks a copy of the program indicated by the `execVector` attribute. At regular intervals (or at the request of the system administrator), *iaed* will consult the Directory to see if anything has changed, and if so, *iaed* will re-configure itself accordingly.

So, the obvious question is: how is the local portion of the DIT populated with these entries? The answer is that the system administrator runs a program to configure this information for each service that *iaed* should invoke. For other services, the program which implements that service can bind to the Directory, and provide the information. Note however that entries created in this fashion must not belong to the `iSODEApplicationEntity` object class — otherwise, *iaed* will start listening for those services as well.

5.3.3 The Directory Assistance Service

In order to be truly useful, a White Pages Service should export its service to the widest collection of platforms (the so-called "universal deployment" argument). Once again, it should not be surprising that the complexity of implementing the DAP along with various interrogation algorithms may make it difficult to realize a user-interface for a White Pages service on computationally-limited devices.

One solution is to split the DUA into two parts and then connect those parts with a smaller, gentler, protocol. Let's call this a split-DUA architecture, and the protocol in between the two parts the *Directory Assistance Protocol*.[7] One half will focus primarily on user-interface issues, and the other will deal with the interrogation algorithms and the DAP. Figure 5.20 shows such an architecture.

In order to maximize coverage, the DA-protocol will be mapped onto the Internet suite of protocols, namely over the Transmission Control Protocol (TCP). Further, the protocol interactions will be textual in order to minimize the amount of serialization mechanisms required at the DA-client. The DA-service uses two TCP connections. In the Directory-Assistant, there are two logical processes, each listening to one of these connections, as shown in Figure 5.21. The DA-

---

[7]So named because it gives assistance in using the Directory, not in finding things in the Directory. Although it is tempting, one never abbreviates the name of this protocol — for the obvious reason.

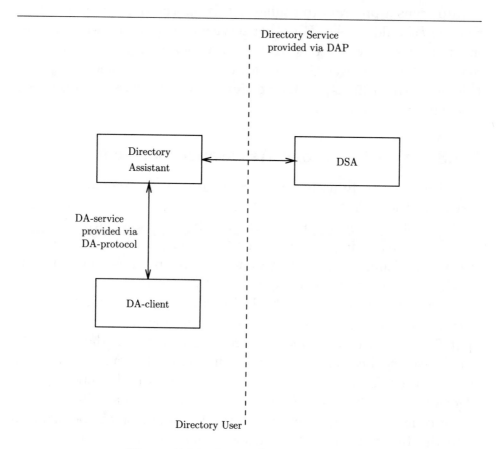

Figure 5.20: Split-DUA Architecture

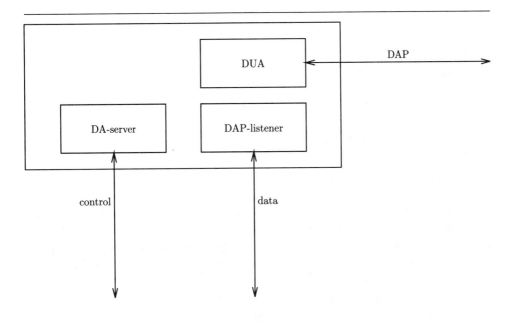

Figure 5.21: The Directory Assistant

server listens to the control-connection, whilst the DAP-listener deals with the data-connection. The syntax of the control-connection is the typical NVT-style enjoyed by many of the Internet applications. (This style of interaction was introduced earlier in Section 2.2.3 on page 46.) In contrast, the syntax of the data-connection is "home-grown" and largely non-intuitive (it evolved from a long line of internal protocols used in QUIPU).

DA-server

The protocol begins when the DA-client(C) establishes a connection to TCP port 411 at the IP-address where the DA-service resides:

```
S: <wait for connection on TCP port 411>
C: <open connection to DA-server>
L: <wait for connection>
S: +OK 192.33.4.21 32867
```

The DA-server(S) responds by indicating the address where the DAP-listener(L) resides.

From this point, the control-connection is only used:

- to ask the DA-server to interrupt the DAP-listener if the latter is taking too long to process a request;

- to check on the status of the DAP-listener; and,

- ultimately, to release the DA-service.

DAP-listener

The DAP-listener serially executes DAP-transactions, one per connection. The full DAP is available, using the syntax defined in QUIPU's *dish* command. For example, the DA-client(I) opens a TCP connection to the DAP-listener(L) and asks to bind to the Directory.

```
I: <open connection to DAP-listener>
I: bind -simple -user "@c=SE@cn=Manager"
```

The DAP-listener responds asking for a simple-authentication password, to which a response is given:

```
L: pc=SE@cn=Manager
-- client asks user for password for "c=SE@cn=Manager"
I: psecret
L: <closes connection, signaling success but no response>
```

This sample protocol interaction only touches on the possible interactions between the DA-client and the DAP-listener. Using the DA-service the DA-client can, among other things:

- expand non-leaf entries in the DIT, in order to present the user with a browsing paradigm;

- invoke an interrogation algorithm, in order to perform White Pages searching; and,

- read entry information from the DIB, in order to display it to the user (including support of pictures).

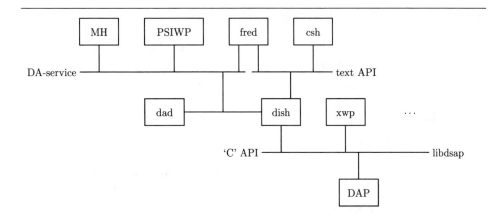

Figure 5.22: White Pages Pilot Interfaces and the QUIPU DUA

5.4   White Pages User-Interfaces

Recall that earlier it was noted that the White Pages abstraction consisted of two parts: an administrative discipline, and a set of user-interfaces. It is now time look at the latter!

As shown in Figure 5.22 (a repeat of Figure 4.9), there are several user-interfaces available. In this section, we'll briefly consider these.

For the White Pages Pilot, the two primary interfaces are available via anonymous network access. This allows users who do not have the White Pages Pilot software installed at their site to still make use of the service. It should be noted that the basic interface, and the DA-service, are a part of the openly-available White Pages Pilot software. The remaining two interfaces are proprietary to Performance Systems International (PSI). They are discussed here because they represent good examples.

5.4.1   The Basic Interface

The basic interface, *fred*, is text-based, and supports all of the interrogation algorithms described earlier in Section 5.2. Typical search
directives to *fred* are:

kille, cs, ucl, gb: tries to resolve the purported name using the
UFN-algorithm.

schoff: looks for some person named "`schoff`" in the default
area (the actual interrogation algorithm invoked is based
on user-preference)

jpo@xtel.co.uk: looks for someone with the given mailbox using the Mailbox-mapping algorithm.

goodfellow -org anterior: looks for some person named
"`goodfellow`" at some organization called "`anterior`" using the Simple Naming algorithm.

rose -title scientist: looks for someone named "`rose`" in the
default area whose title is "`scientist`" using the Simple
Naming algorithm.

-title janitor: looks for everyone in the default area whose title
is "`janitor`" using the Simple Naming algorithm.

Figure 5.23 shows an example of a session with *fred.*

Depending on how *fred* is configured, it can either access *dish*, the
QUIPU DUA, locally; or, it can access the DA-service at a remote
site.

Because *fred* provides a basic level of service, it is not only available via anonymous *TELNET* and *rlogin*, but also via electronic mail.
Messages sent to a special address are examined by *fred* for queries and
the responses mailed back. Further, *fred* is also able to masquerade
on the network as the older Internet *whois* service.

```
% telnet wp.psi.net
Trying 192.33.4.21 ...
Connected to wp.psi.net.
Escape character is '^]'.


SunOS UNIX (wp.psi.net)

login: fred
Last login: Tue Feb 13 18:34:43 from esoteric.cc.sfu.
SunOS Release 4.0.3 (ALEXANDER) #1: Mon Aug 7 11:44:08 EDT 1989


Welcome to the PSI White Pages Pilot Project

Try  "help" for a list of commands
     "whois" for information on how to find people
     "manual" for detailed documentation
     "report" to send a report to the white pages manager

To find out about participating organizations, try
    "whois -org *"

  accessing service, please wait...

fred> whois -org *
70 matches found.
  1. Advanced Decision Systems                     +1 415-960-7300
  2. Alfred University                             +1 607-871-2222
  3. Anterior Technology                           +1 415-328-5615
  4. Bell-Northern Research                        +1 613-763-2211
  5. City College of CUNY                          +1 212-690-6741
  6. Clarkson University                           +1 315-268-6400
  7. Columbia University                           +1 212-854-1754
  8. Corporation for National Research Initiatives +1 703-620-8990
  9. Dana Farber Cancer Institute                  +1 617-732-3000
 10. Defense Communications Agency                 +1 703-692-2788
 11. DMD                                           +1 415-961-3380
 12. Eastman Kodak Co.                             +1 716-724-4000
 13. GTE Laboratories, Inc.                        +1 617-890-8640
 14. Hewlett-Packard                               +1 415-857-1501
 ...
```

Figure 5.23: A Session with Fred

```
fred> whois goodfellow -org anterior
Trying @c=US@o=Anterior Technology ...
Geoffrey Goodfellow (2)          Geoff@Fernwood.MPK.CA.US
     aka: Geoffrey S. Goodfellow

President
Anterior Technology
  POB 1206
  Menlo Park, CA   94026-1206

Telephone: +1 415 328 5615
FAX:       +1 415 328 5649
TELEX:     number: 650 103 7391, country: US, answerback: MCI UW

Mailbox information:
  MCI-Mail: Geoff
  Internet: Geoff@Fernwood.MPK.CA.US
  UUCP: fernwood!Geoff

Drinks:   chilled water

Name:     Geoffrey Goodfellow,
            Anterior Technology,
            US
```

Figure 5.23: A Session with Fred (cont.)

5.4.2   An Interface for the X Window System

Although the *fred* interface appears adequate for dumb-terminal applications, a window-based interface has much appeal. The interface, *xwp*, implements the White Pages abstraction using a windowing paradigm for user-interaction.

When *xwp* starts, its top-level window appears as:

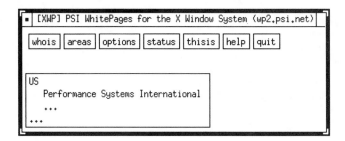

To search, click on the [WHOIS] button, fill-in a name, e.g.,

    schoffstall, psi

Depending on the number of matches found, the user may be presented with a list of possibilities, e.g.,

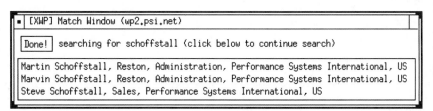

Clicking on any of them will yield additional information, e.g.,

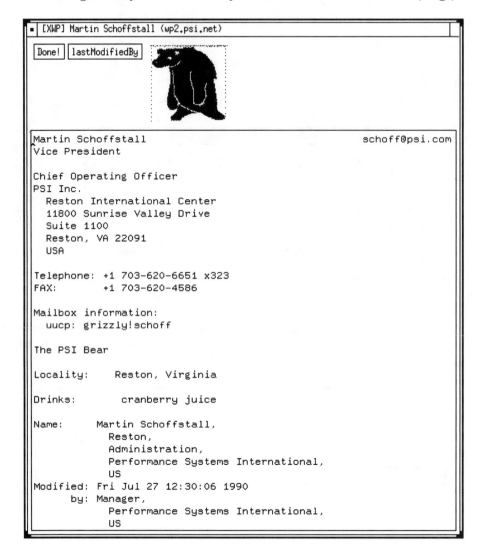

To browse, simply click on a line in the top-level window, which *xwp* maintains as it learns about things in the White Pages, e.g.,

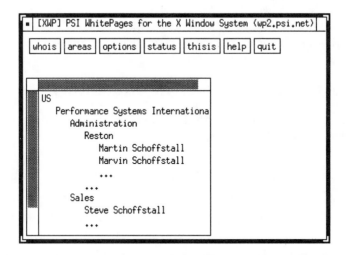

Of course, no computer-communications tradeshow is complete `soap...` without a demonstration that draws a crowd, but has no real substantive value. Because of their "sex and sizzle" appeal, graphical-user interfaces seem destined to fill this well-needed gap.[8] Not even the author is above a little shameless hype from time to time. At the INTEROP® conference and tradeshow in October of 1990, the *xmw* program, shown in Figure 5.24 was unveiled.

The interrogation algorithm used by this program is simple: it starts at a user-selected portion of the DIT and performs a whole-subtree search looking for entries containing a `photo` attribute. It then displays these in a fashion not unlike that used by the Federal Bureau of Investigation in US Post Offices. The user can click on a photo and information about that entry appears in a separate window. Further, if *xwp* is running on a sound-capable computer, and the entry has an attribute containing digitized sound, then this is played when the entry is displayed.

---

[8]The term "fill a well-needed gap" is a *Farberism*, one of many such expressions attributed to Professor David J. Farber. The author recalls Professor Farber first using this particular Farberism when referring to running OSI applications over TCP/IP networks. However, the author's favorite farberism is: "we'll burn that bridge when we get to it," a philosophy which reflects much thinking throughout the computer-communications industry.

The best part is that *xmw* can retrieve frames from a video camera, and add entries to the Directory containing the picture along with any information typed by the user.

It's not clear that *xmw* is a worthwhile use of technology, but it was a really big draw at the INTEROP® '90 tradeshow.

...soap

5.4.3   An Interface for the Macintosh

With the introduction of the DA-service described earlier in Section 5.3.3, a White Pages interface for the Macintosh®, *PSIWP*, was developed.

Figure 5.25 gives a brief flavor of this Macintosh® application. Although there are superficial similarities to *xwp*, the internal construction and look-and-feel of the two interfaces are entirely different. The similarities come from the fact that both interfaces employ the same interrogation algorithms. However, *xwp* does this by direct access of `libdsap`. In contrast, *PSIWP* uses the DA-service to realize the interrogation algorithms and deal with the complexity of the X.500 service and protocols; this leaves *PSIWP* to implement the user-interface paradigms that users of the Macintosh® expect and love!

5.4.4   An Interface for MH

Users of the system, can use the White Pages automatically to lookup the electronic mail addresses of their correspondents.

Rather than specifying an address, the user specifies a name by bracketing a White Pages query between "<<" and ">>" using the user-friendly naming syntax, e.g.,

```
To: << rose, psi, us >>
```

At the **What now?** prompt, the user invokes **whom** to have the names expanded into addresses. Alternately, the **send** option can be used as well.

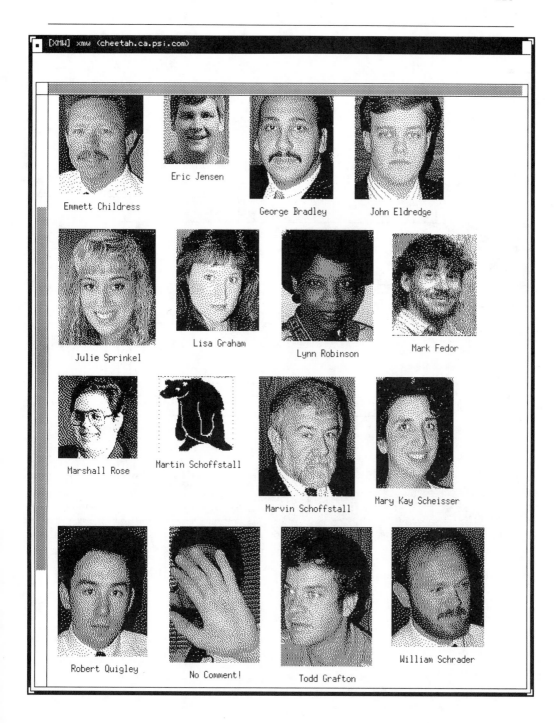

Figure 5.24: XMW - A Real Crowd Pleaser

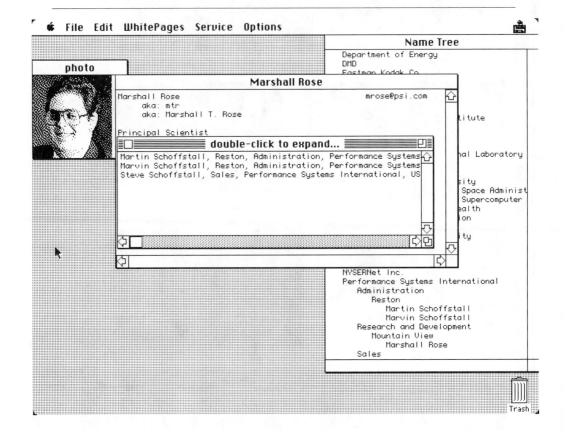

For each query appearing between "<<" and ">>", the DA-server will be asked to perform a White Pages resolution. All matches are printed and the user is asked to select one, e.g.,

```
What now? send

[ Expanding rose,psi,us ]

Please confirm use of the following:
Marshall Rose, ... Systems International, US [y/n] ? y

...
```

This feature is available only to interactive users of MH. Because of the potentially disastrous consequence of sending a message to the wrong recipient, MH requires user-confirmation of the answer given by the White Pages service.

Of course, there are many other mail applications that can make use of the White Pages service. For example, some sites have modified their local MTA to use the White Pages when generating certain kinds of "failed mail" notices: when a remote site asks the MTA to deliver a message to a mailbox which doesn't exist, the MTA will use the local portion of the mailbox as input to an interrogation algorithm and then append the resulting information to the notice. When the notice is returned to the originator, the information provided likely contains the "correct" mailbox to use.

5.5   Beyond the White Pages

The author feels that an X.500–based White Pages service has great potential as an early-entry. However, the Directory is intended to, and likely can, support a much wider range of applications than White Pages service. The unfortunate part, is that it is anyone's guess as to what some of the applications will look like. Rather than dwell on the "far out" possibilities, let's look at some other applications, which can be realized in the short-term, but which don't expressly deal with the White Pages.

5.5.1   Use of Directory to Support MHS

An O/R-address is a combination of several components, taken from a fixed list. In the 1984 standards on Message Handling Systems (MHS), the components available are:

Country (C): identifies the country associated with the mailbox.

Administrative Management Domain (ADMD): identifies the public-carrier associated with the mailbox.

Private Management Domain (PRMD): identifies the private-carrier associated with the mailbox. (See the soapbox on page 66 for a description of the difference between an ADMD and a PRMD.)

X.121 Address: identifies the X.121 address of the mailbox.

Terminal Identifier: identifies the terminal address of the mailbox.

Organization (O): identifies the organization associated with the mailbox.

Organizational Unit (OU): identifies the organizational unit associated with the mailbox.

Unique User-Agent Identifier: identifies the user-process associated with the mailbox.

Personal Name (PN): identifies the personal name associated with the mailbox, a combination of first initial, given name, surname, and generational-qualifier.

Domain-Defined Attribute (DDA): provides an "escape mechanism" by allowing arbitrary key/value strings to be associated with the mailbox. These pairings are meaningful in some other context.

Only a few combinations of these are allowed:

- C, ADMD, and any of: PRMD, O, OU, PN, and DDA

- C, ADMD, X.121 address, and optionally DDA

- C, ADMD, Unique User-Agent Identifier, and optionally DDA

- X.121 address, and optionally Terminal Identifier

The 1988 standard on MHS added more components, to support addressing of processes (which have a common, rather than a personal, name) and physical-delivery addresses.

Regardless of whether one takes the perspective of the 1984 or 1988 standards, O/R-addresses are procrustean, particularly in comparison to format of Internet mailboxes. Although it is difficult to characterize a typical address, consider:

```
/C=GB/ADMD=" "/PRMD=X-Tel Services Ltd/O=XTel/I=J/S=Onions/
```

(Yes, the value of the ADMD component is a single blank-character!) Clearly, an application of a White Pages service is to keep track of X.400 O/R-addresses for a user, and supply them as needed.

Use of Directory to Support 1988 MHS

However, the 1988 standard on MHS goes further in its use of the Directory. Briefly, a recipient of a message is known by an O/R-name, which is either an O/R-address or a Directory Name. If a

Directory Name is supplied by the user, the message transfer system will use the Directory to retrieve the **mhsORAddresses** attribute of the corresponding entry. As shown in Figure 5.26, there are several object classes defined for use by 1988 MHS.

Of these, perhaps the most interesting feature is support for distribution lists. The lists are managed in the OSI Directory, and are referenced using an O/R-address. When referenced, the message transfer system will examine the corresponding Directory entry. For example, on submissions,

- the message transfer system will verify that the originator has permission to send messages to the list; and if so,

- the message transfer system will determine which O/R-names are the list's recipients.

Depending on the authorization policy used by the Directory, users can see which lists they are on, and possibly even add or delete their own mailboxes.

Finally, as mailboxes move, aliases can be temporarily placed in the Directory to ensure continued mail service to a user.

More Use of Directory to Support MHS

In mail systems, the routing problem is concerned with taking a recipient's address and determining which message transfer agent should be used for the next hop. In MHS, routing is troublesome as it is performed almost entirely on the basis of local tables (perhaps maintained at various sites). One possibility to add more flexibility to MHS routing is to use the Directory to map an O/R-address into the name of a message transfer agent at the next hop.

For example, suppose were are only interested in O/R-addresses of the form:

C, ADMD, and any of: PRMD, O, OU, PN

The first step is to introduce an object class which represents objects served by message transfer agents, e.g.,

```
mhsDistributionList OBJECT-CLASS
        SUBCLASS OF top
        MUST CONTAIN { commonName,
                    mhsDLSubmitPermissions,
                    mhsORAddresses }
        MAY CONTAIN { description,
                    organizationName,
                    organizationalUnitname,
                    owner,
                    seeAlso,                                        10
                    mhsDeliverableContentTypes,
                    mhsdeliverableEits,
                    mhsDLMembers,
                    mhsPreferredDeliveryMethods }
        ::= { mhsObjectClass 0 }

mhsMessageStore OBJECT-CLASS
        SUBCLASS OF applicationEntity
        MAY CONTAIN { description,
                    owner,                                          20
                    mhsSupportedOptionalAttributes,
                    mhsSupportedAutomaticActions,
                    mhsSupportedContentTypes }
        ::= { mhsObjectClass 1 }

mhsMessageTransferAgent OBJECT-CLASS
        SUBCLASS OF applicationEntity
        MAY CONTAIN { description,
                    owner,
                    mhsDeliverableContentLength }                   30
        ::= { mhsObjectClass 2 }

mhsOrganizationalUser OBJECT-CLASS
        SUBCLASS OF top
        MUST CONTAIN { mhsORAddresses }
        MAY CONTAIN { mhsDeliverableContentLength,
                    mhsDeliverableContentTypes,
                    mhsDeliverableEits,
                    mhsMessageStoreName,
                    mhsPreferredDeliveryMethods }                   40
        ::= { mhsObjectClass 3 }

mhsUserAgent OBJECT-CLASS
        SUBCLASS OF applicationEntity
        MAY CONTAIN { owner,
                    mhsDeliverableContentLength,
                    mhsDeliverableContentTypes,
                    mhsDeliverableEits,
                    mhsORAddresses }
        ::= { mhsObjectClass 4 }                                   50
```

Figure 5.26: MHS Object Classes

```
mtaServedObject OBJECT-CLASS
    SUBCLASS OF top
    MUST CONTAIN { mhsMTAName }
    ::= { -- tbd -- }

aDMD OBJECT-CLASS
    SUBCLASS OF mtaServedObject
    MUST CONTAIN { admdName }
    MAY CONTAIN  { -- unimportant -- }
    ::= { -- tbd -- }
```

```
-- and so on...
```

The next step is to populate the DIT with these, e.g., we might create an entry

```
c=GB
    @admdName=" "
    @prmdName=X-Tel Services Ltd
    @o=XTel
```

which contains a `mhsMTAName` attribute containing the name of the MTA which services mailboxes associated with this prefix. Later on, when a message is to be delivered to the O/R-address

```
/C=GB/ADMD=" "/PRMD=X-Tel Services Ltd/O=XTel/I=J/S=Onions/
```

the message transfer agent attempts a Directory read operation on

```
c=GB
    @admdName=" "
    @prmdName=X-Tel Services Ltd
    @o=XTel
    @initial=J
    @sn=Onions
```

asking that the value of the `mhsMTAName` attribute be returned. If this entry doesn't exist, the message transfer agent attempts a read operation on

```
c=GB
    @admdName=" "
    @prmdName=X-Tel Services Ltd
    @o=XTel
```

asking for the same information. This process continues until either the name of a servicing MTA is determined (success), or the Distinguished Name is exhausted (failure).

As can be seen from these few examples, the Directory can provide a powerful infrastructure, not only for users of MHS, but also for the message transfer system itself.

5.5.2   Use of Directory to Support Bibliographic Retrieval

As a final example, let's briefly consider a topic outside of message handling.

In many research communities, it is useful to maintain one or more documents series, each pertaining to a particular area of discourse. Depending on the community, a series might contain on the order of a few thousand documents. In the Internet community, the *Request for Comments* (RFC) series is a good example.

Although there has been some work in providing an information retrieval protocol for bibliographic retrieval, it is natural to consider if the Directory could serve in this area, and if so, what its limitations would be.

Looking back to page 148, two simple object classes were defined, one for a document series and the other for a document within a series. A document is named by its `documentIdentifier` attribute, which provides a distinguished attribute value, but little in terms of useful searching. Thus, searching must occur on the basis of other attributes, such as:

```
documentTitle
documentVersion
keywords
subject
authorCN
```

Developing an interrogation algorithm which uses these attributes is only a part of the problem however. Traditional approaches to bibliographic retrieval also involve combining the results of one search with another.

That is, in addition to directives such as:

find all entries in a document series which satisfy this criteria

a likely follow-up directive is:

of the following entries, which resulted from a previous interrogation, find those entries which satisfy this new criteria

The Directory search operation does not directly support this style of interaction as its `baseObject` parameter is a DN, not a collection of DNs. Thus, the DUA must emulate this behavior by either performing a Directory search operation for each entry in the previous result set, or by performing the Directory search on the entire document series, and then intersecting the results of the search with the entries in the previous result set. Neither approach is particularly appealing if either the previous result set or the document series is large.

Let's consider a prototype of a tool which might be used to retrieve bibliographic information, The tool is called *barney*, and Figure 5.27 shows an example of a session with the tool. The user invokes *barney* and issues the `series` commands to find out which document series have been configured by the system administrator.

Next, the user directs *barney* to:

- look for any documents with any author whose name ends in `rose`;

- place the matching documents in a result set called `mtr`; and,

- then display one line of information about each document in the result set.

To fulfill the first part, *barney* performs a whole-subtree search at the base of the document series, looking for entries satisfying the filter:

$$\texttt{authorCN} = \texttt{"*rose"}$$

Once this is done, *barney* creates an internal data structure to represent a result set (simply a list of DNs), and then uses the cached information from the Directory search to generate the one-liners.

```
% barney
barney: connected to '0101'H/Internet=192.70.139.20+17007
barney> series
Current document series is rfcs
        fyi residing at FYI Documents, Internet
        rfcs residing at RFC Documents, Internet

barney> look -browse -sequence mtr author=*rose
20 matches found.
    1. RFC886  Dec83 M.T. Rose      Proposed standard for message header munging
    2. RFC934  Jan85*M.T. Rose      Proposed standard for message encapsulation
    3. RFC983  Apr86*D.E. Cass      ISO transport arrives on top of the TCP
    4. RFC1006 May87*D.E. Cass      ISO transport services on top of the TCP: Ver
    5. RFC1065 Aug88*K. McCloghrie  Structure and identification of management in
    6. RFC1066 Aug88*K. McCloghrie  Management Information Base for network manag
    7. RFC1081 Nov88 M.T. Rose      Post Office Protocol - version 3
    8. RFC1082 Nov88 M.T. Rose      Post Office Protocol - version 3: Extended se
    9. RFC1085 Dec88 M.T. Rose      ISO presentation services on top of TCP/IP ba
   10. RFC1086 Dec88*J.P. Onions    ISO-TP0 bridge between TCP and X.25
   11. RFC1070 Feb89*R.A. Hagens    Use of the Internet as a subnetwork for exper
   12. RFC1155 May90*K. McCloghrie  Structure and identification of management in
   13. RFC1156 May90*K. McCloghrie  Management Information Base for network manag
   14. RFC1158 May90 M.T. Rose      Management Information Base for network manag
   15. RFC1161 Jun90 M.T. Rose      SNMP over OSI
   16. RFC1187 Oct90*J.R. Davin     Bulk table retrieval with the SNMP
   17. RFC1202 Feb91 M.T. Rose      Directory Assistance service
   18. RFC1212 Mar91*K. McCloghrie  Concise MIB definitions
   19. RFC1213 Mar91*K. McCloghrie  Management Information Base for network manag
   20. RFC1215 Mar91 M.T. Rose      Convention for defining traps for use with th
barney> look -browse -seq new mtr and "date=*, 199*"
9 matches found.
    1. RFC1155 May90*K. McCloghrie  Structure and identification of management in
    2. RFC1156 May90*K. McCloghrie  Management Information Base for network manag
    3. RFC1158 May90 M.T. Rose      Management Information Base for network manag
    4. RFC1161 Jun90 M.T. Rose      SNMP over OSI
    5. RFC1187 Oct90*J.R. Davin     Bulk table retrieval with the SNMP
    6. RFC1202 Feb91 M.T. Rose      Directory Assistance service
    7. RFC1212 Mar91*K. McCloghrie  Concise MIB definitions
    8. RFC1213 Mar91*K. McCloghrie  Management Information Base for network manag
    9. RFC1215 Mar91 M.T. Rose      Convention for defining traps for use with th
```

Figure 5.27: A Session with Barney

Then, the user directs *barney* to:

- look for those documents in the result set called `mtr` which were published in the '90s.

- place the matching documents in a result set called `new`; and,

- then display one line of information about each document in the result set.

To fulfill the first part, *barney* performs a whole-subtree search at the base of the document series, looking for entries satisfying the filter:

```
documentVersion = "*, 199*"
```

and then intersects the results with the DNs contained in the sequence named `mtr`. The intersection is then placed in a new result set, which is browsed.

Of course, the user could have simply directed *barney* as:

```
look -browse -seq new author=*rose and "date=*, 199*"
```

to have achieved the same end-result. In this case, *barney* would have performed a single whole-subtree search with the filter:

```
authorCN = "*rose"
  ∧  documentVersion = "*, 199*"
```

Of course, with the first approach, the result set `rose` can be used for other purposes later on.

Finally, once a basic framework is established for bibliographic retrieval, it is a relatively simple step to extend this to document retrieval: once the entries in the Directory corresponding to the desired documents have been identified, those entries can be examined for a `documentStore` attribute indicating where and how the documents can be retrieved. Of course, the Directory wouldn't be used to perform the document retrieval, a different protocol would be employed, such as FTAM, the OSI file service, or FTP, the File Transfer Protocol in the Internet suite.

Chapter 6

Directory System Agents

Discussion now turns to how the Directory is provided through the cooperation of Directory System Agents. First, consideration is given to how DSAs *know* where entry information (either an entry's attributes or the RDNs of its immediate subordinates) is kept. Then, a very brief overview of the Directory System Protocol (DSP) is presented. Following this, the QUIPU DSA is examined in considerable detail to see one practical realization of these concepts. Implementation experience is emphasized as it often provides great insight into the concepts of a DSA, much more so, in the author's opinion, than any sophisticated re-phrasing of the standards. Next, the problem of distributing information about a single entry amongst several DSAs is briefly introduced, and an innovative solution using naming is suggested. Then, the White Pages Pilot is revisited to present some of its less-than-sterling experiences. Finally, some additional references are given.

6.1   Knowledge

If a single DSA implements the DIT, then the problem of knowledge is
trivial: the one and only DSA knows that it contains each and every
entry in the DIT. Of course, use of a single DSA is unacceptable
in terms of reliability, coverage, performance, and ownership. In a
distributed Directory, there must be a mechanism for determining
which DSA holds information about a given entry.

To understand the Directory Knowledge Model, it is useful to
think of the DIT as being composed of several non-overlapping subtrees, and to think of each entry in the DIT as being entirely contained
in exactly one of these subtrees. Given this set of divisions, we can
say that a *naming context* consists of a non-empty subtree of the DIT
which is viewed as one of these regions. The name of the root of a
naming context is termed a *context prefix*. Consider the skeletal DIT
shown in Figure 6.1. It shows three naming contexts, one containing but a single entry. There are three naming contexts shown, with
context prefixes c=XX, c=XX@o=O_1, and c=XX@o=O_N.

Because replication is outside of the scope of the 1988 standard,
each naming context is entirely held in exactly one DSA master. Thus,
a DSA must have knowledge information which identifies the naming
contexts which compose the DIT, along with the addresses of the
corresponding DSAs which master that information.

Although essential to provide an interoperable service, the 1988
Directory standards did not present a concrete representation of how
DSAs communicate knowledge information, beyond the most rudi-
mentary referral information.[1] As with so many topics, this was
deemed to be outside of the scope of the work, due to time considerations.

Before delving into the details, let's introduce a useful convention:
the term *superior* refers to the immediate superior of an entry, whilst
the term *subordinate* refers to an immediate subordinate of an entry.

---

[1]Don't be fooled by the "selected" attribute type termed knowledgeInformation
by the standard. This is a descriptive string meaningful to people, not DSAs!

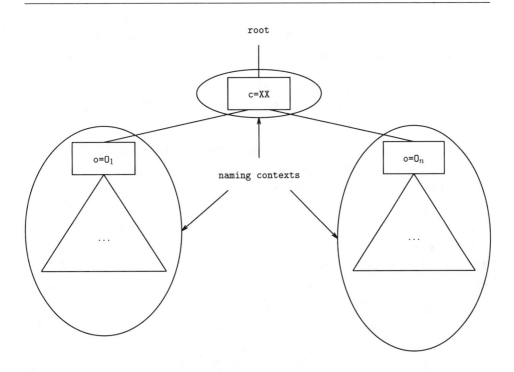

Figure 6.1: A Skeletal DIT divided into Naming Contexts

6.1.1   The DSA Information Tree

For our purposes, it is useful to consider a model being developed in the newer standardization work. Each naming context held by a DSA can be represented within a DSA *Information Tree*, an example of which is shown in Figure 6.2. This illustrates three points:

- because the DSA knows the context prefix, the DSA knows the RDNs of all the entries between the root and the naming context;

- because the DSA masters the naming context, the DSA has complete information about the entries within the subtree; and,

- because naming contexts must be non-overlapping and remain so, the DSA must have knowledge of the DSAs which hold the entries that are subordinate to the naming context.

In context of the Directory, the phrase "knowledge of a DSA" is more precisely stated as *access-point*. An access-point consists of the Distinguished Name of the DSA and its presentation address.

soap...   This definition is quite telling: simply put, DSAs do not trust the Directory! By including the presentation address, use of the DSA's name is optional, and less likely to be used as it will be simpler for implementors to use the presentation address directly. But, if the DSA changes its address, an uncommon, but possible, occurrence, then *all* knowledge information which refers to the DSA must be changed as well. Instead, if the definition of an access-point were simply the Distinguished Name of a DSA, then the Directory could be used to determine the corresponding presentation address and the only thing that need happen when a DSA moves is for its entry in the Directory to be updated — no knowledge pointers have to be tracked down and ...soap   changed.

6.1.2   Knowledge Information

This leads us to consider what kinds of knowledge a DSA might have of the naming contexts which it doesn't master. Well, if the DSA doesn't have knowledge of the immediate subordinates of the root, then it needs to know:

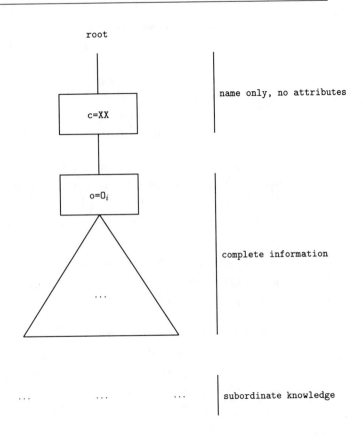

Figure 6.2: Information Tree in one DSA

- A *superior reference* (SUPR), which is a DSA access-point that is knowledgeable about entries higher up in the DIT. When a DSA needs to "move up" or "move up and over," it contacts its superior reference for help.

- For each naming context mastered by the DSA, some kind of *subordinate knowledge*. There are two kinds, either:

  - a *subordinate reference* (SUBR), which consists of a DSA access-point along with a context prefix indicating which subordinate that DSA masters; or,

  - *non-specific subordinate references* (NSSRs), a set of DSA access-points, each of which has some (unspecified) information about a subordinate.

Obviously, the kind of knowledge available has a tremendous impact on the response to an operation which requires that the DSA "move down." If only subordinate references are present, the DSA can select the correct one(s) and act accordingly. If any NSSRs are present, the DSA must often multicast, either serially or in parallel in order to process the request. Because some view non-determinism as generally a bad thing in computers, NSSRs can be seen as anathema.

- Optionally, one or more *cross-references* (CROSSRs), which is a DSA access-point along with the context prefix of the naming context that it masters. This is an optimization which allows a DSA to "move over" without having to contact its superior reference.

To illustrate the different kinds of knowledge information, consider the example given in Figure 6.3 which shows how a DSA for the Freedonian province of Calafia (FIPS numeric province code 06) might be configured.

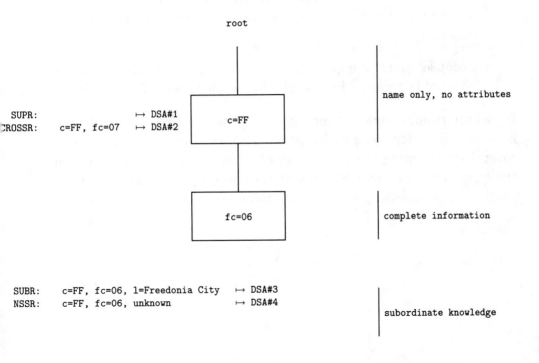

Figure 6.3: Information Tree in DSA for Calafia

6.1.3 First-Level DSAs

A first-level DSA is one which holds a naming context which is immediately subordinate to the root. These DSAs have special knowledge, different than that of other DSAs:

- For each entry immediately subordinate to the root, a first-level DSA knows the DSA access-point which masters the corresponding naming context. That is, all the first-level DSAs are well-known to each other. (One could say that a first-level DSA has a cross-reference for each entry under the root which it does not master.)

- Because of this complete knowledge of the immediate subordinates of the root, a first-level DSA needs no superior-references.

It is important to understand that, in practice, the first-level DSA is a virtual entity. For each (large) country, there are likely to be several DSAs acting in the capacity of a Level-1 DSA. Providing that the operators of these DSAs coordinate accordingly, this should not result in any problems with distributed operations.

6.2 The Directory System Protocol

When a DSA must contact another for information, it chains. The protocol used between DSAs when they chain, the Directory System Protocol (DSP), is largely uninteresting in this discussion, as the DSP contains only slight differences from the Directory Access Protocol which was discussed earlier.

The DSP resides at the OSI application layer, uses ACSE to establish and release associations, and ROSE to carry protocol interactions. As with the DAP described earlier in Section 4.3.1, a DSA supporting distributed operations may consume the services made available at three ports:

- a chained read port, which allows the chaining of the Directory read, compare, and abandon operations;

- a chained search port, which allows the chaining of the Directory search and list operations; and,

- a chained modify port, which allows the chaining of the Directory add entry, remove entry, modify entry, and modify RDN operations.

Figure 6.4 on page 244 shows the application layer structure of such a DSA (or a DSA which communicates with a DUA). Note that these ports are different than those offered to DUAs.

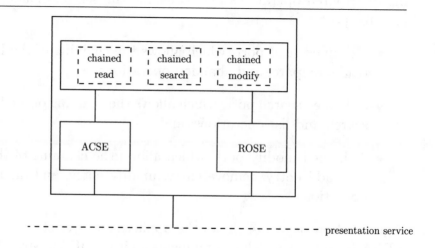

Figure 6.4: Application Layer Structure of a DSA supporting Distributed Operations

6.3   Implementation Focus

The QUIPU DSA is a complete implementation of the 1988 standards, and supports both the Directory Access Protocol and the Directory System Protocol.

> **NOTE:** In reading this section, it must be emphasized that a QUIPU DSA goes to great length to exhibit the external behavior of a DSA, as specified in the Directory standard. As such, a non-QUIPU DSA should not be able to determine, without outside help, whether it is talking to a QUIPU DSA. However, QUIPU DSAs have a means of identifying each other, and if two QUIPU DSAs communicate, they are able to implement several refinements beyond 1988 Directory standards.

The QUIPU database is memory-based, it uses the native UNIX file-system to provide stable-storage between reboots, but otherwise maintains most data in program memory. As might be expected, providing that the DSA avoids paging, execution of the retrieval and interrogation facilities of the Directory can be realized in a timely fashion. Naturally, when an update operation occurs, the copy on disk is modified and a journal entry written before the update is acknowledged. The disk copy is stored in a textual format to facilitate examination. As this copy is read only once — when the DSA starts, typically when UNIX goes multi-user — the cost of such a strategy is believed to be relatively small if properly implemented and tuned.

In order to speed interrogation, QUIPU uses an AVL-like data structure for Directory entries.[2]

---

[2]An AVL tree is a special case of a "balanced tree." These are data structures which are used to permit fast lookup of an entry (if N entries are in the data structure, then, on average, it should take no more than $logN$ operations to find a given entry). Because entries may be inserted or removed, the data structure may need to be re-balanced to retain this retrieval property. An AVL tree contains special mechanisms to reduce the need and expense to perform this re-balancing.

As might be expected, this has good search properties for initial-substring searches, e.g.,

`surName = rose*`

Work continues in tuning both the AVL-like data structure and interrogation algorithms described earlier throughout Section 5.2, in order to achieve a more optimal balance between capability and performance.

We now consider the QUIPU DSA in considerable detail. Initially, we shall see how a QUIPU DSA represents the DIT in stable-storage, and what other bootstrapping information is necessary. Following this, the operational attributes particular to a QUIPU DSA are examined. These operational attributes control the behavior of the DSA, but are kept in the Directory. This avoids the need for having a second information infrastructure to support QUIPU DSAs — the Directory is used both by DUAs and DSAs! Next, the three kinds of replication used by a QUIPU DSA are explored, along with how a QUIPU DSA deals with OSI addresses. Following this, information on how a QUIPU DSA uses knowledge to traverse the DIT is examined, along with the factors affecting the decision to chain or refer. Finally, information on how QUIPU DSAs are named in the DIT, and how they are externally managed, is presented.

6.3.1   Representing the DIT in stable-storage

Since the QUIPU DSA uses the UNIX file-system to model its portion of the DIT, some mapping between the two is needed. This is achieved by dividing up the DIT into manageable units. Think of the entire DIT as being decomposed into discrete units of information termed *entry data blocks* (EDBs), or simply *blocks*. A block consists of a small portion of the DIT: the RDNs and attributes (types and values) of *all* the immediate subordinates of a particular entry. Thus the phrase "this DSA holds a copy of the block for c=NO" means that the QUIPU DSA in question has information about all the *attributes* of all the entries which exist immediately below the c=NO entry, such as

```
c=NO
    @o=Universitetet i Trondheim
```

The phrase does not imply that the QUIPU DSA has any information, whatsoever, about more distant subordinates, e.g.,

```
c=NO
    @o=Universitetet i Trondheim
    @ou=Institutt for Datateknikk og Telematikk
```

(Of course, this is a limitation over the entry-level knowledge granularity in the Directory standard. Skipping ahead a bit to page 257, an exception mechanism for QUIPU's approach is introduced.)

There are three kinds of blocks that a QUIPU DSA might hold:

- a *slave* copy refers to complete, authoritative information of a block: for the entry corresponding to that block, the DSA knows the RDNs of all of the immediate subordinates along with all of their attributes. Slave copies are regularly updated (shadowed) by contacting an *upstream* DSA, and comparing timestamps associated with the two copies of the block. Note that the upstream DSA needn't be the master of the data.

- a *cache* copy refers to possibly partial information that a DSA has received during its execution lifetime, or has been "primed" by the system administrator: the DSA may know about some of the immediate subordinates and some of their attributes. Rules for when that information can be used are discussed later in Section 6.3.4.

- the term *master* copy is self-evident. Only a single DSA may hold the master copy for any portion of the DIT.

Regardless of the categorization, the key concept here is that the QUIPU views the DIT as being broken up into discrete EDBs, and it is these EDBs which are kept in stable-storage, and which are exchanged by the shadowing algorithm.

Mapping EDBs to Disk

Each UNIX directory corresponds to a non-leaf entry, and, within that entry, the file *EDB* has information on the immediate subordinates of that entry.

For example, information on the immediate subordinates for

```
c=AU@o=Commonwealth Scientific and Industrial Research Organisation
```

is kept in the file:

```
.../c=AU/o=Commonwealth Scientific and Industrial Research Organisation/EDB
```

Note that the embedded spaces from the RDN are present in the UNIX filename. In order to shorten type-in, a mapping file, *EDB.map*, can be used. For example, if the file `.../c=AU/EDB.map` contains a line:

```
o=Commonwealth Scientific and Industrial Research Organisation#csiro
```

then the EDB previously referenced is named as

```
.../c=AU/csiro/EDB
```

This facility is particularly useful for variants of UNIX which do not support long filenames. It is also useful because some UNIX variants do not allow spaces in filenames.

When expressed in textual form, the first line of an EDB file identifies its type, either MASTER, SLAVE, or CACHE. The second line is a timestamp, used for opaque comparison by QUIPU's shadowing algorithm. Following this are one or more entries. Each entry contains:

- the RDN;

- all attribute values; and,

- a blank line.

A simple EDB file with one entry might look like:

```
MASTER
900506161200Z
cn=Manager
acl= self # write # entry
acl= others # read # entry
description= (haggard) Manager of the US DMD
cn= Manager
aliasedObjectName= c=US@o=DMD@cn=Manager
objectClass= alias & organizationalRole
```

(Remember that the first occurrence of cn= is the RDN, the second is the actual attribute value.)

Due to the structuring of the textual format used by the DSA, execution of Directory modification operations are slow, since more than the single entry being modified is written back to stable-storage. As a compile-time configuration option, the DSA can use a binary format instead for the disk-copy. This has the advantage of allowing faster updates (only entries modified are actually written), but at the expense of losing the ability to examine the files with UNIX's text-handling tools.

6.3.2 Local Configuration Information

The QUIPU DSA looks for a file, *quiputailor*, which contains boot-strapping information. A fragment of this table is shown in Figure 6.5 on page 251. The configuration options include:

oidtable: the location of the object tables described earlier in Section 4.1.8.

mydsaname: the name of this DSA.

parent: the superior reference for this DSA.

preferDSA: the name of the DSA to be favored when selecting among a list of DSAs which are chaining candidates.

shadow: attributes which should be "spot-shadowed." This is explained later on in Section 6.3.4.

optimize_attr: attributes which should be used as keys for the AVL-like data structure.

index_subtree: non-leaf entries which should be indexed to allow fast traversal.

update: indicates whether this DSA should regularly execute QUIPU's shadowing algorithm. If disabled, the DSA administrator must manually inform the DSA to execute the algorithm.

searchlevel: how deep in the DIT the base-object of a Directory search operation must be before whole-subtree searching is allowed.

adminsize/admintime: the maximum number of entries that may be returned by a Directory search or list operation, along with the maximum number of seconds which may be spent processing such an operation.

cachetime: the cache invalidation time, in seconds.

conntime: the maximum length of time, in seconds, which should be spent trying to establish a connection to a given DSA.

nsaptime: the maximum length of time, in seconds, which should be spent trying to establish a connection to a given NSAP. If the DSA is not multi-homed, effectively, the minimum of `conntime` and `nsaptime` is used.

retrytime: the length of time, in seconds, in between retrying a connection to an unreliable or unavailable DSA.

slavetime: the interval, in seconds, between each execution of QUIPU's shadowing algorithm, if the DSA is enabled for auto-execution of the algorithm.

```
oidtable     oidtable

mydsaname    "c=US@cn=Condor"
parent       "cn=Alpaca"      '0101'H/Internet=192.33.4.20+17007

shadow       aliasedObjectName

optimize_attr commonName
optimize_attr surName
index_subtree "c=US@o=Performance Systems International"

treedir      /usr/etc/quipu/condor/

dsaplog      level=exceptions file=dsap.log
stats        level=all        file=stats.log
logdir       /usr/etc/quipu/condor/

update       on
searchlevel  2

adminsize    50
admintime    300
cachetime    21600
conntime     300
nsaptime     45
retrytime    3600
slavetime    21600
```

Figure 6.5: Partial Listing of a QUIPU DSA's Configuration File

6.3.3   Operational Attributes

Whenever possible, the QUIPU DSA relies on information stored in the Directory for configuration. Once a DSA has "bootstrapped," emphasis is placed on using the Directory to control the behavior of the DSA.

Towards this end, the QUIPU DSA makes use of several *operational attributes*. The concept of an operational attribute, one which controls the operation of the Directory, rather than being intended for users of the Directory, was alluded to in the 1988 standards, and is currently being formalized in new standardization work.

Because attributes belong to objects, it is easiest to explain the operational attributes in terms of the object classes to which they belong.

quipuObject

Each entry which is mastered by a QUIPU DSA contains the value `quipuObject` as one of its `objectClass` values:

```
quipuObject OBJECT-CLASS
    SUBCLASS OF top
    MUST CONTAIN { accessControlList }
    MAY CONTAIN  { lastModifiedBy,
                   lastModifiedTime,
                   entrySecurityPolicy }
```

The key requirement is that an access control list must be present. All QUIPU DSAs understand the semantics of this attribute, and therefore, two QUIPU DSAs can optimize performance using caching whilst enforcing an authorization policy.

The `accessControlList` attribute consists of zero or more positive-access rules, each indicating which users may perform what actions, e.g.,

```
acl= others # read # entry
```

Each site configures its entries accordingly. It should be noted that in the absence of strong authentication, an authorization policy provides little confidence. The source for QUIPU is delivered only with simple authentication. However, QUIPU also supports the simple protected model of authentication, and work is continuing on strong authentication.

When an entry mastered by a QUIPU DSA is modified, the DSA will update two attributes indicating when the modification occurred (`lastModifiedTime`) and which Directory User (DN) initiated the modification (`lastModifiedBy`).

quipuNonLeafObject

Each non-leaf entry which is mastered by a QUIPU DSA contains the value `quipuNonLeafObject` as one of its `objectClass` values:

```
quipuNonLeafObject OBJECT-CLASS
    SUBCLASS OF quipuObject
    MUST CONTAIN { masterDSA }
    MAY CONTAIN  { slaveDSA,
                    treeStructure,
                    inheritedAttribute }
    ::= { quipuObjectClass 6 }
```

The key requirement is that each non-leaf entry must contain knowledge information indicating which DSA is authoritative for all the subordinates of that entry. (Again, QUIPU does allow exceptions, as noted later on on page 257.) Unlike the Directory standard, which represents knowledge information with a presentation-address and an optional DSA name (DN), the single-valued `masterDSA` attribute used by QUIPU is simply the Distinguished Name of the DSA. This eases management considerably.

In addition, QUIPU DSAs may participate in a shadowing algorithm. So, the optional, but multi-valued, `slaveDSA` attribute contains the names of those DSA which shadow authoritative information for the subordinates of an entry.

In order to enforce a DIT structuring scheme, a multi-valued `treeStructure` attribute may be used, the syntax of which is shown in Figure 6.6. Each attribute value imposes structuring requirements (in terms of both naming and schema) on the subordinates of an entry which is mastered by a QUIPU DSA. Of course, the presence of this attribute is optional: in the absence of local policy, QUIPU DSAs may

```
TreeStructureSyntax ::=
  SET {
     mandatoryObjectClasses[1]
        SET OF
          OBJECT IDENTIFIER,

        -- at present, not supported in QUIPU
        optionalObjectClasses[2]
           SET OF
             OBJECT IDENTIFIER                              10
             OPTIONAL,

        -- at present, not supported in QUIPU
        permittedRDNs[3]
           SET OF
              SET OF
                 AttributeType
  }
```

Figure 6.6: QUIPU's Schema Syntax

store arbitrary information. Further, a QUIPU DSA will attempt to
enforce the structuring requirements only if it is the actual master
of the information — replicated information is not checked for conformance to structuring constraints. As might be expected, checking
occurs not only when a DSA starts, but also when the **treeStructure**
attribute is changed in a parent. (The QUIPU DSA should also check
whenever a subordinate is modified, but this check cannot be performed atomically if the subordinates are kept in another DSA.)

Regardless of whether the **treeStructure** attribute is present,
when a QUIPU DSA masters an entry, it computes the mandatory
and optional attributes allowed for that entry by taking the union of
the properties of each **objectClass** value for the entry. Therefore,
QUIPU DSAs do not allow so-called *free extension*, in which arbitrary attribute values may be present in an entry, regardless of its
objectClass values. The one exception is for alias entries, in which
a QUIPU DSA will allow any kind of attribute values to be present.
(This is necessary for an RDN to be associated with the entry!)

soap...   The problem with free extension is that it is inconsistent with
schema enforcement. If the Directory standard defined a special
objectClass value that permitted free extension, then both could
coexist. However, given a lack of authoritative indication that free

extension is enabled for an entry, support of free extension is inconsistent with schema in the Directory.

...soap

Finally, the QUIPU DSA supports an inherited attribute value scheme, which allows one or more attribute values to be inherited by the immediate subordinates of an entry. Although, this was primarily included to reduce the size of the internal structures of the DSAs, it has many uses. For example, associated with an organizational unit may be a single postal address. It is often desirable for each subordinate entry to have the same address.

The syntax for QUIPU's multi-valued `inheritedAttribute` attribute type is shown in Figure 6.7 on page 256. For each attribute value present in a non-leaf entry, inherited attributes for a subordinate may be provided in addition to existing attributes (`always`), or only if the specified attribute is not present (`default`). Further, the attribute values may be taken either from the parent entry (`typeOnly`), or may be independent of those values in the parent entry (`typeAndValues`). Attribute inheritance is done on the basis of object class: for each object class which is to inherit attributes, exactly one attribute value of type `inheritedAttribute` exists in the parent entry. Because the object class component may be omitted from the attribute value, this provides a convenient means for subordinates to inherit an object class.

Although QUIPU's scheme is aimed at single-level inheritance, it can easily be used for multi-level inheritance, simply by including the `inheritedAttribute` in the list of inherited attributes. For example, suppose you have an organization which is arbitrarily structured using only organizational units, and you want to make sure that the entry for each person has a default telephone number. The entry for the organization contains two attribute values: the first indicates that subordinate `organizationalUnit` entries, by default, will inherit `inheritedAttribute` values; and, the second indicates that subordinate `person` entries, by default, will inherit a specific `telephoneNumber` value.

Although there are some limitations with QUIPU's approach to inherited attributes, these are all common-sensical, e.g., subordinates may not inherit distinguished attributes.

```
InheritedAttributeSyntax ::=
    SET {
        -- default which can be overriden in subordinate entry
        default[0]
            InheritedAttributes
            OPTIONAL,

        -- always present in subordinate entry
        always[1]
            InheritedAttributes                                        10
            OPTIONAL,

        -- object class to inherit to
        -- if not present,
        --     then objectClass attribute is also inherited
        objectClass
            OBJECT IDENTIFIER
            OPTIONAL
}
                                                                       20
InheritedAttributes ::=
    SET OF
        CHOICE {
            -- take value(s) from the entry
            typeOnly
                AttributeType,

            typeAndValues
                Attribute
        }                                                              30
```

Figure 6.7: QUIPU's Inherited Attribute Syntax

quipuExternalObject

Of course, all DSAs are not necessarily QUIPU DSAs! So, there must be a means for QUIPU DSAs to be told that an entry is mastered by a non-QUIPU DSA:

```
quipuExternalObject OBJECT-CLASS
    SUBCLASS OF quipuObject
    MAY CONTAIN  { subordinateReference
                   crossReference
                   nonSpecificSubordinateReference }
    ::= { quipuObjectClass 9 }

subordinateReference ATTRIBUTE
    WITH ATTRIBUTE-SYNTAX AccessPoint
    SINGLE VALUE
    ::= { quipuAttributeType 25 }

crossReference ATTRIBUTE
    WITH ATTRIBUTE-SYNTAX AccessPoint
    SINGLE VALUE
    ::= { quipuAttributeType 26 }

nonSpecificSubordinateReference ATTRIBUTE
    WITH ATTRIBUTE-SYNTAX AccessPoint
    ::= { quipuAttributeType 27 }
```

Values from only one of these three attribute types should be present in an `quipuExternalObject` entry.

When a QUIPU DSA masters an EDB with an entry containing this `objectClass` value and either a subordinate-reference or cross-reference value, it maintains a "spot-shadow" of the actual entry, which allows most interrogation operations to proceed without delay. In contrast, when a QUIPU DSA slaves an EDB containing such an entry, it does not spot-shadow, relying instead on the upstream DSA (if the upstream DSA masters the EDB, then this information is determined via spot-shadowing, otherwise the upstream DSA simply passes along the EDB).

Regardless, if asked to navigate into a portion of the DIT below that entry, a QUIPU DSA will follow the value(s) in the refer-

ence attribute, and chain or refer accordingly. If the reference attribute is a non-specific subordinate-reference, then a QUIPU DSA
uses application-layer multicasting to process the request.

quipuDSA

Finally, because QUIPU DSAs implement several refinements beyond
the 1988 Directory standards, it is important for QUIPU DSAs to
be able to recognize each other and use these enhanced features. As
such, each QUIPU DSA is represented by:

```
quipuDSA OBJECT-CLASS
    SUBCLASS OF dSA
    MUST CONTAIN { accessControlList,
                   eDBinfo,
                   userPassword,
                   manager,
                   quipuVersion }
    MAY CONTAIN  { description,
                   lastModifiedBy,
                   lastModifiedTime,
                   dsaDefaultSecurityPolicy,
                   dsaPermittedSecurityPolicy,
                   relayDSA,
                   listenAddress }
    ::= { quipuObjectClass 1 }
```

In addition, the `supportedApplicationContext` attribute of a DSA
contains a third value, besides the DAP and DSP configurations,
namely, `quipuDSP`. When a `quipuDSA` must contact another DSA,
and several choices are available, it tends to favor those DSAs of the
`quipuDSA` object class. For example, caching cannot occur without
an understanding of the authorization policy (access control) being
applied to an entry. (This innocent observation introduces a very important characteristic of caching between DSAs — see Section 6.3.4
on page 262 for the details!)

Shadowing information between QUIPU DSAs is represented with
the multi-valued `eDBinfo` attribute. For each portion of the DIT
for which this QUIPU DSA is authoritative, this attribute contains

the names of the upstream DSA and/or downstream DSAs which participate in the shadowing algorithm. (Note that even if a QUIPU DSA does not participate in a shadowing relationship, it has a single "dummy" attribute value, since this attribute is mandatory.)

The `userPassword` attribute is currently not used, but is present in the definition because earlier (and still running) versions of the QUIPU DSA did make use of it.

The `manager` attribute is used to identify the DSA's super-user. The super-user is allowed to invoke operations available on the DSA's management port. These are described later on in Section 6.3.10 on page 276.

It is possible that a DSA may have very limited connectivity to other DSAs. In this case, it is desirable to identify one or more DSAs which have agreed to relay Directory traffic. This is represented by the multi-valued `relayDSA` attribute. Although a QUIPU DSA uses a complex set of rules in determining its mode of operation, this attribute focuses the decision nicely. This provides a nice lead-in as to how a QUIPU DSA navigates the DIT.

6.3.4 Replication

A QUIPU DSA can utilize three replication techniques: shadowing, spot-shadowing, and caching. These are discussed in turn.

Shadowing

Cooperating QUIPU DSAs can participate in a shadowing algorithm. A QUIPU DSA contains zero or more `eDBinfo` attribute values, each containing:

- the name of an EDB;

- optionally, an upstream DSA;

- optionally, one or more downstream DSAs.

In QUIPU, shadowing is based on a "pull-through" model: a downstream DSA contacts its upstream peer by establishing an association using the `quipuDSP` application context. In addition to offering all of the DSP services on this application context, there is an additional operation, `getEDB`, which is invoked by the downstream DSA. The argument to this operation contains the name of the EDB and a version string. The upstream DSA verifies that the downstream DSA is authorized (by checking the appropriate `eDBinfo` attribute value in the entry for the upstream DSA), and if so, compares the supplied version string to the one currently associated with the EDB. If there is a mismatch, the entire EDB and the new version string is returned as the result of the operation.

If the EDB contains an entry which is being spot-shadowed, then the upstream DSA includes this information with the EDB it sends. As a result, downstream DSAs do not have to spot-shadow such entries.

The scheme has a nice quality in that Directory information is used to capture all of the relationships in the shadowing algorithm. However, there are at least three weaknesses to QUIPU's approach to shadowing:

- first, it cannot handle whole-subtrees — the DMD manager must create an `eDBinfo` attribute value for each EDB to be shadowed, and then keep this information up to date if the DIT structure changes;

- second, it cannot handle individual entries — if any entry in an EDB changes, then the entire EDB must be sent, even if only one attribute value in a single entry had changed; and,

- third, the entire EDB is sent as a single operation. When sending large EDBs over some network infrastructures (most notably those running TP0 over X.25), this puts too much strain on the system, resulting in a truncated EDB being received which must then be discarded. A future release of the software will allow incremental transmission of an EDB.

Of these, the first is considered a critically needed extension, and will probably be implemented in a future release.

Spot-Shadowing

Under three circumstances, a QUIPU DSA will decide that an entry should be spot-shadowed:

- it masters an EDB with an entry with an `objectClass` value of `quipuExternalObject` and either a subordinate-reference or a cross-reference value — this indicates that the entry is actually mastered by another DSA, a non-QUIPU DSA;[3]

- it masters an EDB containing an entry that has an `objectClass` value of `quipuDSA` — this indicates that the QUIPU DSA masters the EDB containing the entry for another QUIPU DSA; or,

- a DN-valued attribute has been flagged as being a candidate for spot-shadowing in the QUIPU configuration file, so the entry named by the attribute value is spot-shadowed.

When an entry should be spot-shadowed, a QUIPU DSA will intermittently attempt to contact another DSA and perform a read operation on the entry.

It turns out that the reason for spot-shadowing is different in all three cases. Respectively, the reasons are:

- for a `quipuExternalObject` object, this allows the DSA to find out about all of the attributes associated with that entry;

- for a `quipuDSA` object, this allows the target DSA to master its own entry; and,

- for flagged DN-valued attributes, this can lead to substantive performance improvements since these attributes are likely to be used by DUAs as the arguments to subsequent Directory operations.

---

[3]If a QUIPU DSA masters an EDB containing an entry with an `objectClass` value of `quipuExternalObject` and a non-specific subordinate-reference, then the QUIPU DSA believes that it masters that entry, and therefore need not employ spot-shadowing. Otherwise, the QUIPU DSA would have to spot-shadow the entry by consulting all of the DSAs indicated by the NSSRs and then correlate the results — an impractical approach at best.

Caching

Much earlier it was noted that the QUIPU DUA can maintain a cache of the information provided by a DSA. Looking back to Figure 4.11 on page 113, it seems that a DUA caching strategy must keep track of:

- the name of the entry to be cached;

- whether attribute values are being added to the cache; and,

- whether all of the entry's attribute values are being added to the cache.

This is straight-forward. Further, a DUA that requests information that is likely to change should employ the `dontUseCopy` service control accordingly: initially, a DUA needn't specify this service control and tries to use the information returned. If the information proves faulty (e.g., a presentation address is retrieved but could not be associated with), then the request is re-issued, with the `dontUseCopy` service control.[4]

In the case of a DSA, the choices are harder. Whenever a DSA chains a request, it has the opportunity to cache the information returned by the other DSA. However, there are two problems which DSAs must cope with:

- deciding when to invalidate the cached information (in general, DSA processes are much more long-lived than DUA processes); and,

- deciding whether the cached information can be used to process requests from a DUA (given that the DUA indicates that "copy" data may be used).

A simplistic solution to the invalidation problem is to assign a relatively small time-out value for cached information, e.g., on the order of six hours. However, if a QUIPU DSA has need to make use of the

---

[4]Neither the AE-lookup algorithm nor the split-DASE protocol described earlier in Sections 5.2.4 and 5.3.1, respectively, currently make use of such a policy, though they certainly should.

cached information itself, e.g., using a cached presentation address for a DSA, and the information proves valid, then the cached information is marked as being freshly cached, and thus, gets a new lease of life.

The DUA-usage problem is harder, since the DSA needs to apply the authorization policy of the DMD which owns the data that was cached. Because the Directory standard does not provide a means for DSAs to exchange this kind of information, a QUIPU DSA will cache information only if it is obtained via a `quipuDSP` association (i.e., from another QUIPU DSA). Further, when information about an entry is sent over a `quipuDSP` association, the `accessControlList` attribute of that entry is always sent. Because this attribute captures the authorization policy used by a DMD utilizing QUIPU DSAs, the receiving DSA can verify that a DUA is entitled to make use of cached information.

6.3.5 OSI Addressing

It is important to appreciate that OSI applications are implemented on a wide range of end-to-end protocol combinations. Since the value of the Directory increases as its coverage increases, it is desirable to offer the Directory service on as many of these combinations as possible.

In Section 5.6 of *The Open Book*, the concept of an OSI *community* was introduced. This refers to a collection of OSI systems sharing both connectivity and a common TS-stack (some combination of end-to-end protocols). Since the same TS-stack must be used to achieve interworking within the OSI model (i.e., in the absence of transport-layer relays), it is possible that two DSAs which share connectivity may still be unable to communicate because they support different TS-stacks.

A QUIPU DSA is knowledgeable about the OSI communities of which it is a member, and, as we shall see, uses this information as a part of its algorithm when deciding whether to chain or refer.

Network Addresses

In Section 4.1 of *The Open Book*, OSI network addressing is considered. Because the choice of OSI network address is related to the TS-stack chosen, the QUIPU DSA must have some knowledge of addressing. Rather than repeat *The Open Book*'s treatment of this topic, let's just consider the basics.

The International standard [39] defines OSI network addressing, and provides an optimized scheme to facilitate allocation of network addresses, through the use of a hierarchical structure. OSI defines several addressing *domains* and then delegates administration of these domains to their respective *addressing authorities*. These authorities may create sub-domains and further delegate authority, and so on.

The responsibility of an addressing authority is to define the structure of an addressing domain and then to allocate values within that domain. The structure is termed an *abstract syntax*. This means that the addressing authority is interested only in the conceptual aspects of the structure and not the actual encoding, the *transfer syntax*, used by the network protocols that carry those addresses.

At the top-level, an address is divided into two parts:

- an *initial domain part* (IDP); and,

- a *domain specific part* (DSP).

The IDP is further subdivided into two parts:

- the *authority and format identifier* (AFI) that is assigned by the ISO/IEC for a particular format to be used by an addressing authority; and,

- the *initial domain identifier* (IDI).

Thus, a network address looks like this:

IDP		DSP
AFI	IDI	

The authority and format identifier specifies how the initial domain identifier is interpreted, both in syntax and semantics. The AFI indicates if the IDI is of variable length, whether leading zeros have significance, and also defines the abstract syntax associated with the domain specific part. In particular, the AFI indicates whether the DSP is formatted using decimal digits or binary information.

The initial domain identifier indicates the entity allowed to assign values to the domain specific part of the address. This is where the first level of delegation from the ISO/IEC occurs.

Finally, the DSP has no pre-defined semantics, per se. It is entirely up to the entity indicated by the IDI to allocate DSP values and assign meaning to those values.

Let's look at two simple examples: An X.121 address may be encoded using:

$$\text{AFI} = 36$$
$$\text{IDI} = \text{X.121 address (up to 14 digits)}$$

as shown here:

36	23421920030013	null DSP

A US GOSIP version 2 address may be encoded using:

$$\text{AFI} = 47$$
$$\text{IDI} = 0005$$

as shown here:

47	0005	DSP					
		vrsn	authority	reserved	domain	area	end-system	nsel
		80	fffc00	0000	0001	0002	0123456789ab	00

Skipping ahead a bit, to Figure 6.8 on page 269, we see that the Directory views an OSI network address as simply a string of octets, expressed in concrete binary notation.

OSI Communities and Network Addresses

An OSI community can be represented as a collection of NSAP prefixes (usually there is a single prefix). So, to determine which community an OSI network address belongs to, simply find the community with the longest prefix that entirely matches. As far as this test is concerned, the AFI, IDI, and DSP are just octets strung together.

Looking back at the two examples, one could imagine that a system attached both to the International X.25 network and the (eventual) US OSI Internet, might have a community table with three entries:

NSAP prefix	Community	TS-stack
36	International X.25	TP0/CONS
470005	US OSI Internet	TP4/CLNS
	other	

soap... Of course, we should be keep in mind that OSI communities are something outside the scope of OSI standardization. They are used to reflect the shortcomings of OSI internetworking as currently standardized. In a more perfect world, the concept of an OSI community wouldn't be needed, in the absence of administrative control, all OSI end-systems would be able to communicate! In the meantime, it is necessary to play little games such as these to allow OSI systems in
...soap different communities to internetwork.

Interim Communities

For OSI communities using standardized TS-stacks, generating and interpreting these octet strings is straight-forward. However, many OSI application processes use non-standard TS-stacks, such as RFC-1006 over TCP[40].[5] A related problem is that some communities might use standardized TS-stacks, but run them over private networks using a different addressing scheme.

There must be a means whereby addresses used in either situation can be stored in the Directory and subsequently interpreted by entities with knowledge of these non-standard communities. A mechanism for solving both problems defined in [41], which is commonly known as "Kille's Interim Addressing scheme." Under this interim solution, non-OSI addresses are encoded in the OSI addressing sub-domain assigned to a given organization by virtue of its Telex address. The

---

[5]Indeed, as of this writing, it is the author's opinion that many more OSI application processes are running over non-standard TS-stacks, such as RFC1006 over TCP, than are running over standardized TS-stacks, such as TP4 over CLNP.

assumption, of course, is that Telex devices will never be upgraded to run OSI. At present, five interim communities are well-known under the UCL Telex prefix:

NSAP prefix	Community	TS-stack
540072872201	International X.25	TP0/X.25(80)
540072872202	UK Janet	TP0/X.25(80)
540072872203	Internet	RFC1006/TP0
540072872205	loopback TCP	RFC1006/TP0
540072872206	International X.25 Interconnection	TP0/X.25(80)

(JANET is the UK academic X.25-based network, often referred to as "envy of the world networking," at least by the UK academic community. International X.25 Infrastructure, or IXI, is a cooperative effort sponsored by the European Academic Research Community to achieve X.25 networking between academic sites throughout Europe.)

Of course, other sites are free to use these conventions, with a different Telex prefix, for their own private networks or non-standard TS-stacks.

Since these conventions do not conflict with "real" OSI addresses (even though they adhere to the OSI address syntax), naive application processes will simply treat these communities as unknown.

OSI application processes which understand these conventions are able to make use of these non-standard communities. In ISODE, a local table is maintained which contains information about all the OSI communities known to the local end-system (including any which the end-system is not a member of). When OSI network addresses are encountered, either via communication with an OSI application process or locally, an internal representation is substituted. Similarly, when a network address must be communicated to another OSI application process, the corresponding concrete binary representation is sent.

The C definition of this internal representation is fairly simple as it contains information about the TS-stack used in the community, an index into the community table, and community-specific address information:

```
struct NSAPaddr {
   long   na_stack;              /* identifies TS−stack */
#define NA_NSAP 0               /*   TP4/... */
#define NA_TCP  1               /*   RFC1006/TCP */
#define NA_X25  2               /*   TP0/X.25(80) */

   long   na_community;         /* identifies community */
/* choice based on value of na_stack */
   union {                                                              10
     /* ... */
   }    na_un;
};
```

As might be imagined, the community table is little more than a list of NSAP prefixes and associated TS-stacks, as shown earlier. When an OSI network address is to be transformed, a determination is made as to which entry contains the longest NSAP prefix that entirely matches. For example, here's how a few network addresses might be transformed:

| | | struct NSAPaddr | |
network address	TS-stack	community	value
4700602001234	tp4	realNS	4700602001234
540072872203010000000006	rfc1006/tcp	Internet	IP 10.0.0.6
54007287220223137039150000002340555	tp0/x.25(80)	Janet	DTE 00002340555 CUDF 892796

Presentation Addresses

The Directory syntax for the `presentationAddress` attribute is shown in Figure 6.8. With this, OSI systems can unambiguously transmit corresponding ASN.1 values across the network using the BER or some other encoding mechanism.

Just as real implementations of the Directory need a textual notation for writing Distinguished Names, for expository (and local) purposes it is important to have a concise textual notation for presentation addresses. [42] defines such a notation. The BNF for this notation is shown in Figure 6.9 on page 270. Because the notation

```
PresentationAddress ::=
      SEQUENCE {
          -- presentation selector
          pSelector[0]
             OCTET STRING
             OPTIONAL,

          -- session selector
          sSelector[1]
             OCTET STRING                                    10
             OPTIONAL,

          -- transport selector
          tSelector[2]
             OCTET STRING
             OPTIONAL,

          -- network addresses, unordered
          nAddresses[3]
             SET OF (1..MAX)                                 20
                OCTET STRING
      }
```

Figure 6.8: Presentation Address Attribute Syntax

must be able to support all forms of OSI addresses, it appears cumbersome. Fortunately, a macro facility is used in conjunction with the BNF so that commonly used address formats can be concisely written. Consider a simple example of a network address written using the format:

`Internet=192.33.4.21+17007`

Here, `Internet=` is a macro which expands to

`TELEX+00728722+RFC-1006+03+`

So the address in the example can be read as belonging to:

> *an OSI system using RFC-1006 over TCP as its TS-stack, residing at IP-address 192.33.4.21 and TCP port 17007.*

As can be seen, with the judicious use of macros, user type-in and display can be considerably shortened. Regardless, the notation is able to handle the full range of OSI addressing formats.

```
<presentation−address>
                ::= [[[ <psel> "/" ] <ssel> "/" ] <tsel> "/" ]
                        <network−address−list>

<network−address−list>
                ::= <network−address> "|" <network−address−list>
                  | <network−address>

<psel>          ::= <selector>
<ssel>          ::= <selector>                                               10
<tsel>          ::= <selector>

<selector>      ::= '"' <otherstring> '"'         −− IA5 repertoire
                  | "#" <digitstring>             −− US GOSIP
                  | "'" <hexstring> "'H"          −− arbitrary
                  | ""                            −− empty

<network−address>
                ::= "NS" "+" <hexstring>          −− concrete binary
                  | <afi> "+" <idi> [ "+" <dsp> ]                            20

<idi>           ::= <digitstring>
<afi>           ::= "X121" | "DCC" | "TELEX" | "PSTN" | "ISDN"
                  | "ICD" | "LOCAL"

<dsp>           ::= "d" <digitstring>             −− abstract decimal
                  | "x" <hexstring>               −− abstract binary
                  | "l" <otherstring>             −− local form
                  | "RFC-1006" "+" <prefix> "+" <ip>
                        [ "+" <port> [ "+" <tset> ]]                        30
                  | "X.25(80)" "+" <prefix> "+" <dte>
                        [ "+" <cudf−or−pid> "+" <hexstring> ]

<prefix>        ::= <digit> <digit>
                                                  −− dot−notation
<ip>            ::= <otherstring>                 −− (e.g., 10.0.0.6)
<port>          ::= <digitstring>
<tset>          ::= <digitstring>

<dte>           ::= <digitstring>                                           40
<cudf−or−pid>   ::= "CUDF" | "PID"

<digitstring>   ::= <digit> <digitstring> | <digit>
<digit>         ::= [0−9]

<otherstring>   ::= <other> <otherstring> | <other>
<other>         ::= [0−9a−zA−Z+−.]

<hexstring>     ::= <hexdigit> <hexstring> | <hexdigit>
<hexdigit>      ::= [0−9a−f]                                                50
```

Figure 6.9: BNF for a String Encoding of Presentation Addresses

6.3.6   DIT Navigation

When a DUA requests some action from a DSA (e.g., to read an entry), the DSA may not have that information resident. In this case, the DSA has a choice: it may either contact another DSA which is "closer" to the information and propagate the request (i.e., *chain*), or it may return information about this "closer" DSA to the DUA, and let the DUA re-issue its request accordingly (i.e., *refer*). Of course, when DSAs communicate between themselves, they may also chain or refer requests.

The key issue is to understand what the term "resident" means with respect to information held by a QUIPU DSA. As noted earlier, QUIPU DSAs employ both shadowing and caching of information in the Directory. Thus, the *residency requirement* is simply enumerated as:

Operation Requested	EDB Required for Residency
read, compare	master, slave, or cache
list, search	master, or slave
update	master

(Actually, a cached copy might be used to satisfy a list request, depending on the service controls used with the operation.)

Hence, whilst a collection of co-operating QUIPU DSAs relies primarily on shadowing (slave blocks) to speed queries, updates still rely on a centralized entity (containing the master block) being available. (This is the best compromise that can be taken without making the system tremendously more complex, e.g., introducing distributed database technology.)

Finally, it should once more be emphasized that QUIPU's EDB approach to knowledge is more coarse than the Directory standard, which suggests that the discrete unit of knowledge information is at the entry-level.

6.3.7   Choice of DSA

If a QUIPU DSA decides to chain a request, there is a possibility that several DSAs might be available. In this case, the DSAs are ordered by operational quality, and an association is attempted to the DSA of highest quality. If an association cannot be established to this DSA, the next DSA in the list is tried, and so on, until either an association is established or the list of DSAs is exhausted.

In early implementations of QUIPU, the list of candidate DSAs was ordered pseudo-randomly and this resulted in truly suboptimal behavior. In order to avoid this, each QUIPU DSA now attempts to determine the "operational quality" of a DSA and maintains this information throughout its execution lifetime. Five sort keys are used to achieve the ordering. These are listed in order of significance:

existing associations: since the DSP allows either the initiator or responder to invoke operations, a QUIPU DSA can always chain new requests on an existing DSP association.

membership in the `quipuDSA` object class: QUIPU DSAs share a common authorization mechanism and are a known quantity.

reliability: a QUIPU DSA keeps track of when it last attempted to associate with another DSA, whether that attempt was successful, and if not, how many failures have occurred since the last successful association.

locality: a QUIPU DSA checks to see if it is in the same OSI community as another DSA, and if not, a check is made to see if the two DSAs are named under the same country.

administrative preference: The local configuration file for a QUIPU DSA described earlier in Section 6.3.2 allows one or more `preferDSA` directives which can be used by the local DMD manager to indicate "favored" DSAs.

Experience has shown that the choice of these sort keys gives a reasonable estimate of operational quality. It should be noted that when things are running well, choice of DSA is largely unimportant; however, when transient network outages and software instability occur, ordering by operational quality is essential if good service is to be maintained in the short-term.

6.3.8 Chaining or Referral

The final set of issues dealing with DIT navigation fall into the area of how a QUIPU DSA decides whether to chain or refer. There are basically three areas to consider:

- whether OSI connectivity exists between the requestor and the target DSA;

- whether a target DSA can "trust" the requestor and the chaining DSA; and,

- whether cached information can be used to satisfy the request, thereby eliminating the need to either chain or refer.

These are now discussed in turn.

Use of Presentation Address

Only within a single OSI community can interworking be achieved. Hence, in order to provide homogeneous service to the user, the DSAs must be able to compare two OSI presentation addresses and determine if an association can be established directly between the two. This need arises in two cases, which are handled by a QUIPU DSA in this fashion:

First, a DSA wishes to perform an operation and then realizes that it must either chain or refer. A QUIPU DSA compares the presentation address of the application entity on whose behalf it is performing the operation, with the presentation address of a DSA which is closer to the information.[6] If the two addresses belong to the same "community" (i.e., are compatible), the DSA knows that it is safe to return a referral. If not, the DSA realizes that, barring service controls to the contrary, it should chain.

Second, a DSA might wish to contact another DSA. In this case, a QUIPU DSA sees if the presentation address of the other DSA is in

---

[6]If the application entity is a DSA, then a QUIPU DSA will look up the entity's presentation address in the Directory; otherwise, if the application entity is a DUA, the QUIPU DUA will make the pessimistic assumption that the DUA belongs to only one community, namely the one which supports the DUA's association to the DSA.

one of the communities of the local end-system. If so, the DSA knows that it is possible to chain operations to that DSA. Otherwise, in the absence of transport-level bridging, the DSA knows that it cannot reach the other DSA.

Use of Simple Authentication

Strong authentication has the promise to provide an effective means for certain identification of the entity which requests a Directory operation. However, implementation experience with strong authentication is limited. Therefore, a DSA must be able to cope in an environment where use of simple authentication is dominant. In the context of QUIPU, an "untrusted DSA" is one which chains a request to another DSA, but does not use strong authentication to identify itself.

If an untrusted DSA chains an interrogation request to a QUIPU DSA, the QUIPU DSA verifies to see that both the originator of the request and the chaining DSA are allowed read access to the information. If not, a QUIPU DSA will return a security error, *inappropriate authentication*, to the chaining DSA. If the chaining DSA happens to be a QUIPU DSA, upon receipt of this error, a referral is given back to the DUA, which may then contact the target DSA directly.

As a consequence of this policy, in the case of a whole-subtree search operation, if portions of the subtree are spread over multiple DSAs, then, only world-readable entries and attributes are returned in the search results.

If an untrusted DSA chains a modification request to a QUIPU DSA, the QUIPU DSA verifies to see that public-writable access is allowed for the entry in question. If not, a security error is returned to the chaining DSA. Because little, if any, information should be public-writable, a QUIPU DSA which must chain a modification request, instead will, if possible, return a referral to the DUA.

6.3.9   Naming DSAs

As noted earlier, if a quipuDSA does not have information resident to satisfy a request, it identifies, to its local knowledge, the deepest non-leaf entry along the DIT path to the desired entry. The `masterDSA` and `slaveDSA` attributes of this entry are consulted to derive the DNs of DSAs which are more likely to be able to perform the desired operation.

Obviously, in order to resolve the `presentationAddress` attribute of the entries corresponding to the closer DSAs, additional retrieval in the Directory is needed. Thus, a DSA should be at the same level in the DIT as the highest EDB for which it holds authoritative information.

To see why this is so, consider a DSA named:

```
c=CA@o=University of Toronto@cn=losing
```

which, according to the entry for

```
c=CA@o=University of Toronto
```

is a `masterDSA`, and there are no `slaveDSAs` for that entry. Now suppose another DSA, called "naive," with knowledge only of `c=CA`, wishes to satisfy a request for a (possibly distant) subordinate of

```
c=CA@o=University of Toronto
```

In order to satisfy the request, the "naive" DSA must know the address of the "losing" DSA, which can obviously not be determined.[7]

Of course, this naming scheme implies that a QUIPU DSA may not master its own entry. For example, if the DSA named

```
c=CH@cn=chaos
```

does not master the EDB for `c=CH`, then some other DSA must master the former's entry. A drawback of this is that the DSA can't easily modify its own entry. This has long been a limitiation of QUIPU's scheme for naming DSAs. Fortunately, in early 1991, a solution was introduced.

A QUIPU DSA, in its home directory, maintains a special file containing its own actual entry. Whenever that DSA receives a read

---

[7]Of course, under some circumstances, it is possible to circumvent this if knowledge references contain the presentation address in addition to the name of the "losing" DSA.

request for that entry, it uses the information in the special file, rather
than any other information it may have (i.e., a slave EDB). As noted
earlier, any QUIPU DSA which finds that it masters an EDB containing entries for other QUIPU DSAs, will spot-shadow those entries by periodically connecting to those DSAs and asking information about them. If this information differs, the mastering DSA will
update its EDB accordingly. Of course, when the entry corresponding
to a QUIPU DSA is to be modified, that modify operation is always
referred to the QUIPU DSA whose entry is to be modified.

6.3.10   DSA Management

In order to provide a management capability for these refinements, a
new attribute type, `control`, is defined for use over the DAP. When
a DUA is bound as the DSA's manager, it may issue the modify
operation to add a value of type `control`. This is interpreted by the
DSA rather than being applied to the DIT.

The operations of interest are:

- abort DSA;

- restart DSA;

- refresh EDB from local stable-storage;

- rewrite EDB to local stable-storage;

- mark EDB as read-only (lock EDB);

- unlock EDB;

- initiate EDB shadowing algorithm with upstream DSA (either
  for all EDBs or a particular EDB);

- initiate spot-shadowing procedure.

For example, if it is necessary to make a substantive change to an
EDB for which the DAP is inappropriate, a DSA manager tells the
DSA to lock the EDB, edits the EDB on local stable-storage, tells the

DSA to re-read the EDB from local stable-storage, and then tells the DSA to unlock the EDB.

Instead, if a DUA issues a read for the `control` attribute of an entry, the value returned consists of a string containing information about:

- the number of entries and EDBs mastered by the DSA;

- the number of entries and EDBs slaved by the DSA; and,

- the number of entries cached by the DSA.

And that concludes our implementation focus on the QUIPU DSA.

6.4   Shared Namespaces

In a commercial environment, no single entity can claim the sole right to manage all the information corresponding to a given real-world object. In particular, if there are competing directory services which cooperate in the DIT, there is no natural administrator for many of the entities named in the DIT. One possible solution is to distribute subordinate and attribute information amongst the DSAs of different service-providers. If information about the RDNs of the immediate subordinates to an entry is distributed amongst DSAs, this is termed the "distributed subtree" problem, and, in theory, non-specific subordinate references provide a solution. In contrast, if an entry's attribute information is distributed amongst DSAs, then this is termed the the "distributed entry" problem. New work has been introduced in the standards process to address these concerns. However, some feel that the distributed entry approach is intractable as it has too many ramifications on the knowledge infrastructure of the Directory.

Recent work by Anthony E. Hodson of ICL, which has been subsequently refined in the North American Directory Forum, has led to an innovative solution based on the naming infrastructure of the Directory, rather than the knowledge infrastructure. This is particularly attractive since it requires no changes to X.500 models, services, procedures, or protocols. Let's consider this solution in the context of the hypothetical country of *Freedonia*.

The *shared namespace* approach relies on the notion of naming links and administrative cooperation. The basic idea, as shown in Figure 6.10 for Freedonia, is that service-providers agree to cooperatively manage a shared space, termed a *shared DIT domain*.[8] The structure of the shared domain is published, and the entries contained therein contain only public information. Because of this, this portion of the DIT is available for interrogation only (modifications occur in an off-line fashion). Further, this information is highly-replicated amongst service-providers.

In addition to a single shared DIT domain, each service-provider

---

[8]The term "DIT domain" is being formalized in new standardization work. It refers to a collection of subtrees in the DIT which are under a common management domain.

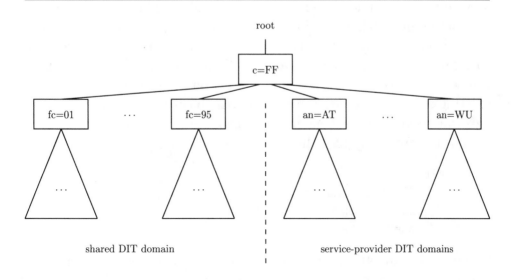

Figure 6.10: A Shared Domain in the DIT

maintains its own private information which is protected by whatever administrative policies it sees fit to impose. Each service-provider DIT domain is autonomously operated by that service-provider and need not have a published structure.

The key aspect of this approach is the information which is kept in the shared DIT domain. Each entry in the shared space contains four kinds of information:

- distinguished attribute values which are necessary to form the RDNs of the entries (and thereby give structure to that portion of the DIT);

- non-distinguished attribute values to aid interrogation (these are critical if the public area is to be meaningfully searched);

- management information which allows the service-providers to coordinate off-line modification of the shared space; and,

- naming links which point into the service-provider DIT domains.

These naming links are simply Distinguished Names found in the service-provider spaces.[9] The agent for a real-world object (e.g., a citizen acting on his/her own behalf, or an officer of a corporation acting on its behalf) enters into a private agreement with a service-provider to establish an entry in the shared DIT domain and a naming link to the service-provider's DIT domain. New naming links are added, or existing naming links are removed, on the basis of subsequent private agreements between the agent and various service-providers.

For example, suppose the person corresponding to

```
c=FF
    @fipsProvNumericCode=06
    @fipsPlaceNumericCode=37000
    @cn=Vera Marcal
```

wishes to be known in the Public Directory. The person enters into a private agreement with a dialtone provider, AT, to have an entry established both in the shared namespace and in the provider's namespace. Two entries are created.

In the shared namespace, the entry

```
c=FF
    @fipsProvNumericCode=06
    @fipsPlaceNumericCode=37000
    @cn=Vera Marcal
```

is created. Among other things, this entry contains a **namingLink** attribute value of

```
    c=FF@addmdName=AT@l=415@cn=Vera Marcal
```

In the service-provider AT's namespace, the entry

```
    c=FF@addmdName=AT@l=415@cn=Vera Marcal
```

is created.

At some time in the future, the person contracts with another service-provider, WU, for X.400 mailbox services, and another entry,

```
    c=FF@addmdName=WU@l=FC@cn=Vera Marcal
```

---

[9]Unlike the **aliasedObjectName** attribute found in an alias entry, a naming link may be multi-valued. Otherwise, this would be a fine use of aliases.

is created containing the O/R Address of the user.

The person decides that this mailbox should be associated with the person's entry in the shared namespace, so the person enters into a private agreement with WU.

In the shared namespace, the entry

```
c=FF
    @fipsProvNumericCode=06
    @fipsPlaceNumericCode=37000
    @cn=Vera Marcal
```

is given a second `namingLink` attribute value

```
c=FF@addmdName=WU@l=FC@cn=Vera Marcal
```

Given that the schema for a service-provider's portion of the DIT is unlikely to be published, it should be clear that the shared namespace must be structured to facilitate interrogation. Given previous discussions on the nature of user-friendliness in the Directory, it is important that DUAs have detailed knowledge of the schema used in the shared namespace!

Typically, a user will employ a public DUA to find an entry in the shared namespace. Depending on the outcome of the interrogation algorithm used by the DUA, the user will be presented with one or more matching entries in the shared DIT domain. At the option of the user, one or more of these entries may be expanded to provide information. In this case, the DUA, when it encounters a `namingLink` attribute value, may query the user to see if the link should be followed.

Continuing with the earlier example, suppose a user at a public DUA asks for information about

> *someone named "Vera Marcal" in someplace called "Freedonia City"*

By applying an interrogation algorithm, the DUA informs the user that the likely answer is

```
c=FF
    @fipsProvNumericCode=06
    @fipsPlaceNumericCode=37000
    @cn=Vera Marcal
```

(but not using this particular string!) and that additional information is available. The user indicates that this should be pursued, and the DUA displays information about the entry

```
c=FF@addmdName=AT@l=415@cn=Vera Marcal
```

and the entry

```
c=FF@addmdName=WU@l=FC@cn=Vera Marcal
```

by following the namingLink attribute values.

In retrospect, it should be observed that this approach has the potential to solve both the distributed entry and distributed subtree problem. The distributed entry problem is solved by using the naming links which offer different views of the same real-world object. The distributed subtree problem is (arguably) solved by simply replicating the shared DIT domain. Distribution with a private DIT domain can be solved in a private fashion by that service-provider!

6.5 A White Pages Pilot Revisited

The White Pages Pilot introduced back in Section 5.1 went from ground-zero to approximately 200,000 entries in a period of about eighteen months. The richness of the service has been attractive, and as more user-interfaces and interrogation algorithms are developed, user interest increased. However, the Directory is a complex technology and it is difficult to adequately educate a UNIX system manager in the nuances of the Directory, through no fault of the system manager.

Let's now consider the two largest problems which were encountered in the first year of operation.

6.5.1 Uniformity of Service

In the first year, the largest problem was uniformity of service: not all DSAs were consistently available, and of those which were available, some were sparsely populated (of the 70 participating organizations, 22 were sparse). Thus, even if a DSA was available, it is quite possible that it did not contain the information it was expected to hold.

This problem is one which is inherent in the approach taken by the pilot, and is largely administrative, not technical, in nature. Fundamentally, the problem with an X.500 Directory is that it requires the construction of a *new* infrastructure: data must be loaded into the Directory, and once loaded, it must be kept consistent with the real-world.

In brief, for a new service like the X.500 Directory to work, one needs an information economy that works. Part of this can be viewed as a supply and demand problem, but the mechanisms must be in place to allow for easy maintenance of the information in the system.

In contrast, other efforts to introduced a White Pages service to the Internet have attempted to leverage existing infrastructure:

- Dr. Ralph Droms of Bucknell University is working on a program which knows about the various White Pages services in the Internet (e.g., *whois*, network *finger*, *profile*, etc.), and simply contacts those services, issuing service-specific queries and then filters the output into a uniform presentation for the user.

- Dr. Michael F. Schwartz at the University of Colorado at Boulder is researching resource discovery tools for internets[43]. As part of this, he has developed a facility which maintains a database that is incrementally built by scanning the "Organization:" fields in public *netnews* messages, and then maintains relationships between domain and organization names. When a user invokes the facility, it consults the database and issues network *finger* commands as appropriate.

Both of these approaches *leverage* existing infrastructure and do not require explicit site administrator action — at the target site — in order to provide the service. Although such services are generally limited to persons with computer accounts, they cleverly avoid the problem of building new infrastructure.

Although some steps have been taken by the pilot sponsors (e.g., a script is run each evening to find DSAs which are unavailable), the administrators of unavailable DSAs do not seem motivated to fix the problems.[10]

The solution to these problems is one of demand: if applications can be provided which use the White Pages, then the service will be in larger demand, and site administrators will be more likely to populate and maintain their DSAs. In brief, one must rely on the superior quality-of-service of the X.500 approach to motivate the community to take on the added expenses of building a new infrastructure.

Unfortunately, this may very well be the proverbial chicken-and-egg problem: coarse statistics monitoring shows comparatively little use of the White Pages service, presumably because little information is stored there!

In order to provide a more realistic level of expectation, in the future the pilot will associate "quality of service" attributes with both DSA and organizational entries. For DSAs, an attribute will indicate what kind of use the DSA supports, one of experimental, pilot, or production. For organizational entries, an attribute will indicate how much data is used to populate the subtree under the entry, one of

---

[10]This suggests that the pilot administrators should consider removing DMDs which are largely sparse or frequently unavailable. Experience in the GB pilot suggests that this strategy can be effective!

sparse, selected, substantial, or full.

6.5.2 Access Control

The existing access control mechanism has proven sub-adequate in providing the authorization policy desired by many potential participating organizations. The access control list attribute allows an administrator to specify, with a subtree-level granularity, as to which DNs may perform what Directory operations on an entry or its immediate subordinates.

The problem is that most organizations would like to allow public search access, but only for reasonable search filters. Since QUIPU's access control list mechanism does not limit the size of a result which might be generated by a Directory search operation, some other means is required to enforce "reasonableness." This is currently accomplished through the use of an administrative limit: a DSA manager instructs the DSA to return at most "n" entries for a Directory search or list operation. Hence, most sites can achieve their desired policy by setting "n" to an appropriately low level.

This has an unfortunate side-effect: most sites also wish to permit unlimited local browsing access. Since browsing is accomplished through either the Directory search or list operation, the administrative limit necessary to enforce the public search access negatively impacts local browsing access.

A second limitation of QUIPU's authorization policy is that it is history-insensitive. If a search operation succeeds with only partial results, then by recursively retrying the operation with an incrementally refined filter, the administrative limit can be (slowly) bypassed. This technique is sometimes called "attack dialing."

In a subsequent release of QUIPU, the authorization policy will be augmented in two respects:

- first, an administrative limit will be present at the attribute level; and,

- if this administrative limit is reached, the operation will return no result, rather than a partial result.

It is hoped that these enhancements will address the current short-comings and make the White Pages Pilot more attractive to potential participants.

6.5.3 The Right Choice?

Providing a White Pages Service using the OSI Directory requires an extensive investment in terms of programming, coordination, and management. Although the payoff is attractive, the cost of providing an entirely new infrastructure is simply *enormous*. Unfortunately, it will be several years before the real payoff of such an approach can even be imagined.

It must be emphasized however that there are other ways to provide a White Pages Service, using architectures, models, protocols, and mechanisms other than those provided by the Directory. Although not intended to support this thesis, the report [44] provides excellent insight in this area. Frankly, had the author not already had a heavy investment in OSI technology prior to the start of the PSI White Pages Pilot Project, it is likely that he never would have undertaken such a project using the OSI Directory as the underlying technology!

6.6 For Further Reading

The base series of International standards on the Directory is defined in [30]. These are technically aligned with the corresponding 1988 CCITT recommendations [31]. The differences between the International standard definition and the CCITT definition are quite small, and should not affect interoperability between implementations written against either document.

There are 8 parts to the Directory standard:

ISO/IEC 9594	Contents
Part 1	Overview of Concepts, Models, and Service
Part 2	Models
Part 3	Abstract Service Definition
Part 4	Procedures for Distributed Operations
Part 5	Protocol Specifications
Part 6	Selected Attribute Types
Part 7	Selected Object Classes
Part 8	Authentication Framework

6.6.1 on the White Pages Pilot

There have been numerous reports prepared in relation to, or in support of, the White Pages Pilot. Here are some of the more relevant ones:

- The QUIPU User's Manual[45]

- The Thorn X.500 Naming Architecture[35]

- The PSI White Pages Pilot Project Administrator's Guide[46]

- Directory Navigation in the QUIPU X.500 System[47]

- The Directory Assistance Service[48]

Chapter 7

The Future

It would certainly be novel for the author to produce a book in which   `soap...`
the final chapter consists of something other than a lengthy soapbox.
So, inasmuch as this is going to be the last book I write for a long
while, I simply couldn't pass up the opportunity for my final, and
perhaps best, shot.

In this chapter, we'll try to forecast the future of not only Directory, but open systems in general, for the remainder of the '90s.
We begin by looking at OSI and Internet standardization, and then
proceed to focus on the Directory.

7.1   A Long Dark Night for Open Systems

In the final soapbox of *The Open Book*, the problems with the standards process, ranging from standards organizations which are sadly detached from reality, to functional profiles written by marketeers rather than implementors, to the folly of conformance testing, were examined. The purpose of that soapbox was to reinforce the notion that the promise of open systems can be achieved *only* through implementation. Indeed, the first soapbox of *The Little Black Book* (starting way back on page 7) continued in this vein. Perhaps my opinion in this area is somewhat biased since I prefer to be an implementor rather than either a diplomat or a *provocateur*. Regardless, the standards process is not a pretty picture by any means.

7.1.1   The Never-Ending Standard

Perhaps one of the biggest costs of the way the standards process works is that the standard is never quite done.

Consider: In 1980, CCITT produced a recommendation on a network protocol called X.25. It was widely implemented, and in 1984, some modest extensions were added. However, this second version did not receive rapid implementation. In fact, the majority of X.25 implementations, to the author's knowledge, are still based on the 1980 recommendations. This is unfortunate since, in order to use X.25 to provide the OSI connection-oriented network service, one either needs to implement X.25(84) or a special protocol on top of X.25(80).

In 1984, CCITT produced a recommendation on Message Handling Systems called X.400, which received some implementation. However, few significant implementations of this standard had reached the market by the end of 1988, when CCITT introduced a vastly modified version of X.400. So, here's a situation where implementors are still struggling to get the first standard off the ground, and out pops something an order of magnitude more complex (in order to add still more generality). Needless to say, implementations of the 1988 standard for X.400 are somewhat rare. Further, given the expense incurred by organizations which transitioned to X.400(84), and the corresponding installed-base, suggestions of yet another transition are usually met with jeers. Although the 88 version of X.400 is meant to be upwards compatible with its predecessor, transition is not easy.

And this brings us to the Directory. In 1988, CCITT in joint work with ISO produced a recommendation on Directory called X.500, which is receiving some implementation. But, the standards process is hard at work in making things more general and adding more capabilities, as we speak

Perhaps CCITT's four-year study period has become a great hindrance to OSI, particularly considering that ISO must operate in lockstep fashion for any joint work to occur. One can argue that it is a forcing function for the groups to get serious and produce something by a deadline. However, because the groups can keep working after that, the four-year study period does little more than fragment the technology being produced. In the market, it causes either early adoption by the enthusiastic few, or late adoption by the majority. In many cases, it's simply easier to put off acquiring the technology because there's never an end to the changes. This has led the well-known *Cynic of the Internet*, Dr. Paul V. Mockapetris, to observe:

Q: Why are Standards preferable to Communism?

A: Communists make 5 year plans.

Some, including the author have been pushing the Internet community to be an early adopter, emphasizing use of the 1988 recommendations on Directory, and then adding the minimal set of refinements necessary to produce a working system. Stephen E. Kille of University College London, has been leading the effort to reach technical agreement in the Internet Engineering Task Force (IETF). This has two key advantages: first, the majority of the benefits of adoption can be realized quickly; and, second, one can always say that the refinements are "interim," awaiting standard solutions some time in the future. Of course, it is anyone's guess as to the likelihood that the ever-more-complicated work being produced by the standards process will be usable. In the meantime, the Internet community can enjoy a powerful new information infrastructure as a pilot, and eventually production, service.

7.1.2   So Many Standards, So Little Time

Obviously, the pace of standardization (as slow as it is) has out-stripped the ability (or perhaps the inclination) to produce implementations, and, the gap appears to be widening at an alarming pace! This is true not only of OSI technology, but also in the Internet suite, particularly in the network management area. The problem of course is that:

> *It is easier to write and agree on standards that it is to develop products which implement those standards.*

Because of this, implementation experiences becomes further and further "removed from the loop." The downside is that in the absence of implementation experience, it is difficult to place confidence in the final results. Indeed this is well-illustrated by the tremendous mismatch between the resource requirements of the OSI network management protocol (CMIP) and the resource capabilities of routers, bridges, and the like. But, there is a second, more insidious, downside: users are becoming disallusioned. More and more OSI standards are produced, many product announcements are made, but few products follow.

Framing a solution to this problem is made difficult by the fact that the standards process is based on pseudo-democracy, not fascism. It is unfortunate that things can't be weighted on the basis of the technical competence of the participants, but frankly the cost of "making the trains run on time" (i.e., produce workable technology) may simply not be worth the cost.

However, the Internet community has long held the view that final standardization status can be granted only in the light of considerable implementation and interoperability. Perhaps this perspective provides a positive direction for OSI standardization.

The author personally favors declaring a four-year moratorium on the standards process. During this time, the focus will be on implementing the OSI standards produced thus far. At the end of this time, we'll have a better idea as to what works, and then the standards process can be re-started, first by fixing the things which didn't work as expected! Of course, it is unlikely that anyone actually involved with the ponderous standards process would favor this idea.

After all, the process is currently a powerful weapon — against the market!

7.1.3 The End-Effect of the OSI Standards Process

Although only a few of the individuals participating in the standards process are actually malicious towards users, the process has an inherent flaw which does work against users. To see this, consider an interpretation of the standards process, that shows it to be a "layered defense" against users.

First, we produce standards that are so large that no one could possibly implement them fully. Officially, we claim this is in the name of generality and extensibility, but we really do it this way because it allows us to reach a political consensus, albeit at the expense of the technical quality. Second, we arrange for several regional groups to create profiles of these standards. Officially, we claim this is to make the standards easier to implement and to foster interoperability, but we really do this to allow for regional differences. Of course, for either of these two steps, any vendor who has a proprietary technology which competes with a standard is given many opportunities to sabotage or delay the development of the standard or its profile.[1] Third, we create conformance tests for profiles. Officially, we claim this is to prove that the implementations will interoperate, but we really do this because everyone is fearful to commit publically that that their products will interoperate with the others. Throughout this whole process we can talk about how hard everyone is working to bring standards-based solutions to the user, and this, in some small way, allows us to prepare the users for the outrageous amount of money they'll have to pay for

---

[1]One reviewer suggested there is a powerful analogy between this activity and the behavior of lobbyists and political action groups in government. Past performance does suggest that this is an amazingly clear analysis. However in the case of OSI standardization, the author is more likely to recall that "one should never attribute to malice that which can be adequately explained by incompetence." As such, an alternate interpretation is that OSI standardization presents a great opportunity for individual vendors to get their worst people out of the office and make them someone else's problem for a while.

the products. But, since we deeply care about open systems, we can now use a new marketing *slogo* (slogan+logo):

> *The more you spend the more we care!*

7.1.4 Malicious GOSIP

Unfortunately, the situation is worsening. Open systems were intended as a means of expanding markets and providing useful service to users. Instead, OSI has now become a focal point for inverting market forces.

In a robust market, competition between products is an important catalyst. Unfortunately, there are always those who would attempt to change the market's course by using *outside* influence. In the OSI world, the well-intentioned, but certainly ill-conceived, government mandates for OSI, serve to invert forces in the market. If OSI is to survive and prosper, it should do so on the merit of the products which implement its services. By arbitrarily requiring that enterprises procure OSI products, there is less incentive for vendors to offer products which are truly competitive with other open systems technologies (e.g., products implementing the Internet suite of protocols). Indeed, in the long-term, it is likely that these mandates will do more harm than good, by prolonging the "childhood" of the OSI market.

It should be noted that in 1990, two years after the publication of the US GOSIP document, a "clarification" statement was issued, allowing US Government agencies more leeway to not purchase OSI technology. This was certainly a positive development in that procurement policy was taking note that "OSI was not ready" despite the earlier mandate!

To add litigation to injury, the author has received an unconfirmed report that one OSI consortium is offering its members legal advice so that they may challenge procurements in which OSI offerings are bid but not selected. To rephrase an 18th century witticism:

> *It has been suggested that litigation is the last refuge of the scoundrel; I submit that it is also the first.*

Once again, if OSI is to achieve the promise it made back in 1978, then it should do so because its products are superior, and not because its litigious proponents were able to amass more billable hours than the supporters of other technologies. In a strange way, these mandates for OSI do little more than motivate vendors of the Internet suite of protocols to strive harder to maintain superiority over their OSI competitors.

Well, that about wraps up my meager thoughts on the OSI standards process, now let's turn to "the other side."

7.1.5 The Changing Nature of the Internet Standardization Process

The final soapbox in the *The Open Book*, also detailed problems with the Internet standardization process, with an emphasis on its treatment of OSI topics. Over the last two years or so, the Internet Engineering Task Force has undergone a startling metamorphosis: it now appears to be largely a venue for education, along with some business negotiations. The IETF is much better managed, most working groups are better organized, and Internet pre-standards are still being produced, but with a disturbing trend towards more specification before implementation. Much to the author's shame, as chair of the SNMP working group, he is guilty of having overseen the largest number of such pre-standards by a single working group. Rather than dwell on the author's embarrassment, let's look at the educational component.

Because of the significant success of the Internet suite of protocols, there is a great demand for Internet educational services. Some organizations provide this as a part of their business charter, with two-day intensive courses as the norm. However, the registration fees for such courses are relatively high (on the order of US$1000), and the courses are offered only a few times a year. In contrast, there are three IETF meetings held each year, each a week long. The registration fee is much cheaper (on the order of US$100), and there is access to a large number of Internet gurus and wheels. So, in addition to the usual reasons for sending people to a standards meeting, the educational potential becomes quite attractive to many organizations.

Unfortunately, this trend has served to only further alienate the true experts of the Internet. It has always been difficult for leading-edge companies (particularly small ones) to justify their engineers participating in the IETF when technology must ultimately be shared with competitors if it is to be advanced. Now however, in addition to having to give away technological insight, the experts have to act as tutors to a growing collection of professionals who, by and large, have not read the documents being discussed, and have not come up to speed on the technology.

In fact, the tutorial analogy is more apt that it might seem: at a tutorial, the students wear badges and pay to attend, whilst the tutors wear different badges and perhaps get paid; at an IETF meeting, everyone wears badges and pays to attend, regardless of whether they are acting as a student or a tutor. Of course, this criticism isn't being made against those trying to come up to speed on Internet technology. We *need* more Internet-capable professionals! But, in fairness to people trying to service the Internet community by contributing their expertise, the IETF should be a place to advance Internet engineering, not provide tutorial services.

To exacerbate matters, vendors looking to acquire Internet technology have started to attend, so as to maximize the number of business contacts they can make. At one IETF, a representative from a company looking to purchase network management software was able to have lunch with one vendor, dinner with another, and breakfast with a third vendor the next morning! The author has it on good authority that the dinner was particularly fine. Of course, this criticism isn't being made against those trying to acquire Internet technology. But, in fairness to people trying to service the Internet community by contributing their expertise, the IETF should be a place to advance Internet engineering, not a meeting place for business deals.

7.1.6   The Barbarians at the Gates

These factors, combined with the fact that now everyone wants to be involved with the making of Internet technology, has led to a severe lapse in the effectiveness of the Internet standardization process. The amount of effort required to "get good work through" in many working groups is simply astronomical, whilst in other working groups, the average level of technical competence is so low as to rival that of some of the standards people producing OSI.

I am quite truthful when I say that this is breaking my heart. Instead of being able to focus on good engineering solutions to the problems of the Internet community, which has given myself and others such wonderful opportunities, far too much time is spent doing damage control and preemptive strikes. As chair of the SNMP working group, a lot of my time is spent running around the city walls, keeping the barbarians from achieving a breach. (That is, I try to prevent market-damaging or technically-inept proposals from advancing. The former are put forward by competent people who have a view of the world which is contrary to the management philosophy adopted in the Internet; whilst the latter are put forward by incompetent people who simply don't know any better, sometimes who have been sent to the IETF by their management to slow down the process, thereby allowing them to do more maneuvering with their proprietary plans.) Occasionally, one or two barbarians avoid the molten lead being poured down and manage to get a ladder up on the wall (i.e., one of these losing proposals gets through). I then sprint over there to push the ladder away before they can climb up. (That is, I have to get some competent people to come-up with a counter-proposal, one that would actually work. Then we have a political slugfest, in which the technically-capable people know what the correct choice is, but we still have to convince all the wanna-be's, hanger's-on, and goer's, which make up the majority of the working group.)

This may all seem egotistical and self-serving, and perhaps it is. However, experience shows that the only reliable predictor for future success is past success, and once an approach (such as the one taken in Internet network management) has proven successful, it is important to continue using the same philosophy when extending the system. Thus, it is a prudent strategy to rely on the people who forged the past successes to provide continued technical guidance. So, perhaps it is not egotism but commonsense to say that:

> *you are more likely to win if you associate with winners rather than losers*

7.1.7   An Error in Judgement

Of course, not all meetings of a working group have to occur during an IETF, but owing the increasing political pressure that decisions appear to be made in the open, a working group must meet during an IETF to ratify important documents. As chair of the SNMP working group, I made a disastrous error in judgement in the fall of 1990, when I decided to hold a working group meeting a month before the IETF met, in order to hammer down the final details of an important document. The first meeting was well-attended by several competent engineers, and there were relatively few distractions. Unfortunately, few of these professionals attended the second meeting at the IETF, under the mistaken impression that all the work was done. Instead, at the second meeting, a large crowd, consisting of several political factions and many novices, had a jolly time re-thinking solutions and making a few pernicious changes, despite the best efforts of the chair and three network management gurus! This resulted in the final document being less capable than it could and should have been, though it was still credible.

To add ingratitude to injury, the chair had gone out of his way, prior to the second meeting, to mend fences and do favors for the various political factions, so as to "grease the path" for the document. For example, one of the competent-but-misdirected participants was unable to attend the first meeting but wanted a few things added. The chair went out of his way to put forth these changes, and argued them forcibly, even if he didn't agree with all of them. They were accepted at the first meeting, after which, some noted that had the actual author of the changes been present, he likely wouldn't have gotten all of them, since some find that person rather unpleasant to deal with. You can imagine the chair's surprise when, at the second meeting, the competent-but-misdirected participant was the most disruptive person present, doing the most harm to the document.

This may all seem anecdotal, but these kind of things repeat themselves constantly. As such, the standardization of Internet network management technology has become a particularly *ugly* business. Network management isn't the only area in serious trouble in the IETF, but it is clearly one of the most visible.

In the interests of fairness (and also to preempt some "ballistic behavior" on the part of certain persons), it should be noted that the Internet management structure recognizes the problem. There have been several suggestions that the IETF should sponsor some form of educational activity immediately prior to working group meetings. This would allow the chairs to prohibit tutorial periods within their working groups. However, the problem with this approach is that, for the most part, the Internet gurus and wheels attend IETF meetings to solve critical problems, not necessarily to educate others.

However, the true problem with the current Internet standardization process is its new emphasis on being "open." Although it is a noble effort to maximize participation, the simple fact is that not all participants are able to make worthy contributions. Further, the larger the venue, the harder to reach agreement on technical issues, and the easier to emphasize political consensus instead. Perhaps there are no solutions to the problem of success. Certainly neither the OSI nor Internet communities have found them.

7.1.8 Internet v. OSI Revisited

As of this writing, the Internet Activities Board (IAB), the technical body overseeing the development of the Internet suite of protocols, has expanded its membership to include three members with considerable OSI experience. Despite this, the author feels that very little "official" support for use of OSI in the Internet has been forthcoming from the Internet management structure. This is unfortunate since use of OSI in the Internet represents a phenomenal opportunity. The Internet community is large and hungry for new services. OSI may be able to provide some of those services, and could certainly benefit from being used in real, instead of "toy," networks. However, there seem to be three stumbling blocks.

First, as of this writing the IAB seems to be hesitant in issuing Internet-standards which detail the use of OSI technology in the context of an Internet-setting. For example, some four years after its publication, RFC1006, a method for running OSI applications on top of TCP, has yet to receive any standardization status. Perhaps the author is biased because he is co-author of that document. If so, one can instead consider other documents dealing with OSI-in-the-Internet, such as one describing how NSAP addresses should be allocated, which are still waiting to be published as RFCs. Perhaps this lack of action is merely conservatism on the part of the IAB: because parts of OSI are radically different than the Internet suite, they are unwilling to seriously consider these documents due to the potential ramifications of their use in the Internet. This is understandable given the lack of stability of OSI technology, and the numerous "gang territories" that exist for OSI (national standards bodies, national profiling groups, etc.) Regardless, use of OSI in the Internet suffers through a preponderance of inaction.

Second, although many computer-communication vendors belong to the Internet community, there doesn't seem to be a lot of OSI software being produced for use in the Internet. (Actually, there's not a lot of OSI software period, but that's part of a larger problem.) The OSI Directory and MHS pilots taking place in the Internet are using only a few different implementations — indeed, there is only one implementation presently used in the White Pages Pilot. Whilst this is probably okay for pilot usage, more implementations are needed to provide both wider coverage and testing. Perhaps some of this is due to the frenzy for more and more "pure" Internet applications as the Internet community continues to grow. As a result of this, vendors often cut back on their OSI development teams, moving more resources to work in the increasingly competitive market for products in the Internet suite.

Third, there is still a subliminal academic tone to the Internet, in that the people who work on the Internet suite are doing "research" and this is "good," whilst the people doing OSI are doing "something else" and this is "bad." Certainly, the Internet is a marvelous platform for doing internetworking research, and the Internet suite may provide a good foundation for that research. However, it is probably not optimal to treat *every* problem as a research problem, possibly in some attempt to assure continued research funding through academic snobbery. No one argues the importance of doing research on information infrastructure, and no one argues that research, any research, should be given strong funding and encouragement on the basis of its merits. What is questionable is arguing that deploying outside technology should not be encouraged because research is being done in that area, and clearly the research, when completed, will be better.

7.2   The Painful Dawn of Directory

The author views the Directory as the platform for bringing OSI into the Internet in a big way, as there is a tremendous "opportunity for synergy" between the Internet and the Directory. A public Directory service with deep-Internet coverage will offer a lot of information services to the community. Current Internet information services (with the exception of the DNS) are largely centralized in both administration and location. These services, such as the Internet WHOIS database, providing information on the various on-line document series and the like, can be placed into an X.500 framework. In turn, this would allow the development of a new generation of powerful interrogation and retrieval applications for information resources. A White Pages service, is useful, but only one candle of potentially many, on the proverbial cake. In brief, the author sees the Directory as providing the next-generation information infrastructure for the Internet.

Of course, the Directory is hardly problem-free, and is worthy of many, many soapboxes — indeed, it has received quite a few! For now, let's just look at two of the biggest problems:

7.2.1   National Coverage

The paternal influence of the PTTs is quite clear in the Directory standard. In particular, the hierarchical structure is developed just enough to foster a PTT-view of international connections, but is not developed enough to allow naming policies to be developed independent of these connections. That is, the lack of policy on a DIT structure seems tailor-made to allow a national PTT authority to enforce its own naming policy on its national constituency. The concessions made for commercial competition at the national level are a step forward from this, but still are not developed enough, in the author's opinion, to foster a PTT-free national decision. Talk of NSSRs and distributed entries are fine on paper, but cannot be used to realize a production service within a meaningful time-frame.

For those countries in which competition is mandated, this provides quite a problem. In the US, the North American Directory Forum (NADF) was formed to address these issues and make public Directory Service a reality. Surprisingly, progress is being made in this forum, albeit at a pace much slower than the author would prefer. But perhaps this is the nature of such industry cooperative-efforts.

Here again, the traditional no-nonsense "let's field it and see what works" attitude of the Internet community may help tremendously. If, in a few years, the Internet community is able to deploy an operational X.500 service containing some thousands of PRDMDs, then this will go along way towards providing the public Directory for which many hunger.

7.2.2 A Competitive Market for Interrogation Algorithms

Imagine the difficulty a simple DUA would have in finding things in Freedonia, given their "avant garde" but nonetheless legitimate national decision. Is it possible for DUAs to be able to search effectively in other countries or even other regions within a country? There are many possibilities, but the spectrum lies between two points:

- regional DUAs will dominate, and the market will fragment to support this; or,

- intelligent DUAs will dominate, and the market will support brisk competition.

Until products containing DUAs become a commodity item, the Directory will not achieve a high degree of usefulness, hurting OSI in general. This is unfortunate, since the highly competitive nature of the market segment for the Internet suite of protocols has already forced commodity pricing for some classes of products.

Of course, the pressure on DUAs can be traced back to the generalized DIT structure and object schema of the Directory standard. So, this is yet another indication of the damage done by the OSI standards process.

7.3 In Conclusion

Despite this rather pessimistic view, the author is still enthusiastic about the Directory. The core ideas are sound, even if the actual details could use a lot of work. In the end, all of these technologies, Internet or OSI, succeed or fail on the basis of their implementations, on how useful the community finds the services that are actually delivered. Indeed, in my book, it's axiomatic that:

A technology is indistinguishable from its implementation.

For the Directory to succeed in the Internet community, it must be implemented well and provide a useful service. To date, we have had only minimal pilot experience, but that experience has been generally positive. As the Directory gains acceptance, it seems clear that the next generation of information-infrastructure is being ushered in!

| ...soap |

And that concludes *The Little Black Book*.

Appendix A

Toward a US national decision

The North American Directory Forum (NADF) is a collection of organizations which offer, or plan to offer, public Directory services in North America, based on the CCITT X.500 Recommendations. The NADF has been developing implementation agreements for public Directory service provision, schema definitions, and mapping procedures. NADF documents are openly available — they are not copyrighted. Distribution of NADF documents, with attribution, is unlimited.

For further information on the North American Directory Forum, please contact:

Postal: North American Directory Forum
            c/o Theodore H. Myer
            Rapport Communication, Inc.
            3055 Q Street NW
            Washington, DC 2007
            US

Telephone: +1 202 342 2727

As a part of its charter, the NADF must reach agreement as to how entries are named (using DNs) in the public portions of the North American Directory. NADF-123 is a scheme proposed for this purpose. The NADF has circulated NADF-123 widely, for the purpose of gathering comments.

As of this writing, NADF-123 has received several comments, which will likely lead to numerous revisions. So, rather than reproduce NADF-123 here, let's take a step back and look at the large issues involved in reaching a national decision.

It must be emphasized that the text which follows is a "snapshot." As such, it will likely be refined by the NADF and others. Further, the text which follows was developed by Einar A. Stefferud of Network Management Associates and the author, after several discussions within the NADF, and after having received several comments on NADF-123.

A.1 Approach

It should be observed that there are several different naming universes that could be used in the Directory Information Tree (DIT). For example, geographical naming, community naming, political naming, organizational naming, and so on. The choice of naming universe largely determines the difficulty in mapping a user's query into a series of Directory operations to find useful information. Although it is possible to simultaneously support multiple naming universes with the DIT, this is likely to be unnatural. As such, this scheme focuses on a single naming universe.

The naming universe in this scheme is based on *civil authority*. That is, it uses the existing civil naming infrastructure and suggests a (nearly) straight-forward mapping on the DIT. An important characteristic is that entries can be listed wherever searches for them are likely to occur. This implies that a single object may be listed as several separate entries.

A.1.1 Names and User-Friendliness

It must be emphasized that there are two distinct concepts which are often confused when discussing a naming scheme:

user-friendly naming: a property of a Directory which allows users to easily identity objects of interest; and,

Distinguished Name: the administratively assigned name for an entry in the OSI Directory.

It must be emphasized that Distinguished Names are not necessarily user-friendly names, and further, that user-friendly naming in the Directory is a property of the Directory Service, not of Distinguished Names.

A.1.2 Choice of RDN Names

The key aspect to appreciate for choice of RDNs is that they should provide a large name space to avoid collisions: the naming strategy must provide enough "real estate" to accommodate a large demand for Distinguished Names. This is the *primary* requirement for RDNs. A *secondary* requirement is that RDNs should be meaningful (friendly to people) and should not impede searching.

However, it is important to understand that this second requirement can be achieved by using additional (non-distinguished) attribute values. For example, if the RDN of an entry is

`organizationName is Performance Systems International`

then it is perfectly acceptable (and indeed desirable) to have other values for the `organizationName` attribute, e.g.,

`organizationName is PSI`

The use of these abbreviated names greatly aids searching whilst avoiding unnecessary Distinguished Name conflicts.

In order to appreciate the naming scheme which follows, it is important to understand that wherever possible it leverages existing naming infrastructure. That is, it relies heavily on non-OSI naming authorities which already exist. Note that inasmuch as it relies on existing naming authorities, there is little chance that any "final" national decision could obsolete this scheme.[1] (To do so would require a national decision that disregards existing national and regional infrastructure, and establishes some entirely new and different national naming infrastructure.)

---

[1] Any naming scheme may be subject to the jurisdiction of certain national agencies. For example, the US State Department is concerned with any impact on US telecommunications treaty obligations.

A.1.3 Outline of the Scheme

The naming scheme is divided into four parts:

- a discussion of the right-to-use, registration, and publication concepts;

- a discussion of objects with national, regional, local, and foreign standing;

- a discussion of objects which may be listed at national, regional, and local levels; and,

- a discussion of how RDNs are formed for entries at each different level.

A.2   The Naming Process

There are three stages to the naming process.

A.2.1   Right-To-Use

First, a naming authority must establish the *right-to-use* for any name to be used, within the jurisdiction of the given naming authority. Names that are used in public are generally constrained by public laws. Names that are only used in private are a private matter. We are primarily concerned here with public names because these are the names that are most interesting to enter into directories where we can search for them.

There is a global governmental/civil/organizational infrastructure already in place to name and number things like people, cars, houses, buildings and streets; localities like populated places, cities, counties, states, and countries; organizations like businesses, schools, and governments; and other entities like computers, printers, ports, routers, processes, files, filesystems, networks, management domains, and so on. There are also naming (and numbering) authorities for various standards and for networks (e.g., ISO/IEC, CCITT, IANA) which depend on acceptance by their constituent communities for their authority.

This collective infrastructure is comprised of a very large number of authorities that we will call *naming authorities*. Naming authorities tend toward hierarchical organization. Parents have authority (granted by government) to choose the names of new-born children, the courts have authority to change a person's name, car makers have authority to name the models of cars they build (within the limits of Trademarking Law), and they are obligated to assign unique serial numbers to each car. Cities assign names to their streets and districts, states assign city, county, and township names, and so on. State governments also assign names to "registered" organizations that operate under state charters, which in turn name their own suborganizations. Cities and Counties license businesses to use their chosen (unambiguous) names "in association with" the city and county names. Companies name and number the computers and communications devices they make and sell. There are many many name spaces, some of which are subordinate to others, and some of which are independent.

Public names must be "registered" in some "public record" to record the fact of the assignment of the right-to-use to specific "owners." In general, this is to prevent collisions of the right-to-use assignments in public shared name spaces. For example, unique names given to corporations are registered by the state of incorporation. A request to use a new name for any corporation must not conflict with the name of any other corporation registered in the same state. The same applies for businesses licensed within cities and counties.

Establishment of the right-to-use for a name is not a Directory Service. The right-to-use for a name is always derived from some other (non-directory) source of authority because of the legal aspects of intellectual property rights which are entirely outside the scope of directory service specifications. People and organizations attach great value to the names they are allowed to associate with their lives and businesses, and intellectual property law protects their interests with respect to these values.

This is not to say that directory service designers and providers have no interest in the processes and procedures for establishment of the right-to-use for the names that will be entered into any directory. Indeed, without a supply of rightfully-usable names, there cannot be any directory. But, given an adequate supply of registered names, the directory service is not otherwise concerned.

We should note here that some naming authorities must deal with name spaces that are shared among large communities (such as computer networks) in which collisions will occur among applicants for desired name assignments, while other name spaces (such as for given names of children in a family) are not shared outside the family. Sharing is always a problem, which has led to trademarking laws, business license laws, and so on. Naming within organizations should be easier, because it is "in the family," so to speak. Hierarchical naming schemes facilitate distribution of naming authority.

A.2.2   Registration

Second, a name may be *bound* (as a value) to some object attribute.

Given the right to use a name, a Naming Authority, such as a family which has an inherited surname and, more or less, has the right to use any names it pleases for its children's given names, must bind selected names to selected object attributes (e.g., firstname=Einar). Note that this same name might also be used as the first name or middle name of other children, as long as each sequence of given names of each family member is distinguished (i.e., none are duplicates) within the family. Wise families do not bind the same sequence of given names to more than one child. Some avoid any multiple use of a single name. Some use generational qualifiers to prevent parent-child conflicts.

The Internet Domain Name System (DNS) names top level domains which are then free (within some technical limits) to chose and bind names to entries which are subordinate to a given named domain, and so forth down the DNS name tree. The ISO/CCITT naming system serves the same purposes in other separate name spaces.

A.2.3   Publication

Third, after binding, a name must be advertised or *published* in some community if it is to be referenced by others. If it is not advertised or published, then no one can refer to it.

This publication stage is what the Directory Service is all about. The Directory contains entries for "listed" names (or numbers) that are bound to the attributes of the entries in the directory DIT. Historically speaking, the directory business is a subclass of the publishing business, serving to dereference names into knowledge about what they stand for.

It is important to keep in mind that a directory "listing entry" is not a "registration" unless a particular segment of the directory also just happens to be the authoritative master register of some naming authority. Registration and listing are very different service functions, though it is conceivable that they might be combined in a single DIT.

For example, in the United States of America, each state name is registered by the Congress by inclusion of the name in the legislation that "admits each State into the Union." Note however that the name is also then published in many places (such as on maps and in directories), while the master "register" is kept with the other original records of laws enacted by the Congress and signed by the President.

Also, the name is then entered (listed) in many directories, in association with the name "The United States of America." And so on down the civil naming tree, with entities named in each state, etc.

It is certainly not the case that the American National Standards Institute (ANSI) registers the names of the States in the United States of America! That right and duty is clearly reserved to the Government of the United States of America.

On the other hand, in the Internet DNS, the act of inserting a given rightfully-usable name and address entry into a nameserver constitutes simultaneous registration and directory publication. (Insertion of an entry with duplicate name and a different meaning is problematic.)

A.3   Structuring Objects

The first step in providing a civil naming infrastructure is to model the geographical/governmental entities which provide a basis for the assignment of public names.

A.3.1   The National Level

The *nation* is modeled with an object of class `country`, subordinate to the root of the DIT, and has an RDN consisting of a single attribute value assertion:

```
countryName= US
```

The entry (minimally) contains these attributes:

```
objectClass= country
description= United States of America
```

A.3.2   The Regional Level

Within the nation, there are *regions*. Each region corresponds to a state or state-equivalent as recognized by the US Congress. The list of these is maintained is US FIPS 5. A sample entry from this FIPS document looks like this:

FIPS-5 Name	State Numeric Code	State Alpha Code
California	06	CA

Each region is modeled with an object of class `usStateOrEquivalent`, which is defined thusly:

```
usStateOrEquivalent OBJECT-CLASS
    SUBCLASS OF locality, nadfObject
    MUST CONTAIN { localityName,
                   fipsStateNumericCode,
                   fipsStateAlphaCode,
                   stateOrProvinceName }
```

Each entry is subordinate to c=US, and has an RDN consisting of a single attribute value assertion:

```
stateOrProvinceName= <FIPS-5 name>
```

e.g.,

```
stateOrProvinceName= California
```

Each entry (minimally) contains these attributes:

```
objectClass= usStateOrEquivalent
description= <official name of region>
localityName= <FIPS-5 name>
localityName= <FIPS-5 state alpha code>
fipsStateAlphaCode= <FIPS-5 state alpha code>
fipsStateNumericCode= <FIPS-5 state numeric code>
```

e.g.,

```
objectClass= usStateOrEquivalent
description= State of California
localityName= California
localityName= CA
fipsStateAlphaCode= CA
fipsStateNumericCode= 06
```

A.3.3   The Local Level

Within each region, there are *places*. Each place corresponds to a county or county-equivalent as recognized by the regional government. The list of these is maintained in US FIPS 55 as a populated place with a five-digit numeric place code starting with "99." A sample entry from this FIPS document looks like this:

State Numeric Code	Place Numeric Code	State Alpha Code		FIPS-55 Name	
06	99085	CA	...	Santa Clara (County)	...

(Any parenthetical text in the FIPS-55 name is considered a "remark" about the place.)

Each county is modeled with a `usCountyOrEquivalent` object, which is defined thusly:

```
usPlace OBJECT-CLASS
    SUBCLASS OF locality, nadfObject
    MUST CONTAIN { localityName,
                    fipsPlaceNumericCode }


usCountyOrEquivalent OBJECT-CLASS
    SUBCLASS OF usPlace
    MUST CONTAIN { fipsCountyNumericCode }
```

Each entry is subordinate to the entry naming the region which contains the county, and has an RDN consisting of a single attribute value assertion:

```
localityName= <FIPS-55 name without remarks>
```

e.g.,

```
localityName= Santa Clara
```

Each entry (minimally) contains these attributes:

```
objectClass= usCountyOrEquivalent
fipsPlaceNumericCode= <FIPS-55 place numeric code>
fipsCountyNumericCode= <last three digits of FIPS-55 place code>
stateOrProvinceName= <FIPS-55 state alpha code>
stateOrProvinceName= <FIPS-5 corresponding name>
description= <FIPS-55 name with remarks>
```

e.g.,

```
objectClass= usCountyOrEquivalent
fipsPlaceNumericCode= 99085
fipsCountyNumericCode= 085
stateOrProvinceName= California
stateOrProvinceName= CA
description= County of Santa Clara
```

In addition, for each populated place named within the county, a non-distinguished `localityName` attribute value may be present to aid searching, e.g.,

```
localityName= Mountain View
localityName= San Jose
```

and so on.

A.3.4 ADDMD Operators

Also within the nation, there are public Directory service providers. Each service-provider corresponds to an ADDMD operator as recognized by the NADF. Each ADDMD operator is modeled with an object of class `nadfADDMD`, which is defined thusly:

```
nadfADDMD OBJECT-CLASS
    SUBCLASS OF nadfObject
    MUST CONTAIN { addmdName }
    MAY CONTAIN { organizationName,
                  organizationalAttributeSet }
```

Each entry is subordinate to `c=US`, and has an RDN consisting of a single attribute value assertion:

```
addmdName= <NADF registered name>
```

e.g.,

```
addmdName= PSINet
```

Each entry (minimally) contains this attribute:

```
objectClass= nadfADDMD
```

The structure of the subtree below each `nadfADDMD` entry is a matter for that service-provider to establish.

A.3.5 Summary of Structuring Objects

To summarize the naming architecture thus far:

Level	Element	objectClass	Superior	RDN
root	0			
international	1	country	0	countryName
national	2	usStateOrEquivalent	1	stateOrProvinceName
	3	nadfADDMD	1	addmdName
regional	4	usCountyOrEquivalent	2	localityName
local	5	...	4	...

A.4   Entity Objects

The next step in using the civil naming infrastructure is to model the entities which reside within the geographical/governmental structure.

A.4.1   Organizations

Organizations exist at several levels.

Kinds of Organizations

An organization is said to have *national-standing* if it is chartered (created and named) by the US Congress. An example of such an organization might be a national laboratory. There is no other entity which is empowered by government to confer national-standing on organizations. However, ANSI maintains an alphanumeric name-form registration for organizations, and this will be used as the public directory service basis for conferring national-standing on private organizations.

An organization is said to have *regional-standing* if it is chartered by the government of that region. An example of such an organization might be a public university. In addition, private organizations may achieve regional-standing by registering with the "Secretary of State" (or similar entity) within that region — this is termed a "doing business as" (DBA) registration.

> **NOTE:** An organization may have a DBA registration in several states, even though it is incorporated in only one state, and this is largely independent of wherever an organization might choose to incorporate, and where they choose to locate their business operations.
>
> For example, a large organization might have a DBA registration in most of the 50 states, and be incorporated in Delaware. For the purposes of this naming scheme, such an organization is said to have regional-standing in each state where it has a DBA registration. This DBA registration confers the sole right to use the DBA name in association with the named jurisdiction of the registration authority.

An organization is said to have *local-standing* if it is chartered by a local government within that place. In addition, private organizations may achieve local-standing by registering with a "County Clerk" (or similar entity) within that place — this is termed a "doing business as" (DBA) registration. Note that local-standing is somewhat ambiguous in that there may be multiple local governments contained within a county or county-equivalent. Depending on local government rules of incorporation and containment, registering with one entity may prevent others from registering that same name with other entities contained within that place.

Modeling Organizations

In the DIT, an organization is modeled by one of three object classes:

- if an organization has national-standing through ANSI registration, it is modeled with an object of class usOrganization:

      usOrganization OBJECT-CLASS
          SUBCLASS OF organization, nadfObject
          MUST CONTAIN { ansiOrgNumericCode }

- if an organization has foreign-standing, it is modeled with an object of class foreignOrganization:

      foreignOrganization OBJECT-CLASS
          SUBCLASS OF organization, nadfObject
          MUST CONTAIN { countryName }

- otherwise, it is modeled with an object of class organization (including organizations chartered by government at any level).

A.4.2 Residential Persons

Residential persons are naturally thought of as always having local-standing. For a given residential person, it should be possible to identify the entry in US FIPS 55 which corresponds to "smallest" populated place where that person resides.

A residential person is modeled with an object of class residentialPerson.

A.5 Listing Entities

The final step is to define how entities are listed within the context of the civil naming infrastructure. Note than an entity may have several listings (DNs) in different parts of the Directory.

A.5.1 Organizations

The RDN used when listing an organization depends on both the standing of the organization, and where the listing is to be placed:

Entity	Listing (RDN) under c=US	c=US, st=X	c=US, st=X, l=Y
national-standing	organizationName	organizationName localityName=US	organizationName localityName=US
regional-standing	organizationName stateOrProvinceName=X	organizationName	organizationName
... (other region)		organizationName stateOrProvinceName=Z	organizationName stateOrProvinceName=Z
local-standing	organizationName stateOrProvinceName=X fipsPlaceNumericCode	organizationName fipsPlaceNumericCode	organizationName fipsPlaceNumericCode
... (other region)		organizationName stateOrProvinceName=Z fipsPlaceNumericCode	organizationName stateOrProvinceName=Z fipsPlaceNumericCode
foreign-standing	organizationName, ... countryName	organizationName, ... countryName	organizationName, ... countryName

This scheme makes no requirements on the DIT structure within an organization. However, the following naming architecture is suggested:

Level	Element	objectClass	Superior	RDN
listing	11	organization	1,2,4	depends on standing
organizational	12	organizationalUnit	11,12,13	organizational- UnitName
	13	locality	11,12,13	localityName
	14	organizationalRole	11,12,13	commonName
	15	organizationalPerson	11,12,13	commonName
application	16	applicationProcess	11,12,13	commonName
	17	nadfApplicationEntity	14	commonName
	18	groupOfNames	11,12,13	commonName
	19	ediUser	11,12,13	ediName
	20	device	11,12,13	commonName

A.5.2 Residential Persons

Residential persons are identified by the place where they reside, usually with a multi-valued RDN (consisting of a `commonName` attribute value, and some other distinguished attribute value). Although an obvious choice is to use something like `postalCode` or `streetAddress`, it should be noted that this information may be considered private. Hence, some other, distinguishing attribute value may be used — possibly even a "serial number" attribute value which has no other purpose other than to give uniqueness. (It should be noted that an attribute of this kind is not helpful in regards to searching — other attribute values containing meaningful information should be added to the entry and made available for public access, as an aid to selection.)

The RDN used when listing persons depends on where the listing is to be placed:

Entity	Listing (RDN) under		
	c=US	c=US, st=X	c=US, st=X, l=Y
person	commonName, ... stateOrProvinceName=X fipsPlaceNumericCode	commonName, ... fipsPlaceNumericCode	commonName, ... fipsPlaceNumericCode
... (other region)		commonName, ... stateOrProvinceName=Z fipsPlaceNumericCode	commonName, ... stateOrProvinceName=Z fipsPlaceNumericCode

Note that listing of foreign persons is for further study.

A.6 Usage Examples

Organizations with National-Standing

Suppose that the organization

```
Lawrence Livermore National Laboratory
```

has national-standing by virtue of having been chartered by the US Congress. According to the table in Section A.5.1, this organization has the right to list as any (or all) of these names:

```
{ c=US,
          o=Lawrence Livermore National Laboratory }

{ c=US, st=*,
        { o=Lawrence Livermore National Laboratory,
          l=US } }

{ c=US, st=*, l=*,
        { o=Lawrence Livermore National Laboratory,
          l=US } }
```

Suppose that the organization

```
Performance Systems International, Inc.
```

has national-standing by virtue of having an alphanumeric nameform in the ANSI registry. According to the table in Section A.5.1, this organization has the right to list as any (or all) of these names:

```
{ c=US, o=Performance Systems International }

{ c=US, st=*,
        { o=Performance Systems International,
          l=US } }

{ c=US, st=*, l=*,
        { o=Performance Systems International,
          l=US } }
```

Organizations with Regional-Standing

Suppose that the organization

```
Network Management Associates, Inc.
```

has regional-standing by virtue of having a DBA registration with the Secretary of State for the State of California. According to the table in Section A.5.1, this organization has the right to list as any (or all) of these names:

```
{ c=US,
          { o=Network Management Associates,
            st=California } }

{ c=US, st=California,
          o=Network Management Associates }

{ c=US, st=California, l=*,
          o=Network Management Associates }
```

Further, in some state other than California, this organization might also list as:

```
{ c=US, st=*,
          { o=Network Management Associates,
            st=California } }

{ c=US, st=*, l=*,
          { o=Network Management Associates,
            st=California } }
```

Organizations with Local-Standing

Suppose that the tavern and eatery

```
St. James Infirmary
```

has local-standing by virtue of having a DBA registration with the City Clerk for the City of Mountain View in the State of California. According to the table in Section A.5.1, this organization has the right to list as any (or all) of these names:

```
{ c=US,
          { o=St. James Infirmary, st=California,
            fips55=49670 } }

{ c=US, st=California,
          { o=St. James Infirmary, fips55=49670 } }

{ c=US, st=California, l=*,
          { o=St. James Infirmary, fips55=49670 } }
```

Further, in some state other than California, this organization might also list as:

```
{ c=US, st=*,
          { o=St. James Infirmary, st=California,
            fips55=49670 } }

{ c=US, st=*, l=*,
          { o=St. James Infirmary, st=California,
            fips55=49670 } }
```

Organizations with Foreign-Standing

Suppose that the five-star restaurant

```
Erik's Fisk
```

has foreign-standing by virtue of having a DBA registration through-out Sweden. According to the table in Section A.5.1, this organization has the right to list as any (or all) of these names:

```
{ c=US,
        { o=Erik's Fisk, c=SE } }

{ c=US, st=*,
        { o=Erik's Fisk, c=SE } }

{ c=US, st=*, l=*,
        { o=Erik's Fisk, c=SE } }
```

Persons

Suppose that the person

```
Marshall T. Rose
```

residing in the City of Mountain View in the State of California, wishes to be listed in the Directory. According to the table in Section A.5.2, this person might be listed as any of these names:

```
{ c=US,
        { cn=Marshall T. Rose, postalCode=94043-2112,
          st=California, fips55=49670 } }

{ c=US, st=California,
        { cn=Marshall T. Rose, postalCode=94043-2112,
          fips55=49670 } }

{ c=US, st=California, l=Santa Clara,
        { cn=Marshall T. Rose,
          postalCode=94043-2112 } }
```

Further, in some state other than California, this person might also list as:

```
{ c=US, st=*,
        { cn=Marshall T. Rose, postalCode=94043-2112,
          st=California, fips55=49670 } }

{ c=US, st=*, l=*,
        { cn=Marshall T. Rose, postalCode=94043-2112,
          st=California, fips55=49670 } }
```

Appendix B

Ordering ISODE

Reproduced here is the announcement for the ISODE 6.0 Release distribution. Note that information such as this is always out of date. It is best to call one of the phone numbers listed below to determine current ordering information.

Further, you might be interested in getting the ISODE 6.8 Interim distribution, which was released on 11 March, 1991. ISODE 6.8 is available only via the network, from any of the FTP or FTAM sites listed below. The name of the file to retrieve is `isode-interim.tar.Z`.

ANNOUNCEMENT

The most recent release of *The ISO Development Environment* was made available on 24 January 1990. This release is called

ISODE 6.0

This software supports the development of certain kinds of OSI protocols and applications. Here are the details:

- ISODE is not proprietary, but it is not in the public domain. This was necessary to include a "hold harmless" clause in the release. The upshot of all this is that anyone can get a copy of the release and do anything they want with it, but no one takes any responsibility whatsoever for any (mis)use.

- ISODE runs on native Berkeley (4.2BSD and later) and AT&T (SVR2, SVR3) systems, in addition to various other UNIX-like operating systems. No kernel modifications are required.

- Current modules include:

  - OSI transport service (TP0 on top of TCP and X.25; TP4 for SunLink OSI)
  - OSI session, presentation, and association control services
  - ASN.1 abstract syntax/transfer notation tools, including:
    * remote operations stub-generator
    * structure-generator (ASN.1 to C)
    * element-parser (basic encoding rules)
  - OSI reliable transfer and remote operations services
  - OSI file transfer, access and management
  - FTAM/FTP gateway
  - OSI directory services
  - OSI virtual terminal (basic class, TELNET profile)

- ISODE 6.0 consists of final "IS" level implementations with a few exceptions: ROSE and RTSE are current to the last circulated drafts (March, 1988); VT is a DIS implementation. ISODE also contains implementations of the 1984 X.400 versions of ROS and RTS.

- Although ISODE is not "supported" per se, it does have an address to which problems may be reported:

  `Bug-ISODE@XTEL.CO.UK`

Bug reports (and fixes) are welcome, by the way.

- The discussion group `ISODE@NIC.DDN.MIL` is used as an open forum on ISODE. Contact `ISODE-Request@NIC.DDN.MIL` to be added to this list.

- The primary documentation for this release consists of a five volume User's Manual (approx. 1000 pages) and a set of UNIX manual pages. The sources to the User's Manual are in LaTeX format. In addition, there are a number of notes, papers, and presentations included in the documentation set, again in either LaTeX or SLiTeX format.

For more information contact:

Postal:	ISODE Distribution
	X-Tel Services Ltd.
	University Park
	Nottingham University
	Nottingham, NG7 2RD
	UK

Telephone:	+44 602 412648
Fax:	+44 602 790278
Telex:	37346
Internet:	support@xtel.co.uk

DISTRIBUTION SITES

- NORTH AMERICA
  For mailings in NORTH AMERICA, send a check for 375 US
  Dollars to:

Postal:	University of Pennsylvania
	Department of Computer and Information Science
	Moore School
	Attn: David J. Farber (ISODE Distribution)
	200 South 33rd Street
	Philadelphia, PA 19104-6314
	US

Telephone:	+1 215 898 8560

Specify one of:

1. 1600bpi 1/2–inch tape, or

2. Sun 1/4–inch cartridge tape.

The tape will be written in *tar* format and returned with a documentation set. Do not send tapes or envelopes. Documentation only is the same price.

- EUROPE
  For mailings in EUROPE, send a cheque or bankers draft and
  a purchase order for 200 Pounds Sterling to:

  Postal address: Department of Computer Science
                    Attn: Natalie May/Dawn Bailey
                    University College London
                    Gower Street
                    London, WC1E 6BT
                    UK

  For information only:

  Telephone: +44 71 380 7214
  Fax: +44 71 387 1397
  Telex: 28722
  Internet: `natalie@cs.ucl.ac.uk`
               `dawn@cs.ucl.ac.uk`

  Specify one of:

  1. 1600bpi 1/2–inch tape, or

  2. Sun 1/4–inch cartridge tape.

  The tape will be written in *tar* format and returned with a documentation set. Do not send tapes or envelopes. Documentation
  only is the same price.

- EUROPE (tape only)
  Tapes without hardcopy documentation can be obtained via the
  European UNIX User Group (EUUG). The ISODE 6.0 distribu-
  tion is called EUUGD14.

  Postal: EUUG Distributions
            c/o Frank Kuiper
            Centrum voor Wiskunde en Informatica
            Kruislann 413
            1098 SJ Amsterdam
            The Netherlands

For information only:

Telephone:	+31 20 5924121
	(or +31 20 5929333)
Telex:	12571 mactr nl
Telefax:	+31 20 5924199
Internet:	`euug-tapes@cwi.nl`

Specify one of:

1. 1600bpi 1/2–inch tape: 130 Dutch Guilders

2. 800bpi 1/2–inch tape: 130 Dutch Guilders

3. Sun 1/4–inch cartridge tape (QIC-24 format): 190 Dutch Guilders

4. 1600 1/2–inch tape (QIC-11 format): 190 Dutch Guilders

If you require DHL, this is possible and will be billed through. Note that if you are not a member of EUUG, then there is an additional handling fee of 300 Dutch Guilders (please enclose a copy of your membership or contribution payment form when ordering). Do not send money, cheques, tapes or envelopes; you will be invoiced.

- PACIFIC RIM
  For mailings in the Pacific Rim, send a cheque for 250 Dollars Australian to:

Postal:	CSIRO DIT
	Attn: Andrew Waugh (ISODE Distribution)
	55 Barry Street
	Carlton, 3053
	Australia

For information only:

Telephone:	+61 3 347 8644
Fax:	+61 3 347 8987
Internet:	`ajw@ditmela.oz.au`

Specify one of:

1. 1600/3200/6250bpi 1/2–inch tape, or

2. Sun 1/4—inch cartridge tape in either QIC-11 or QIC-24 format.

The tape will be written in tar format and returned with a documentation set. Do not send tapes or envelopes. Documentation only is the same price.

- Internet
  If you can FTP to the Internet, then use anonymous FTP to the host `uu.psi.com` residing at [`192.33.4.10`] to retrieve `isode-6.tar.Z` in BINARY mode from the `pub/isode/` directory. This file is the *tar* image after being run through the compress program and is approximately 4.5MB in size.

- NIFTP
  If you run NIFTP over the public X.25 network or over JANET, and are registered in the NRS at Salford, you can use NIFTP with username "guest" and your own name as password, to access `UK.AC.UCL.CS` to retrieve the file `<SRC>isode-6.tar`. This is a 14MB *tar* image. The file `<SRC>isode-6.tar.Z` is the *tar* image after being run through the compress program (4.5MB).

- FTAM on the JANET or PSS
  The source code is available by FTAM at the University College London over X.25 using JANET (DTE 00000511160013) or PSS (DTE 23421920030013) with TSEL 259 (ASCII encoding). Use the "anon" user-identity and retrieve the `<SRC>isode-6.tar`. This is a 14MB *tar* image. The file `<SRC>isode-6.tar.Z` is the *tar* image after being run through the compress program (4.5MB).

- FTAM on the Internet
  The source code is available by FTAM over the Internet at host `osi.nyser.net` residing at [`192.33.4.10`] (TCP port 102 selects the OSI transport service) with TSEL 259 (numeric encoding). Use the "anon" user-identity, supply any password, and

retrieve `isode-6.tar.Z` from the `pub/isode/` directory. This file is the *tar* image after being run through the compress program and is approximately 4.5MB in size.

For distributions via FTAM, the file service is provided by the FTAM implementation in ISODE 5.0 or later (IS FTAM).

For distributions via either FTAM or FTP, there is an additional file available for retrieval, called `isode-ps.tar.Z` which is a compressed tar image (7MB) containing the entire documentation set in PostScript format.

Appendix C

An Overview of ISODE

The concept of *open systems*, those computer systems which interop- soap... erate, regardless of manufacturer or model, has proven quite popular. The Internet suite of protocols (commonly referred to as the TCP/IP protocol family) demonstrates quite well the demand for interoperable computer-communication products. Indeed, the ARPANET experimental development of the Internet suite of protocols provides the empirical proof of the whole open systems model, and the roots of many OSI tools and services can be found in the ARPANET research literature. Given its deep market penetration, the Internet suite of protocols is often referred to as today's *de facto* standard for computer-communications. It is only lacking formal international standing!

However, for various technical and political reasons, many expect that an *internationally* standardized suite of protocols, based on the Open Systems Interconnection (OSI) model, will join and eventually displace the Internet suite of protocols as the off-the-shelf commodity of choice for building infrastructure in the computer networking world. The fiery debate on this statement generates much heat, but little light: by virtue of its international backing, both in terms of political and marketing support, OSI will most likely be tomorrow's *de jure* standard for computer-communications.

Of course, it not enough to simply *mandate the use* of OSI, as has been done in numerous national and regional contexts. Rather, OSI must be *implemented* before it can be used! Whilst a rather self-evident statement, the history of OSI, starting in the late '70s, has not been particularly successful in this regard. Fortunately, there are some implementations — and this appendix will examine one such effort.

C.1 What is ISODE?

ISODE (pronounced *eye-so-dee-ee*), or *ISO Development Environment*, is a collection of library routines and programs that implements an extensive set of OSI upper-layer services. The ISODE implementation is interesting in four respects: it provides extensive automatic tools for the development of OSI applications; it supports OSI applications on top of both OSI and TCP/IP-based networks; it provides a novel approach to the problems of OSI coexistence with and transition from the Internet suite of protocols; and, it is openly available (non-proprietary).

ISODE was originally developed in 1986 at the Northrop Research and Technology Center as a means to experiment with OSI applications.

The ISODE is an openly available implementation, available for a minimal distribution fee from any of several international distribution sites, via both postal and on-line means. There is an implicit "hold-harmless" clause contained in the software, although no signatures, letters of intent, or other such legal encumbrances need be exchanged in order to receive a source release of the software. Once a copy of ISODE is obtained, any party is free to make use of the software for any legal purpose, including re-selling it for a profit (modified or not), providing that the authors and distribution sites are held harmless from any legal entanglements.

This style of openly available source coupled with contributions from the user community is reminiscent of the early days of DARPA-sponsored networking, when researchers freely exchanged their findings in order to facilitate rapid understanding of the technology. However, the policy is in sharp contrast to the modern trend of so-called "public domain" software that can be used only for non-commercial purposes. The openly-available/no restrictions model is particularly appropriate for ISODE, whose original authors felt that the dearth of OSI implementations combined with the frenzy for OSI-based systems outweighed the potentially huge financial opportunity that could be made with a high-quality, relatively complete implementation of OSI. Northrop management was far-sighted enough to agree with this posture, which in turn set the tone for subsequent sponsors of ISODE.

C.1.1   Overall Organization

Figure C.1 shows the overall organization of ISODE:

- a set of application service elements;

- a collection of ASN.1 tools;

- presentation and session services; and,

- interfaces to transport and network layer realizations.

isode currently reflects the standards as they existed towards the end of 1988.

The modular architecture shown in Figure C.1 bears a close resemblance to the layered divisions of the OSI model, and has proven successful in allowing various organizations to develop their own OSI applications and services on top of ISODE. As a result of continuing development and cooperation, the ISODE now contains implementations of the four main OSI applications: message handling (MHS), file service (FTAM), directory services, and terminal service, plus a gateway between FTAM and the Internet File Transfer Protocol (FTP), and a gateway between MHS and the Internet Simple Mail Transfer Protocol (SMTP). Finally, ISODE contains a network management implementation, but not the OSI network management protocol.

ISODE was initially developed as a tool for studying how OSI applications could be built. However, since then it has grown into a system extensively used in international pilots of OSI services, and it been pressed into service as a reference implementation of the core aspects of OSI.

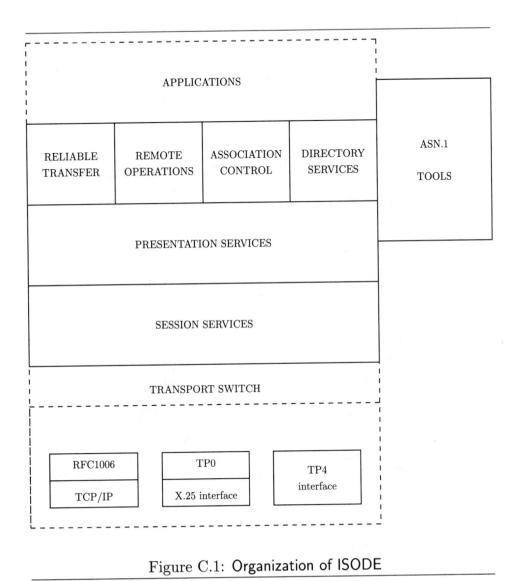

Figure C.1: Organization of ISODE

C.2   ISODE as a Development Environment

ISODE is really a programming kit: the 6.0 release available in January of 1990, contained everything but the message handling software, and consisted of approximately 250,000 lines of C code, along with a five volume user's manual of over 1000 pages. ISODE runs on different variants of the UNIX operating system, and does not require any changes to the operating system.

C.2.1   Building Distributed Applications

Although ISODE can be programmed at several levels, it provides a set of semi-automatic tools, termed *The Applications Cookbook*, which can be used to rapidly construct OSI applications.

In OSI, there is a concise notation for describing programs that use remote operations. ISODE contains a compiler which reads this notation and produces equivalent procedure calls in the *C* programming language. When a program calls one of these routines, a run-time library is invoked which initiates a remote procedure call across the network. Another compiler defines *C* data structures equivalent to the ASN.1 structures defined by the notation. Finally, a third compiler generates *C* code to map between the *C* and ASN.1 structures. These relationships are summarized in Figures C.2 and C.3.

The impact of a system such as the *Applications Cookbook* is that it frees the programmer from worrying about network-specifics: the programmer deals with the application-specific aspects of the system, and the *Cookbook* deals with how the application talks to the network.

C.2.2   Transport-Independence

When ISODE was originally developed in January of 1986, there were very few networks and systems which supported the OSI transport service. In contrast, the Internet suite of protocols, and in particular, its reliable transport protocol, TCP, were widely deployed even at that time (and are even more so today).

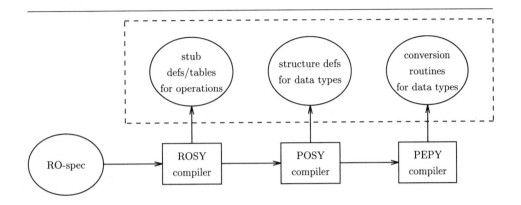

Figure C.2: Static Facilities of the Applications Cookbook

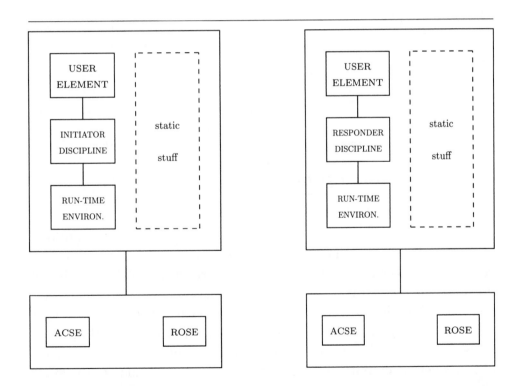

Figure C.3: Dynamic Facilities of the Applications Cookbook

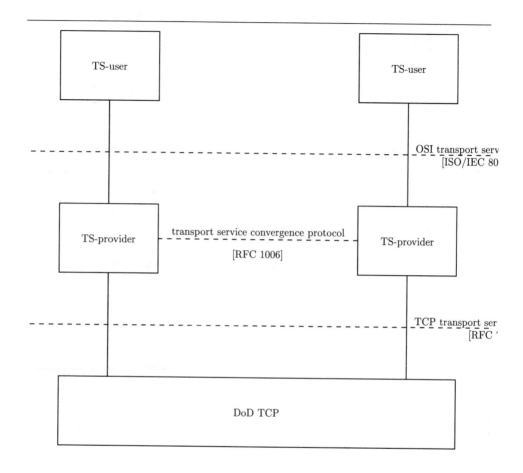

Figure C.4: OSI Transport Services on top of TCP

To solve this problem, a *transport service convergence protocol* (TSCP) between the TCP and the OSI transport service was developed, as shown in Figure C.4. This particular TSCP is a simple protocol that runs over the TCP and makes the service it offers appear to be identical to the OSI transport service. This is an important abstraction in that it allowed the development of native OSI applications, that behaved as if they were running in a pure OSI environment. Later, when some pure OSI environments became available, the same applications ran without even being re-compiled: they were simply reloaded with a new transport library!

This development led to an important abstraction in ISODE called the *transport switch*. When ISODE is configured, one or more transport-stacks are defined. A transport-stack is simply a combination of protocols which offer the OSI transport service, e.g., TP4 over CLNP, or TP0 over X.25, or RFC1006 (the TSCP mentioned earlier) over TCP. When a connection is to be initiated, the transport-switch examines the destination address and automatically invokes the correct transport-stack. Once a connection is established, the appropriate transport-stack is used exclusively for that connection.

Initially, the transport-switch was written with the belief that there would be only a few transport-stacks that it would have to know about. However, many in the new generation of network technologies are likely to use their own transport service. As a result, some predict that by mid-'90s there will be many competing transport services, all useful, but few interworking. In cases such as these, the transport-switch will prove useful in providing a transparent mechanism for OSI applications to run on these new technologies.

C.2.3 Transition to OSI

Being able to run OSI applications over TCP/IP-based networks might be an interesting approach towards the transition to OSI. But, if one site has OSI applications running on top of TP4/CLNP, and another runs the same applications over RFC1006/TCP, then how can these two sites interoperate?

The solution is to provide a device called a *transport-service bridge* (or *active transport layer relay* in ISO parlance). As shown in Figure C.5, this is a device which supports at least two different transport-stacks. When a connection comes in on one stack, it starts a connection with the second stack and then starts shuffling data.

Of course, such a device is outside the scope of OSI as it performs functions which are not allowed within the framework of the OSI model. So, it should not be surprising that this "solution" is not perfect: issues such as accounting, access control, and load balancing have yet to be resolved. But, in many environments, the use of TS-bridges has proven crucial in achieving interoperability between communities. For example, many sites run TCP/IP over their local area network and also have a host with an international-X.25 connec-

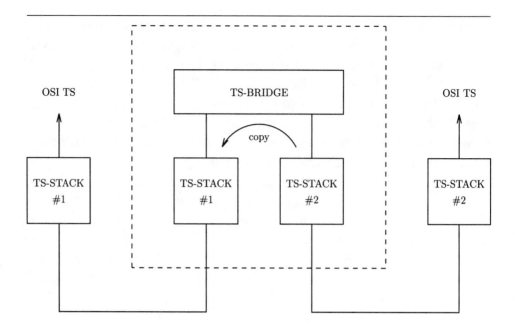

Figure C.5: Transport-Service Bridge

tion. By running a TS-bridge on this host, all of the machines on the
local area network are able to access OSI services available anywhere
in the international-X.25 network.

C.3 Pilot Usage of ISODE

Because ISODE is a high-quality prototype of the core aspects of OSI, it is being used to provide the infrastructure for several OSI related projects, including multi-national pilots of various OSI application services. The PSI White Pages Pilot Project is one such example.

C.4 ISODE as a Reference Implementation

Finally, ISODE has been pressed into service as a reference implementation of the core aspects of OSI. First, ISODE is being used as the foundation for a project that is developing a complete, openly-available OSI implementation for a POSIX-conformant Berkeley UNIX environment. In doing so, its sponsors hope to spur the introduction of OSI into the workplace, by leveraging on the vast deployment of systems based on Berkeley UNIX.

Independent of this, many vendors of computer-communications hardware and software are turning to ISODE as the basis of their future OSI products. For example, in 1990, this year Cray Research announced the availability of an OSI package for the XMP supercomputer that is based on ISODE. By providing a platform which is readily portable to numerous variants of the popular UNIX operating system, ISODE can give commercial and research organizations an early, highly-functional OSI capability. After portation, vendors using such a platform can then customize the software to add value and achieve market distinction.

In brief, leverage can be seen as a key motivating factor: the resource investment required to produce an OSI implementation is quite high, in terms of both personnel and time. By using a reference implementation, and leveraging the work of others, a vendor can achieve a significant savings in developing OSI-based products. At times this savings can be quite dramatic.

For example, consider the case of one particular vendor which has two major product platforms, based on different operating systems. Four years ago, engineers for one of these product platforms began working on OSI products. One year ago, engineers for the other product platform ported ISODE to their platform. Upon doing so, the second group completely leap-frogged the efforts of the first group: they were able to demonstrate a more complete OSI capability (in terms of both protocol and user-interface functionality), than the group which had started from scratch! (It is an exercise for the reader to guess what management's response was to this situation.)

C.5 In Retrospect

Historically ISODE has been an exercise in "technological counter-culture." For example, offering a white pages service using the OSI Directory in a TCP/IP-based environment is an unlikely combination from either an OSI or Internet perspective. However, experience has shown it to be an optimal combination of facilities:

- the sheer size of the Internet, which forms the infrastructure for research, educational, and commercial concerns in the US and elsewhere, provides an excellent testing ground for a White Pages service pilot project;

- the Internet is supported by the stable and widely-implemented Internet suite of protocols, which provide the basic internet-working capability; and,

- the OSI Directory provides a rich environment for building a highly-functional White Pages service.

Having the ability to form combinations such as this was one of the key motivations driving the original authors of ISODE.

Of course, combinations such as this are more often the subject of politics and marketing than technology. Over the past five years, there have been four issues of contention:

C.5.1 Is Unlicensed Software Bad?

It has been pointed out that making an openly available OSI implementation may not be popular with those vendors that have invested considerable resources into developing their own implementations. For third-party software vendors, ISODE might be viewed as a direct commercial challenge (why pay upwards of US$1M for a license when roughly equivalent software can be had for essentially no fee?).

In response, from the historical perspective of the Internet community, we have seen how a *reference implementation* is necessary to help a technology receive multi-vendor acceptance in a marketplace. The inclusion of the Internet protocols in Berkeley **UNIX** demonstrated this quite eloquently: there are now literally scores of vendors offering

TCP/IP-based products on numerous platforms; the majority of these products can trace their implementational roots back to the Berkeley distribution. Indeed, many persuasively argue that inclusion of the Internet protocols in Berkeley UNIX was a significant contributing factor to the creation of the marketplace for Internet technology!

On the other hand, reference implementations are hardly perfect — ISODE certainly isn't! Consider also the cautionary tales contained in the soapbox starting on page 53. (In fairness to the contributors of BSD UNIX, it should be noted that the TCP and IP components are top-notch implementations — it's just the two main applications which are hosed!)

C.5.2   Is Mixing Protocol Stacks Bad?

It has been pointed out that providing a means for running OSI applications over TCP/IP-based networks may not be popular with those parties interested in either "pure OSI" or "pure TCP/IP." The OSI purists feel that ISODE was "committing the terrible crime of diluting the momentum of OSI by doing anything with TCP/IP." In contrast, the Internet purists thought ISODE project was "foolish for doing anything with something that clearly will never work" (OSI). These are actual quotations from "industry experts."

In response, it should be noted that both suites of protocol can capitalize on the strengths of the other. The original authors of the ISODE were less interested in "political correctness" than in simply "making things work." In particular, note that the large installed base of TCP/IP-based networks has an impressively large user community. Today, these TCP/IP-based internets are far larger than any collection of existing OSI networks. The Internet community depends on the production quality of their networks to remain intact. Nonetheless, many users in the community are interested in the power of OSI applications.

C.5.3   Is full transition to OSI really necessary?

It has been pointed out that being able to run OSI applications over TCP/IP-based networks brings into question the whole motivation for ever *fully* transitioning to OSI. If transitioning a network requires changing the software in *all* the routers in addition to changing the operating system and user software in *all* the end-systems, then this is a substantial undertaking. It will require massive synchronization of cutover phases, and would force some work units to convert at unfortunate times. If only changing the user software in the end-systems was required to effect the transition, then many might find this an attractive alternative to wholesale synchronized conversion. Further, by allowing the two communities to achieve applications-level interoperability using *transport-service bridges*, then the transition to OSI can be made on a schedule that is convenient and comfortable for each segment of the total network community.

Once such full application-level interoperability is achieved, there is little reason to transition the remainder of the network, particularly if that network is a production facility whose value lies in its continued stability. Hence, the question of transition to OSI really becomes one of extended coexistence with OSI. If one can coexist well, then transition, per se, becomes a non-issue: transition occurs at the end of the coexistence period, if and when there are no longer any Internet-only systems in the network. Naturally, this will occur only when OSI has proved its worth in the market, with competitive products and services. It needn't occur due to administrative fiat.

C.5.4   Will OSI Network Management ever work?

It has been pointed out that providing an implementation of the Internet Simple Network Management Protocol (SNMP), and not providing an implementation of the OSI network management protocol, CMIP, is rather strange.

The reason for this is two-fold: first, there are many solid technical arguments against the viability of OSI network management, as it is currently standardized (e.g., [49]). Further, there is tremendous field-experience that the Internet-standard network management framework, as embodied by the SNMP and its correspondent technologies, is workable and provides a useful solution.

Second, many believe that the continued survival of the Internet hinges on all nodes becoming network manageable. By including an

SNMP implementation with ISODE, and then distributing ISODE with future releases of Berkeley UNIX, there is some hope that systems, as they upgrade, will also run the network management software.

In order to provide management of "pure" OSI networks, ISODE not only contains support for running SNMP over the OSI transport service, but also can manage the OSI portions of the Berkeley UNIX kernel. Thus, whilst SNMP may not be the "official" OSI network management, as existing networks begin incorporating OSI components, it might become a *de facto* management system for OSI!

C.5.5   In Conclusion

There is much controversy, but few clear answers, to these four issues. Fortunately, by combining a complete set of upper-layer OSI services with the ability to run them over diverse transport services, ISODE has proven itself quite popular, both with a diverse, international user-community, and with several vendors of computer hardware and

`...soap` software.

Glossary

Abstract Syntax Notation One: the OSI language for describing abstract syntax; (imprecise usage) both the OSI language and the Basic Encoding Rules.

abstract syntax: a description of a data type that is independent of machine-oriented structures and restrictions.

acceptor: a user that receives the .INDICATION primitive associated with a service. See *requestor*.

ACK: the *acknowledgement* bit in a TCP segment.

ACSE: see *Association Control Service Element*.

active open: the sequence events of occurring when an application entity directs TCP to establish a connection.

ADDMD: see *Administrative Directory Management Domain*.

address class: a method used to determine the boundary between the network and host portions of an IP address.

address mask: a 32–bit quantity indicating which bits in an IP address refer to the network portion.

Address Resolution Protocol: the protocol in the Internet suite of protocols used to map IP addresses onto Ethernet (and other media) addresses.

address resolution: a means for mapping network-layer addresses onto media-specific addresses.

address: a location; when used in the context of a particular layer (e.g., session address), it refers an instances of a service access point at that layer (e.g., a session service access point).

ADMD: see *Administrative Management Domain.*

Administrative Directory Management Domain: a Directory management domain run by a PTT authority. See *DMD* and *PRDMD.*

administrative framework: a scheme for defining a policy of authentication and authorization.

Administrative Management Domain: an MHS management domain run by a PTT authority. Each ADMD must contain MHS routing information to all other ADMDs.

Advanced Research Projects Agency: see *Defense Advanced Research Projects Agency.*

AE: see *application entity.*

AET: see *application entity title.*

AM: an *amendment* to an International Standard.

American National Standards Institute: the US national standardization body. ANSI is a member of ISO.

ANSI: see *American National Standards Institute.*

AP: see *application process.*

APDU: *application protocol data unit*

API: see *Application Programmer's Interface.*

application context: the collection of application service elements (ASEs) which comprises an application entity (AE) along with the rules defining the interactions between the ASEs.

application entity: the OSI portion of an application process (AP).

application entity title: the authoritative name of an OSI application entity, usually a Distinguished Name from the Directory.

application layer: that portion of an OSI system ultimately responsible for managing communication between application processes (APs).

application process: an object executing in a real system.

application protocol: see *application context.*

application service element: the building block of an application entity (AE). Each AE consists of one or more of these service elements, as defined by its application context.

application services: the services collectively offered by the upper four layers of the OSI model.

Applications Programmer's Interface: a set of calling conventions defining how a service is invoked through a software package.

ARP: see *Address Resolution Protocol.*

ARPA: see *Defense Advanced Research Projects Agency.*

ASDU: *application service data unit*

ASE: see *application service element.*

ASN.1: see *Abstract Syntax Notation One.*

Association Control Service Element: The application service element responsible for association establishment and release.

association: a presentation layer connection augmented with application layer semantics (e.g., application layer naming).

attribute: an attribute type along with one or more associated values.

attribute set: a collection of attributes, useful in some context, e.g., postal-addressing.

attribute type: a definition of the properties of some information, including its abstract syntax, constraints on that syntax, and what kinds of comparisons can be made between two values belonging to the type.

attribute value: an instance of the syntax associated with an attribute type.

Basic Encoding Rules: the OSI language for describing transfer syntax.

BER: see *Basic Encoding Rules.*

bridge: (imprecise usage) an entity responsible for simple mappings at a single layer.

British Standards Institute: the U.K. national standardization body. The BSI is a member of ISO.

broadcast address: a media-specific or IP address referring to all stations on a media.

broadcasting: the act of sending to the broadcast address.

BSI: see *British Standards Institute.*

C: the *C* programming language.

caching: a form of replication in which information learned during a previous transaction is used to process later transactions.

CCITT: see *International Telephone and Telegraph Consultative Committee.*

CD: a committee draft. If ratified, the committee draft advances to Draft International Standard (DIS) status.

Charlie-Foxtrot: (colloquial usage) *seriously* beyond all hope.

checksum: an arithmetic sum used to verify data integrity.

CL-mode: see *connection-less mode.*

CLNS: *connectionless-mode network service*

CLTS: *connectionless-mode transport service*

CO-mode: see *connection-oriented mode.*

connection-less mode: a service that has a single phase involving control mechanisms such as addressing in addition to data transfer.

connection-oriented mode: a service that has three distinct phases: *establishment,* in which two or more users are bound to a connection; *data transfer,* in which data is exchanged between the users; and, *release,* in which the binding is terminated.

connection: a logical binding between two or more users of a service.

CONS: *connection-oriented network service*

COR: a *confirmation of receipt* in the network service.

COTS: *connection-oriented transport service*

DAM: a *draft amendment* to an International Standard. If ratified, the draft amendment advances to Amendment (AD) status.

DAP: see *Directory Access Protocol.*

DARPA Internet: see *Internet.*

DARPA: see *Defense Advanced Research Projects Agency.*

data link layer: that portion of an OSI system responsible for transmission, framing, and error control over a single communications link.

data: (imprecise usage) see *user-data.*

datagram: a self-contained unit of data transmitted independently of other datagrams.

DCS: see *defined context set.*

Defense Advanced Research Projects Agency: an agency of the US Department of Defense that sponsors high-risk, high-payoff research. The Internet suite of protocols was developed under DARPA auspices. DARPA was previously known as ARPA, the Advanced Research Projects Agency, when the ARPANET was built.

defined context set: the set of defined presentation contexts for a presentation connection.

device: a network element of some kind.

DIB: see *Directory Information Base.*

Directory Access Protocol: the protocol used between a Directory User Agent (DUA) and a Directory System Agent (DSA).

Directory Information Base: the collection of information objects in the Directory.

Directory Information Tree: the global tree of entries corresponding to information objects in the Directory.

Directory Management Domain: a collection of DSAs that holds a portion of the DIT. For political reasons, there are two kinds of DMDs: ADDMDs and PRDMDs. This distinction is largely artificial.

Directory System Agent: an application entity that offers the Directory service.

Directory System Protocol: the protocol used between two Directory System Agents (DSAs).

Directory User Agent: an application entity that makes the Directory service available to the user.

DIS: a *draft* International Standard. If ratified, the draft advances to International Standard (IS) status.

Distinguished Name: the global, authoritative name of an entry in the OSI Directory.

DIT: see *Directory Information Tree.*

DMD: see *Directory Management Domain.*

DN: see *Distinguished Name.*

dotted quad notation: a convention for writing IP addresses in textual format, as in "192.67.67.20."

DSA: see *Directory System Agent.*

DSP: see *Directory System Protocol.*

DUA: see *Directory User Agent.*

ECMA: see *European Computer Manufacturers Association.*

End-System to Intermediate-System Protocol: the ISO protocol used for router detection and address resolution.

end-system: a network device performing functions from all layers of the OSI model. End-systems are commonly thought of as hosting applications.

end-to-end services: the services collectively offered by the lower four layers of the OSI model.

ES-IS: see *End-System to Intermediate-System Protocol.*

ES: see *end-system.*

European Computer Manufacturers Association: a group of computer vendors that have performed substantive pre-standardization work for OSI.

Federal Research Internet: see *Internet.*

File Transfer Protocol: the application protocol offering file service in the Internet suite of protocols.

File Transfer, Access and Management: the OSI file service.

FIN: the *finish* bit in a TCP segment.

flow control: the mechanism whereby a receiver informs a sender how much data it is willing to accept.

fragment: an IP datagram containing only a portion of the user-data from a larger IP datagram.

fragmentation: the process of breaking an IP datagram into smaller parts, such that each fragment can be transmitted in whole on a given physical medium.

FTAM: see *File Transfer, Access and Management.*

FTP: see *File Transfer Protocol.*

FU: see *Functional Unit.*

Functional Unit: a grouping of one or more elements of a service that are functionally related. The elements of this group can be enabled or disabled as a unit, by enabling or disabling use of the corresponding functional unit.

gateway: (Internet usage) a router; also, (imprecise usage) an entity responsible for complex mappings, usually at the application layer.

hardware address: see *media address.*

header: (imprecise usage) see *protocol control information.*

host-identifier: that portion of an IP address corresponding to the host on the IP network.

host-number: that portion of a subnetted IP address corresponding to the host-number on the subnet.

host: (Internet usage) an end-system.

IAB: see *Internet Activities Board.*

IANA: see *Internet Assigned Numbers Authority.*

ICMP: see *Internet Control Message Protocol.*

IEEE: see *Institute of Electrical and Electronics Engineers.*

IETF: see *Internet Engineering Task Force.*

IFIP: see *International Federation of Information Processing.*

inheritance: the process whereby the properties of a superior object class are visited upon a subordinate object class.

initiator: a service user that initiates a connection or association. See *responder.*

Institute of Electrical and Electronics Engineers: a professional organization, which, as a part of its services to the community, performs some pre-standardization work for OSI.

interface layer: the layer in the Internet suite of protocols responsible for transmission on a single physical network.

intermediate-system: a real system performing functions from the three lower-layers of the OSI model. Intermediate-systems are commonly thought of as routing data for end-systems.

International Federation of Information Processing: a research organization that performs substantive pre-standardization work for OSI. IFIP is noted for having formalized the original MHS model.

International Organization for Standardization: the organization that produces many of the world's Standards. OSI is only one of many areas standardized by ISO/IEC.

International Standards Organization: there is no such thing. See the *International Organization for Standardization.*

International Telephone and Telegraph Consultative Committee: a body comprising the national Post, Telephone, and Telegraph (PTT) administrations.

Internet Activities Board: the technical body overseeing the development of the Internet suite of protocols.

Internet Assigned Numbers Authority: the entity responsible for assigning numbers in the Internet suite of protocols.

Internet Community: anyone, anywhere, who uses the Internet suite of protocols.

Internet Control Message Protocol: a simple reporting protocol for IP.

Internet Drafts: a means of documenting the work-in-progress of the IETF.

Internet Engineering Task Force: a task force of the Internet Activities Board charged with solving the short-term needs of the Internet.

internet layer: the layer in the Internet suite of protocols responsible for providing transparency over both the topology of the internet and the transmission media used in each physical network.

Internet Protocol: the network protocol offering a connectionless-mode network service in the Internet suite of protocols.

Internet suite of protocols: a collection of computer-communication protocols originally developed under DARPA sponsorship. The Internet suite of protocols is currently the de facto solution for open networking.

internet: (Internet usage) a network in the OSI sense; historically termed a *catenet* — a concatenated set of networks. The Internet is the largest internet in existence.

Internet: a large collection of connected networks, throughout the world, running the Internet suite of protocols. Sometimes referred to as the *DARPA Internet, NSF/DARPA Internet,* or the *Federal Research Internet.*

interpersonal message: a structured message exchanged between two MHS user agents, consisting of a well-defined heading and one or more arbitrary body parts.

IP address: a 32–bit quantity used to represent a point of attachment in an internet.

IP: see *Internet Protocol.*

IPM: see *interpersonal message.*

IS: either *intermediate-system* or *International Standard*, depending on context. In the latter case, such a document is named as either "ISO/IEC number," if it represents work under Joint Technical Committee 1; otherwise, it is named as "ISO number."

ISO Development Environment: a research tool developed to study the upper-layers of OSI. It is an unfortunate historical coincidence that the first three letters of ISODE are "ISO." This is not an acronym for the International Organization for Standardization, but rather three letters which, when pronounced in English, produce a pleasing sound.

ISO/IEC: see *International Organization for Standardization.*

ISODE: see *ISO Development Environment.*

LAN: see *local area network.*

local area network: any one of a number of technologies providing high-speed, low-latency transfer and being limited in geographic size.

maximum transmission unit: the largest amount of user-data (e.g., the largest size of an IP datagram) that can be sent in a single frame on a particular medium.

media address: the address of a physical interface.

media device: a low-level device which does not use a protocol at the internet layer as its primary function.

Message Handling System: a store-and-forward third-party system for delivering arbitrarily structured messages.

Message Store: an entity acting as an intermediary between an MHS user agent and its local message transfer agent.

Message Transfer Agent: an application entity that offers the Message Transfer service.

Message Transfer System: a collection of connected Message Transfer Agents (MTAs).

MHS: see *Message Handling System*.

MS: see *Message Store*.

MTA: see *Message Transfer Agent*.

MTS: see *Message Transfer System*.

MTU: see *maximum transmission unit*.

multi-homed: a host or gateway with more than one attachment to an IP network.

National Bureau of Standards: see *National Institute of Standards and Technology*.

National Institute of Standards and Technology: the branch of the US Department of Commerce charged with keeping track of standardization. Previously known as the *National Bureau of Standards*.

NBS: see *National Institute of Standards and Technology*.

network: a collection of subnetworks connected by intermediate-systems and populated by end-systems; also, (Internet usage) a single subnetwork or a related set of subnetworks in the OSI sense.

network byte order: the Internet-standard ordering of the bytes corresponding to numeric values.

network layer: that portion of an OSI system responsible for data transfer across the network, independent of both the media comprising the underlying subnetworks and the topology of those subnetworks.

network-identifier: that portion of an IP address corresponding to a network in an Internet.

NIST: see *National Institute of Standards and Technology*.

NPSDU: *normal data presentation service data unit*

NS: *network service*

NSAP: *network service access point*

NSDU: *network service data unit*

NSF/DARPA Internet: see *Internet.*

NSF: *National Science Foundation*

NSSDU: *normal data session service data unit*

Open Systems Interconnection: an international effort to facilitate communications among computers of different manufacture and technology.

OSI: see *Open Systems Interconnection.*

passive open: the sequence of events occurring when an application entity informs the TCP that it is willing to accept connections.

PCI: either *presentation context identifier* or *protocol control information,* depending on context.

PDAM: a *proposed draft amendment* to an International Standard. If ratified, the proposed draft amendment advances to Draft Amendment (DAM) status.

PDU: see *protocol data unit.*

PE: see *presentation element.*

physical layer: that portion of an OSI system responsible for the electromechanical interface to the communications media.

port number: identifies an application entity to a transport service in the Internet suite of protocols.

PPDU: *presentation protocol data unit*

PRDMD: see *Private Directory Management Domain.*

presentation context identifier: an integer identifying a particular presentation context active on a presentation connection.

presentation context: a binding between an abstract syntax and a transfer syntax.

presentation element: in ISODE, a *C* data structure capable of representing any ASN.1 object in a machine-independent form.

presentation layer: that portion of an OSI system responsible for adding structure to the units of data that are exchanged.

presentation stream: in ISODE, a set of routines providing an abstraction to provide transformations on presentation elements.

Private Directory Management Domain: a Directory management domain *not* run by a PTT authority. See *DMD* and *ADDMD*.

Private Management Domain: a MHS management domain run by a private organization. Each PRMD must contain MHS routing information to its parent ADMD. In addition, by bilateral agreement, a PRMD may have MHS routing information to other ADMDs and PRMDs.

PRMD: see *Private Management Domain.*

protocol control information: (conceptually) the initial part of a protocol data unit used by a protocol machine to communicate information to its peer.

protocol data unit: a data object exchanged by protocol machines, usually containing both protocol control information and user data.

protocol machine: a finite state machine (FSM) that implements a particular protocol. When a particular input (e.g., user request or network activity) occurs in a particular state, the FSM potentially generates a particular output (e.g., user indication or network activity) and possibly moves to another state.

PS: either *presentation service* or *presentation stream*, depending on context.

PSAP: *presentation service access point*

PSDU: *presentation service data unit*

pseudo-header: a 96–bit quantity used by a transport protocol in the Internet suite to guard against misbehaving implementations of IP.

PTT: a *post, telephone, and telegraph* authority.

QOS: see *quality of service.*

quality of service: the desired or actual characteristics of a service; typically, but not always, those of the network service.

QUIPU: a pioneering software package developed to study the OSI Directory and provide extensive pilot capabilities.

RDN: see *Relative Distinguished Name.*

reassembly: the process of recombining fragments, at the final destination, into the original IP datagram.

Relative Distinguished Name: the final component of an entry's Distinguished Name, consisting of one or more attribute/value pairs.

Reliable Transfer Service Element: the application service element responsible for transfer of bulk-mode objects.

remote operation: an action invoked by one application entity but performed by another.

Remote Operations Service Element: the application service element responsible for managing request/reply interactions.

remote procedure call: a synchronous remote operation.

replication: the process of keeping a copy of data, either through shadowing or caching.

Request for Comments: the document series describing the Internet suite of protocols and related experiments.

requestor: a user that initiates a service by invoking the .REQUEST primitive associated with that service. See *acceptor.*

responder: a service user that responds to a connection or association. See *initiator.*

retransmission: the process of repeatedly sending a unit of data while waiting for an acknowledgement.

RFC Editor: the entity responsible for publishing RFCs in the Internet suite of protocols.

RFC: see *Request for Comments.*

RO-notation: an set of extensions to ASN.1, defined using ASN.1's macro facility, that convey the semantics of remote operations.

RO: see *remote operation.*

ROSE: see *Remote Operations Service Element.*

router: a level-3 (network layer) relay.

RPC: see *remote procedure call.*

RTSE: see *Reliable Transfer Service Element.*

SAP: see *service access point.*

SDU: see *service data unit.*

segment: the unit of exchange in the TCP.

selector: a portion of an address identifying a particular entity at an address (e.g., a session selector identifies a user of the session service residing at a particular session address).

service access point: an artifact modeling how a service is made available to a user.

service data unit: user-data passed through a service access point.

service primitive: an artifact modeling how a service is requested or accepted by a user.

session layer: that portion of an OSI system responsible for adding control mechanisms to the data exchange.

shadowing: a form of replication in which well-defined units of information are copied to several DSAs.

Simple Mail Transfer Protocol: the application protocol offering message handling service in the Internet suite of protocols.

Simple Network Management Protocol: the application protocol offering network management service in the Internet suite of protocols.

SMTP: see *Simple Mail Transfer Protocol.*

SNAcP: see *subnetwork access protocol*.

SNDCP: see *subnetwork dependent convergence protocol*.

SNICP: see *subnetwork independent convergence protocol*.

SNMP: see *Simple Network Management Protocol*.

SNPA: *subnetwork point of attachment*

socket: a pairing of an IP address and a port number.

SPDU: *session protocol data unit*

SSAP: *session service access point*

SSDU: *session service data unit*

stevie-kins: instructions which only make sense if you already know how to do something, e.g., "take the first left; no, not *that* first left, the *next* first left."

subnet mask: a 32–bit quantity indicating which bits in an IP address that identify the physical network.

subnet-number: that portion of an IP host-identifier which identifies a particular physical network within an IP network.

subnet: (most unfortunate Internet usage) a physical network within an IP network.

subnetting: the process of using IP subnetting procedures.

subnetwork: a single network connecting several nodes on a single (virtual) transmission medium.

subnetwork access protocol: a protocol used to access a particular subnetwork technology.

subnetwork dependent convergence protocol: a protocol used to augment the service offered by a particular subnetwork technology to the OSI network service.

subnetwork independent convergence protocol: a protocol used to provide the network service between two end-systems.

SYN: the synchronize bit in a TCP segment.

TCP/IP: see *Internet suite of protocols.*

TCP: see *Transmission Control Protocol.*

TELNET: the application protocol offering virtual terminal service in the Internet suite of protocols.

three-way handshake: a process whereby two protocol entities synchronize during connection establishment.

TLV: *tag, length, and value*

TPDU: *transport protocol data unit*

transfer syntax: a description of an instance of a data type that is expressed as string of bits.

Transmission Control Protocol: the transport protocol offering a connection-oriented transport service in the Internet suite of protocols.

transport layer: that portion of an OSI system responsible for reliability and multiplexing of data transfer across the network (over and above that provided by the network layer) to the level required by the application.

transport-stack: the combination of protocols, at the transport layer and below, used in a given context.

TSAP: *transport service access point*

TSDU: *transport service data unit*

UA: see *User Agent.*

UDP: see *User Datagram Protocol.*

upper-layer protocol number: identifies a transport entity to the IP.

URG: the urgent bit in a TCP segment.

urgent data: user-data delivered in sequence but somehow more interesting to the receiving application entity.

User Agent: an application entity that makes the message transfer service available to the user.

User Datagram Protocol: the transport protocol offering a connection-less-mode transport service in the Internet suite of protocols.

user-data: conceptually, the part of a protocol data unit used to transparently communicate information between the users of the protocol.

virtual filestore: the abstraction provided by FTAM to model a system-independent file service.

Virtual Terminal: the OSI virtual terminal service.

VT: see *Virtual Terminal*.

WAN: see *wide area network*.

WD: a *working document*. If ratified, the working document advances to Committee Draft (CD) status, if relating to a new work item; or, Proposed Draft Amendment (PDAM) status, if relating to an existing standard. As a part of the advancement, a number is assigned to the result CD or PDAM.

well-known port: a transport endpoint which is documented by the IANA.

wide area network: any one of a number of technologies providing geographically distant transfer.

X.121: the addressing format used by X.25–based networks.

X.25: a connection-oriented network facility (some say that's the problem).

X.409: the predecessor to Abstract Syntax Notation One and the Basic Encoding Rules.

Bibliography

[1] Information Processing Systems — Open Systems Interconnection: Service Conventions. International Organization for Standardization and International Electrotechnical Committee, 1987. Technical Report 8509.

[2] Information Processing Systems — Open Systems Interconnection: Basic Reference Model. International Organization for Standardization and International Electrotechnical Committee, 1984. International Standard 7498-1.

[3] Danny Cohen and Jon B. Postel. The ISO Reference Model and Other Protocol Architectures. In *Proceedings of the IFIP Congress*, 1983. Paris, France.

[4] Information Processing Systems — Open Systems Interconnection: Basic Reference Model — Addendum 1: Connectionless-mode Transmission. International Organization for Standardization and International Electrotechnical Committee, 1987. International Standard 7498-1/AD 1.

[5] Information Processing — Open Systems Interconnection — Specification of Abstract Syntax Notation One (ASN.1). International Organization for Standardization and International Electrotechnical Committee, 1987. International Standard 8824.

[6] Information Processing — Open Systems Interconnection — Abstract Syntax Notation One (ASN.1) — Draft Addendum 1: Extensions to ASN.1. International Organization for Standardization and International Electrotechnical Committee, 1987. International Standard 8824/AD 1.

[7] Specification of Abstract Syntax Notation One. International Telegraph and Telephone Consultative Committee, 1988. Recommendation X.208.

[8] Information Processing Systems — Open Systems Interconnection — Service Definition for the Association Control Service Element. International Organization for Standardization and International Electrotechnical Committee, December, 1988. International Standard 8649.

[9] Information Processing Systems — Open Systems Interconnection – Protocol Specification for the Association Control Service Element. International Organization for Standardization and International Electrotechnical Committee, December, 1988. International Standard 8650.

[10] Information Processing Systems — Text Communication — Reliable Transfer Part 1: Model and Service Definition. International Organization for Standardization and International Electrotechnical Committee, November, 1989. International Standard 9066-1.

[11] Information Processing Systems — Text Communication — Reliable Transfer Part 2: Protocol Specification. International Organization for Standardization and International Electrotechnical Committee, November, 1989. International Standard 9066-2.

[12] Information Processing Systems — Text Communication — Remote Operations Part 1: Model, Notation and Service Definition. International Organization for Standardization and International Electrotechnical Committee, November, 1989. International Standard 9072-1.

[13] Information Processing Systems — Text Communication — Remote Operations Part 2: Protocol Specification. International Organization for Standardization and International Electrotechnical Committee, November, 1989. International Standard 9072-2.

[14] Association Control Service Definition for CCITT Applications. International Telegraph and Telephone Consultative Committee, December, 1988. Recommendation X.217.

[15] Association Control Protocol Specification for CCITT Applications. International Telegraph and Telephone Consultative Committee, December, 1988. Recommendation X.227.

[16] Reliable Transfer: Model and Service Definition. International Telegraph and Telephone Consultative Committee, March, 1988. Recommendation X.218.

[17] Reliable Transfer: Protocol Specification. International Telegraph and Telephone Consultative Committee, March, 1988. Recommendation X.228.

[18] Remote Operations: Model, Notation and Service Definition. International Telegraph and Telephone Consultative Committee, March, 1988. Recommendation X.219.

[19] Remote Operations: Protocol Specification. International Telegraph and Telephone Consultative Committee, March, 1988. Recommendation X.229.

[20] Information Technology — Open Systems Interconnection — Application Layer structure. International Organization for Standardization and International Electrotechnical Committee, December, 1989. International Standard 9545.

[21] Information Technology — Open Systems Interconnection — Extended Application Layer Structure. International Organization for Standardization and International Electrotechnical Committee, April, 1991. Proposed Draft Amendment 9545/PDAM 1.

[22] Vinton G. Cerf and Edward A. Cain. The DoD Internet Architecture Model. *Computer Networks and ISDN Systems*, 7(10):307–318, October, 1983.

[23] Jon B. Postel. *Simple Mail Transfer Protocol.* Request for Comments 821, DDN Network Information Center, SRI International, August, 1982. See also MIL-STD 1781.

[24] Craig Partridge. *Mail Routing and the Domain System*. Request for Comments 974, DDN Network Information Center, SRI International, January, 1986.

[25] David H. Crocker. *Standard for the Format of ARPA Internet Text Messages*. Request for Comments 822, DDN Network Information Center, SRI International, August, 1982.

[26] Jon B. Postel. *File Transfer Protocol*. Request for Comments 959, DDN Network Information Center, SRI International, October, 1985. See also MIL-STD 1780.

[27] Jon B. Postel. *TELNET Protocol Specification*. Request for Comments 854, DDN Network Information Center, SRI International, May, 1983. See also MIL-STD 1782.

[28] Paul V. Mockapetris. *Domain Names — Concepts and Facilities*. Request for Comments 1033, DDN Network Information Center, SRI International, November, 1987.

[29] Jeffrey D. Case, Mark S. Fedor, Martin L. Schoffstall, and James R. Davin. *A Simple Network Management Protocol*. Request for Comments 1157, DDN Network Information Center, SRI International, May, 1990.

[30] Information Processing Systems — Open Systems Interconnection — The Directory — Overview of Concepts, Models, and Service. International Organization for Standardization and International Electrotechnical Committee, December, 1988. International Standard 9594-1.

[31] The Directory — Overview of Concepts, Models, and Service. International Telegraph and Telephone Consultative Committee, December, 1988. Recommendation X.500.

[32] Stephen E. Kille. *Implementing X.400 AND X.500: The PP and QUIPU Systems*. Artech House, 1991. ISBN 0-89006-564-0.

[33] Rob Pike and Peter J. Weinberger. The Hideous Name. In *Proceedings, Summer Usenix Conference and Exhibition*, pages 563–568, June, 1985. Portland, Oregon.

[34] Brian W. Kernighan and Dennis M. Ritchie. *The C Programming Language. Software Series*, Prentice-Hall, Inc., Englewood Cliffs, New Jersey, 1978.

[35] Stephen E. Kille. *The THORN X.500 Naming Architecture.* THORN Project Internal Report UCL-45, revision 6.1, University College London, January, 1989.

[36] F. Sirovich and M. Antonellini. The THORN X.500 Distributed Directory Environment. In *Esprit '88: Putting the Technology to Use*, pages 1711–1720, North Holland, November, 1988.

[37] Stephen E. Kille. *Using the OSI Directory to achieve User Friendly Naming.* Research Note RN/90/29, Department of Computer Science, University College London, June, 1990.

[38] Stephen E. Kille. *X.500 and Domains.* Research Note RN/89/47, Department of Computer Science, University College London, May, 1989.

[39] Information Processing Systems — Data Communications — Network Service Definition — Addendum 2: Network Layer Addressing. International Organization for Standardization and International Electrotechnical Committee, June, 1988. International Standard 8348/AD 2.

[40] Marshall T. Rose and Dwight E. Cass. *ISO Transport Services on top of the TCP.* Request for Comments 1006, DDN Network Information Center, SRI International, May, 1987.

[41] Stephen E. Kille. *An interim approach to use of Network Addresses.* Research Note RN/89/13, Department of Computer Science, University College London, February, 1989.

[42] Stephen E. Kille. *A string encoding of Presentation Address.* Research Note RN/89/14, Department of Computer Science, University College London, February, 1989.

[43] Michael F. Schwartz. *Resource Discovery and Related Research at the University of Colorado.* Technical Report CU-CS-508-91, Department of Computer Science, University of Colorado at Boulder, January, 1991.

[44] Michael F. Schwartz and Panagiotis G. Tsirigotis. *Techniques for Supporting Wide Area Distributed Applications.* Technical Report CU-CS-519-91, Department of Computer Science, University of Colorado at Boulder, February, 1991.

[45] Stephen E. Kille, Colin J. Robbins, Michael Roe, and Alan Turland. *The ISO Development Environment: User's Manual, Volume 5: QUIPU.* February, 1990.

[46] Marshall T. Rose. *PSI White Pages Pilot Project: Administrator's Guide.* Technical Report, Performance Systems International, 1990. (living document).

[47] Paul Barker and Colin J. Robbins. *Directory Navigation in the QUIPU X.500 System.* Technical Report, Department of Computer Science, University College London, 1989.

[48] Marshall T. Rose. *Directory Assistance Service.* Request for Comments 1202, DDN Network Information Center, SRI International, February, 1991.

[49] Marshall T. Rose. Network Management is Simple: You just need the "Right" Framework. In *Integrated Network Management, II,* Iyengar Krishnan and Wolfgang Zimmer, editors, pages 9–25, North-Holland, April, 1991.

Index